Dave & Penny

May you have many happy years
in your new home

Bob & Sheely

ABU

Books by A. A. Hoehling

The Last Voyage of the Lusitania (with Mary Hoehling)
Lonely Command
A Whisper of Eternity: The Mystery of Edith Cavell
Last Train from Atlanta
They Sailed into Oblivion
The Fierce Lambs
The Great Epidemic
Who Destroyed the Hindenburg?
The Week Before Pearl Harbor
The Great War at Sea
Home Front USA
The Jeannette Expedition
Vicksburg, 47 Days of Siege
America's Road to War, 1939-1941
Great Ship Disasters
The Lexington *Goes Down*
Disaster: Major American Catastrophes
The Franklin *Comes Home*
Thunder at Hampton Roads
Epics of the Sea
The Day Richmond Died, reissued as *The Last Days of the Confederacy* (with Mary Hoehling)
Lost at Sea

DAMN THE TORPEDOES!

The opposite photograph is an artist's rendering of the *Alabama's* sinking at the hands of the USS *Kearsarge* off Cherbourg, France, in June 1864.

Courtesy of the U.S. Naval Historical Center

DAMN THE TORPEDOES!
Naval Incidents of the Civil War

A. A. Hoehling

GRAMERCY BOOKS • New York

Copyright © 1989 by A. A. Hoehling.
All rights reserved under International and Pan-American
Copyright Conventions.

No part of this book may be reproduced or transmitted in any form or by
any means electronic or mechanical including photocopying and recording,
or by any information storage and retrieval system, without permission in
writing from the publisher.

This 1998 edition is published by Gramercy Books,
a division of Random House Value Publishing, Inc.,
201 East 50th Street, New York, New York 10022,
by arrangement with John F. Blair, Publisher.

Gramercy Books and design are registered trademarks of
Random House Value Publishing, Inc.

Random House
New York • Toronto • London • Sydney • Auckland
http://www.randomhouse.com/

Printed and bound in the United States of America

A CIP catalog record for this book is available from the Library of Congress.

Damn the Torpedoes! Naval Incidents of the Civil War / by A. A. Hoehling
ISBN 0-517-18979-8

8 7 6 5 4 3 2 1

THIS BOOK IS DEDICATED TO
THE BRAVE YOUNG OFFICERS AND MEN OF
THE UNION AND CONFEDERATE NAVIES
WHO SERVED AND FOUGHT ABOARD
MEN-O'-WAR, MANY OF WHICH, BY
LATER STANDARDS, WOULD NOT HAVE BEEN
DEEMED SEAWORTHY, OR SAFE
EVEN AT DOCK.

TABLE OF CONTENTS

Captured Confederate blockade-runner *Robert E. Lee*, renamed USS *Fort Donelson*. With their light hulls and sleek lines, such British-built vessels could outrun most Federal pursuers.

U.S. Naval Historical Center

INTRODUCTION

IT WAS AN UNORTHODOX AND OFTEN WILD naval war, that of the rebellion. The Civil War was waged at sea with more massed violence and with more diversity of ships and weaponry than any previous, sustained naval action. It was pressed with at least the same vigor and passion as on land, and with considerably more improvisation.

Ferryboats were turned by edict into men-o'-war. China and upholstered furniture were trundled off ocean liners as they were converted into warships. To compensate for a lack of naval guns, army field pieces were snatched from forts and wheeled onto tarred deckings, then lashed down.

Iron or tin plating was nailed onto wooden steamships to make them "ironclads" or "tinclads." Still, they took their knocks from Confederate shore batteries and from ingenious mines (or "torpedoes"), since they were not armored below water line. A revolutionary little gunboat flush with the water and sporting but one turret would prove a nemesis for the ponderous Confederate ironclads, whose very avoirdupois damned their maneuverability. At the same time, the noble wooden frigate with multiple banks of cannon met extinction.

The Confederates, not to be outdone, went into battle with "cottonclads" in addition to ironclads, but the former proved as susceptible to fire as dry tinder. The South pioneered in "torpedoes," including some sophisticated models detonated electrically.

With few exceptions, the Civil War's naval actions were fought within sight of the coasts, in bays, or upon the wide rivers, especially the Mississippi. Although fleet or squadron operations continued an historic role, the daring of the individual still possessed the potential to destroy a Goliath. Stealth, deception, and hoax were employed alongside conventional military confrontation.

On occasion, the army's prerogatives became interchangeable with the navy's. Soldiers attacked ships. Sailors raided shore targets. Army officers even had the impertinence to command vessels. And in one coastal city—Portland, Maine—the citizenry mobilized with muskets to repel a one-man invasion from the sea. Although, in retrospect, certain operations might appear to have been curious kinds of games, the participants, to paraphrase an old proverb, "died in earnest."

These shadings, as well as the bold strokes in the War of the Rebellion, the War Between the States, or whatever the Civil War is to be called, make up the canvas of this book. Too often, the naval role has been overshadowed by the scope and casualties of the land battles from Bull Run (or First Manassas) to Cold Harbor and the fall of Richmond. Yet the struggle was carried forth with undiminished ferocity at sea and upon the waterways, and with equal effectiveness. North and South alike exerted immense efforts to control the paths of trade and communication. The outcome would materially effect the conflict's final curtain.

Confrontation on the seas was heralded on April 15, 1861, when President Lincoln declared a blockade of the ports from South Carolina to the Gulf of Mexico. The blockade was soon extended northward to include all of Virginia. "For this purpose," Lincoln stated, "a competent force will be posted so as to prevent entrance and exit of vessels" under pain of capture. Further, any attempt to interfere would be "held amenable to the laws of the United States for the prevention and punishment of piracy." In so doing, the president was invoking one of history's oldest stratagems of warfare: starving the enemy into submission.

"A paper blockade!" howled the secessionists, and at the time it truly was. Foreign nations joined the chorus, especially Great Britain, which was experiencing nightmares about feeding her cotton mills. She needed to keep cargo ships—sail or steam—running to Wilmington, North Carolina; Charleston, South Carolina; Savannah, Georgia; Pensacola, Florida; New Orleans, Louisiana; Galveston, Texas; and even Matamoros, Mexico.

The United States Navy was manifestly unprepared. Easily half of the ninety vessels listed in the 1861 Naval Register either were unfit for sea or were languishing in shipyards while awaiting decommission. Also, some twenty-eight of the so-called active showed the flag off foreign shores. Half a dozen of these lazed at anchor on the popular China station, their crews ashore on historic personal quests.

Left were a meager fourteen, at most, to defend the East Coast and to blockade Dixie.

"After the inauguration of Mr. Lincoln as President," wrote Rear Admiral Daniel Ammen, "a painful lethargy seemed to pervade every branch of the Administration, while the South was arming and organizing with extraordinary activity for the avowed purpose of destroying the Government, which apparently supinely awaited that event."

An "instant navy" was needed, first to seal off the more than three thousand miles of bays, inlets, river mouths, and deltas that stretched from Virginia through the Gulf of Mexico. Such a goal would become known as the Anaconda Plan, aimed at strangling the rebellion.

There appeared but one approach. It entailed the arming of almost anything afloat of reasonable size, including ocean steamers, ferryboats, fishing smacks, river sidewheelers, private yachts, harbor tugs, and barnacled old schooners. If the craft happened to be steam-propelled, that was a plus. Otherwise, if the vessel did not leak too badly, she was expected to slosh off to war. Barges were in demand, since they could carry mortars and all manner of materiel.

The shallow-draft "double-enders" were unique newcomers to the fleet. They were called "ninety-day gunboats" because of their rapid construction from green wood. Their engines were geared to enable them to reverse quickly and thus avoid turning in narrow rivers or channels. They were big, many of them, like the *Shamrock* and *Otsego*, rated at almost 1,000 tons. And they were fast, capable of 12 or 13 knots. The Confederates possessed virtually nothing to match either their speed or agility. Uniquely tailored for a specific role in an unusual conflict, they were forerunners (except for their rapid production) of no future naval vessels. But they exemplified the imagination of their designers.

Even as the United States Navy sought out fast ships to lend meaning to the executive proclamation, a swashbuckling fleet composed largely of British blockade-runners was hauling to sea, manned by river pilots, tugboat captains, grizzled ferryboat masters, and officers from the Royal Navy operating under assumed names.

Great Britain was pragmatic in recognizing Washington's lack of an adequate watchdog fleet. She made no effort to discourage the growing squadrons of merchantmen that were materializing overnight to ply from Liverpool, Southampton, the Thames, and Belfast via the Bahamas, Bermuda, and Havana to the seceded states.

If this was not bold enough, English shipyards heated up their spar-steaming kettles to build warships for the Confederacy. Business was business, even though Richmond's currency was backed by little more than cotton bales, tobacco, and turpentine.

By 1862, although the United States Navy was increasing in size, blockade-running was approximating the frequency, if not the regularity, of the transatlantic steamship lines.

Linked by a brotherhood of peril, the captains were a varied and daring lot. A few names stand out among the hundreds: Louis M. Coxetter, a tough one-time privateer with a price on his head; John Wilkinson, suave, rotund, formerly of the United States Navy, once imprisoned in Fort Warren in Boston Harbor; John Newland Maffitt, also resigned from the United States Navy, among the most innovative; and Augustus Charles Hobart-Hampden, surely the most colorful of the lot, late of Her Majesty's navy and holder of the Victoria Cross. "Lads, sharpen your swords!" was a quote attributed to Hobart-Hampden, who used several names to spare the navy embarrassment—Hewett, Ridge, Gulick, Roberts, and even Hobart-Pasha, during a subsequent stint with the Turkish navy.

Improvisation was a sine qua non. The captains marshaled every ruse known, plus some hitherto unknown. They flashed false signals with lanterns, flew the Stars and Stripes or other national flags, changed nameplates, and even dipped colors to passing Federal men-o'-war. The latter often returned the honor. It is not surprising that the hunted proved more able to capture the world's imagination than did the hunters.

Consider Coxetter's method of keeping crewmen at their posts in times of peril. Wrote James Morris Morgan, a fifteen-year-old midshipman aboard the 562-ton steamer-turned-blockade-runner *Herald*: "[Coxetter] was convinced that the great danger in running the blockade was in his own engine room, so he seated himself on the ladder leading down to it and politely informed the engineer that if the engine stopped before he was clear of the [blockading] fleet, he, the engineer, would be a dead man.

"As Coxetter held in his hand a Colt's revolver, this sounded like no idle threat. . . . We safely bumped our way across the shallows, and plunging and tossing in the gale, this little cockleshell, whose rail was scarcely five feet above the sea level, bucked her way toward Bermuda."

Or consider Wilkinson, commander of the iron-hulled former Glasgow-Belfast packet steamer *Giraffe*, renamed the *R. E. Lee*. To set an example of stealth, the bearded Wilkinson wore slippers on the bridge. In describing one of his twenty-one successful voyages hauling bales of cotton valued at more than $2 million in gold, he wrote: "The breeze was still blowing fresh as in the morning, but we were now running directly away from it, and the cruiser [USS *Iroquois*] was going literally as fast as the wind, causing the sails to be rather a hindrance than a help. . . . Sending for the chief engineer, I said . . . let us try cotton, saturated with spirits of turpentine. There were on board, as part of our deck load, 30 or 40 barrels of 'spirits.' In a very few moments, a bale of cotton was ripped open, a barrel tapped, and buckets full of the saturated material passed down into the fireroom. . . .

"We now began to hold our own, and even to gain a little upon the chaser. . . . I saw the big 'bone in the mouth' of our pertinacious friend, for she was near enough to us at one time for us to see distinctly the white curl of foam under her bows."

Unfortunately, the burned cotton choked the flues. The *Iroquois* appeared to be gaining. Wilkinson ordered kegs of gold brought up to be distributed among the crew. A female passenger, Miss Lucy Gwin, offered to fill a purse and keep it on her person until the danger had passed. Twilight turned into darkness as the officer atop the paddle-wheel housings at last called out: "We have lost sight of her!"

"I remained on deck an hour," Wilkinson continued, "and then retired to my stateroom with a comfortable sense of security. We had fired so hard that the very planks on the bridge were almost scorching hot, and my feet were nearly blistered.

"I put them out of the window to cool, after taking off slippers and socks. While in this position, Miss Lucy came on the bridge in company with her father. Tapping my foot with her hand, she said, 'ah, captain, I see we are all safe, and I congratulate you!'"

The experiences of Coxetter and Wilkinson were familiar ones to blockade-runners. Theirs was a defensive role, often frustrating. For the "hounds," the chasers, it was a different "game" entirely, even though they knew blockade-runners could never fight back, lest their captains be tried as privateers.

Among the blockading fleet, only the methodical, competent Commander John J. Almuzi of the fast, 2,000-ton steamer USS *Connecticut* is much remembered, perhaps because he alone wrote memoirs of

The one-time passenger steamer USS *Connecticut*, Commander John J. Almuzi's ship, was among the few "chasers" that could raise flank speed of 15 knots and overtake the best of the runners.

U.S. Naval Historical Center

any consequence. The *Connecticut* set a record of four runners destroyed and four captured. As Almuzi recalled: "The blockade runners would always select dark nights to run in and out, and certain stages of the moon; generally between the last and first quarters . . . when it set early and rose late. . . . A tolerably high tide also entered into the calculation.

"These blockade runners were all English steamers, and were painted lead color . . . to prevent their being discovered at night, when running close in along the land. The fire and steam arrangements were for burning soft English coal, which always made black smoke, by which they could be discovered a long distance in the day.

"On board the *Connecticut*, when the lookout at the masthead sang out, 'black smoke!' all was commotion. A chase once lasted 15 hours . . . when the blockade runner was lost sight of. She had to throw overboard nearly all her cargo, which comprised English goods, as she was bound in. We passed through and by innumerable boxes during the day, some of which we perceived contained shoes."

In foggy weather, Almuzi and his fellow pursuers often picked up the trail by such jetsam as cotton bales, which bobbed like buoys, boxes containing almost anything, half-empty barrels of turpentine, wine casks, and larger deck cargo such as wagon wheels or even entire wagons.

The blockade-runners bought time for the South and prolonged the Union's effort to crush the rebellion. The battle of Shiloh, for example, would have been more one-sided had not nine hundred barrels of gunpowder been rushed into Wilmington, North Carolina, earmarked for that bloody contest in Tennessee.

The effort—a transfusion—fell far short of a cure. The Anaconda Plan was choking the South.

The course of the war and, indeed, the suicidal path of the Confederacy may have been embodied in a single incident from the blockade that took place on the last day of September 1864. Augustus Charles Hobart-Hampden, this time operating under the name of Ridge, was guiding his blockade-runner *Condor* toward Wilmington through stormy seas. He carried a most important passenger—Rose O'Neal Greenhow. In the North, she was considered notorious, and in the South, a heroine.

With her entrée to Washington society and officialdom, the well-to-do widow Greenhow had been able to learn about early Union strategies, most notably those preliminary to Bull Run. Mrs. Greenhow had passed advance details of troop movements to General Pierre Beauregard, one of President Davis's workhorse commanders. Apparently, the information contributed materially to the Union debacle in northeastern Virginia.

Even terrible-tempered Secretary of War Edwin M. Stanton could not bring himself to do more than incarcerate the widow, first in her own house—"Fort Greenhow," her neighbors quipped—where she blithely continued to convey military information, and then in Old Capitol Prison. Finally, she was deported south. She tarried long enough only to pack her bags for London, where she traveled both to conduct Confederate business and to finish her memoirs. Her flirtation with belles-lettres reached print under the title *My Imprisonment and the First Year of Abolition Rule in Washington*. Neither succinct nor objective, the book was largely a diatribe against the Union and an exhortation for the continuance of slavery. Like the ascetic, withdrawn Jefferson Davis, the widow Greenhow could not fathom why Washington was less than pleased with the South.

Returning to Richmond aboard Hobart-Hampden's *Condor*, she bore undisclosed messages for President Davis and, around her neck, a small drawstring bag containing gold sovereigns. It was speculated that the bag contained some three hundred of the British coins, worth at least two thousand dollars. The sum may have come from either her publisher or some benefactor of the nearly depleted Confederate treasury.

Condor had almost reached the New Inlet channel to the Cape Fear River when she was picked up by a Federal cruiser. In his desire to avoid a nearby wreck, Captain "Ridge" steered hard onto a shoal, cracking the keel. The normally cool and calculating Rose Greenhow panicked. She implored the commander to send her ashore in a small boat, shrilly asserting that she must not be captured.

The daring Hobart-Hampden allowed emotion to prevail over common sense. He ordered a skiff made ready and gallantly assisted Mrs. Greenhow into it, along with the pilot and two strong rowers. Hobart-Hampden had grown up near the wild North Sea, and he should have known better. The sea lanes to Wilmington were lashed by the worst storms that the Gulf Stream, in its collision with Cape Hatteras, could conjure.

The gale did not abate as the little craft bobbed off into the blackness. Halfway to safety, it capsized in the huge combers. The men struggled to the beach, which was not many yards distant. Rose Greenhow, weighted by her gold coins, her flowing skirts, and her coat, sank.

Her body washed ashore with other flotsam. A number of persons would take credit for the somber discovery. Something was wrong, though—the sovereigns and Mrs. Greenhow's dispatch case were missing.

A soldier professing deep remorse did return some gold sovereigns, claiming to have stumbled across the body while on patrol and confessing that he could not resist pilfering the bag of gold. But many questions were left unanswered. Exactly how much money was returned? What became of it? Where was the dispatch case? Had a Federal agent reached the body first and rifled the case's contents? Why didn't the crew of the little boat make more of an effort to save their passenger? And what, if anything, was done with the soldier who stole and returned the coins?

On October 1, Rose Greenhow's funeral was held in Wilmington. She was buried with full military honors in Oakdale Cemetery, her casket draped with the Stars and Bars, the emblem of the cause she so passionately served to her death. Somehow, the sacrificial act of the widow Greenhow, carried out during a brief moment toward the end of the long blockade, seems an epitaph for a Confederacy that was slowly strangling.

The Union had recovered rapidly from its early lethargy. Within eight months of mobilization, morning colors were being sounded on 264 United States Navy vessels, ragtag or otherwise. A year later, the count was 427.

By the last December of the war, that of 1864, 671 ships were on the Navy Department register. A virtual screen of vessels of all sizes, shapes, and types sealed off those Southern ports that had not already fallen to pressure from the sea or to the artillery of conquering armies, especially the forces of General Sherman. By then, the navy boasted the radical class of turreted flush-deckers spawned by the sunken *Monitor*, as well as heavy ironclads and swift gunboats. Big "steam sloops," mounting masts, became the last salute to ships of wood. To compensate for their fragility, most of these draped heavy chain armor over their sides. Nonetheless, their masts were like vestigial tails in the evolution of mammals. All of the new ships could overtake the blockade-runners, and usually did.

The effects were severe. As a case in point, exports of cotton to England shrank from 816 million pounds to 6 million pounds in the first two years of the rebellion. The late author Robert Carse wrote in *Blockade*, published in 1958 by Rinehart & Co.: "There were in England more than 2 million people brought to starvation by the cotton shortage. The mills were closed tight. The millworkers had months ago spent the last of their savings. Then, the pictures had gone from the walls of the workers' homes, and the family trinkets were sold, and clothing, the chests of drawers, the rest of the furniture, the beds, the mattresses, the kitchen utensils. The families slept numb, wretched, on piles of straw. Girls of 14 and 15 went out on the streets. . . . Younger children died of malnutrition."

The people of the South suffered greatly because of the disruption of the grain trade to Australia. Richmond experienced "bread riots" on Easter 1863.

What was the toll on the runners? No one will ever know exactly. The South kept no records. Britain did not care to discuss her major role in the operations. The United States Navy, manifestly exaggerating, claimed that some 1,000 vessels were captured, destroyed, or disabled in attempting to pass the blockade. The navy said that 295 of these were steamers, the others "coasters," such as sailing vessels.

Significant, nonetheless, was the fact that not one captain or officer lost his life on these ships, and very few passengers or crew.

Prize courts placed a $24.5 million price tag on captured ships and their cargoes. Those destroyed were valued at approximately $7 million.

The grave markers of a valiant attempt to break through to a hungry and beleaguered South are yet strewn along the Southeast coast and into the Gulf of Mexico—the rusted, barnacled fittings of such as the *Condor, Little Lila, Will o' the Wisp, Sophia, Georgiana, Night Hawk, Stonewall Jackson, Ruby, Venus, Vesta, Ranger, Fanny and Jenny, Mary Bowers, Lynx, Stormy Petrel* . . .

Scores, perhaps hundreds.

The war at sea was demanding, real, and frightening, even though casualties were dwarfed by those in the great land battles. This backward look at a fiery period of our nation's history focuses upon the people of North and South and their many acts of daring and valor as they fought upon the seas and lesser waters. It is their story, told largely in their own words, always against the backdrop of the blockade.

Drawing of the *Merrimack/Virginia*.

Chapter 1

THE *MERRIMACK* IS COMING!

*"Things began to look vigorous Sunday
morning the 9th of March, [when] the news
of the Merrimack's frolic came here."*
Diary of John Hay

IT WAS ALL TOO TRUE. The monster ironclad *Merrimack*, renamed CSS *Virginia*, had been unleashed, as had long been feared. She was bent, in the words of her commander, Commodore Franklin Buchanan, on "carnage, havoc and dismay!"

On Saturday morning, March 8, 1862, she had accomplished exactly that in Hampton Roads. She sank two frigates, damaged other Union vessels, and caused heavy loss of life. She would certainly have destroyed more of the Federal fleet, including the grounded and helpless flagship *Minnesota*, had she not exhausted her ammunition and the tide begun to ebb. Because of her excessive draft of twenty-two feet, the *Merrimack*'s route past Sewell's Point down the Elizabeth River to the Norfolk Navy Yard was chancy at best.

When word arrived in Baltimore the next morning by the Old Point Comfort steamer *Adelaide*, panic spread quickly south to Washington and north to New York. The single-ship Confederate navy would soon be thundering up the coast, and cities would surely be leveled. Each shot from her "huge" guns, it was asserted, could level any one of the fine buildings on Wall Street. Nothing could stop so impregnable a warship.

As early as the previous October, George Templeton Strong, New York patron of the arts, had noted in his voluminous diary the warning given him by Major General Montgomery C. Meigs, the quartermaster general. "We have only two guns that can make any impression on her," Strong wrote, "the Union Gun at [Fort] Monroe and another . . . not yet mounted. [Meigs] expects [the *Merrimack*] to sally forth 'on the rampage' in a few days, shell the camp at Newport News, pass Fort Monroe, and play the devil. If he is right and she is invulnerable, there is no reason why she should not steam up the Narrows and lay this city [New York] under contribution."

The nation's capital was also believed to be at risk. Washington was serving as a hospital center, with thousands of sick and wounded in scores of wards on the Mall and around the city's perimeter; surgeons made hasty plans for evacuating their patients, and word was passed to quartermasters to have horses and ambulance wagons standing by.

This singular scenario had been ordained on April 21, 1861, with the chaotic abandonment of the Norfolk, or Gosport, Navy Yard by Commodore Charles S. McCauley. Not only did the aging and infirm commandant order the firing of the base's installations, but the scuttling of the warships docked there as well. Turpentine was splashed over the decks and torches applied. Seacocks were opened, and the fleet at the Norfolk Navy Yard settled into the muck of the Elizabeth River. Among those destroyed or badly damaged was the old, 3,000-ton steam frigate *Merrimack*. Mounting almost fifty cannon, she was justifiably rated first-class. She had been in decommission, however, awaiting new engines and a drive shaft.

The yard was relinquished to the Confederacy without a shot. The scuttling was only partially successful. Resting in mud, the *Merrimack* was salvageable. Advised of her availability, Confederate Navy Secretary Stephen Mallory recognized that he now possessed the vehicle that would help him realize his long-held dream of an armored ship.

By the end of 1861, the *Merrimack* emerged phoenixlike from fire and turmoil. Rechristened the *Virginia*, though most even in the South continued to prefer her original name, she bore scant resemblance to her old self. She was sheathed with nearly 800 tons of 1- and 2-inch-thick iron plate hammered onto her 2-inch casemate of oak and pine so as to present a 172-foot housing worked into a thirty-five-degree slope. The *Merrimack*'s overall length remained at 262 feet, though a 2.5-foot, 2,500-pound iron ram was added to the prow 2 feet underwater. Within protected ports, she mounted a main battery of four 7- and 6.40-inch rifled cannon plus six smoothbore 9-inch. The latter, like the ship herself, had been seized from the United States Navy.

Now approaching 4,000 tons, the *Merrimack/Virginia* was as unwieldy as the prehistoric beasts some thought she resembled. She was top-heavy. Her lack of power was inevitable, since needed machinery could not be obtained by the South; engineers had to make do with the old steam engines. The rickety shaft was patched up as best Southern mechanics, unfamiliar with the design, could manage. The

Merrimack, one crewman sniffed, was as maneuverable "as Noah's Ark." Engineers figured her top speed to be about 8 knots under the most auspicious conditions of wind and tide, and they figured her turning circle to be about a mile! Thus, it might require the better part of an hour to alter course and come around to the stern of an opponent, assuming that an antagonist would wait placidly for the *Merrimack* to deliver a broadside into her tail.

Meanwhile, a far more radical warship was taking shape. John Ericsson, Swedish naval architect and inventor and the man who patented the "rotary," or screw, propeller, had sold the navy and President Lincoln on the idea of a moderate-sized armored craft. It would be but 172 feet overall and an estimated 776 tons maximum. The entire decking would be flush with the water. Aside from a novel telescoping funnel, the sole superstructure would be a revolving turret protected by 8 inches of armor plate and twin, mounted, 11-inch, smoothbore "columbiads," or Dahlgren guns, that would fire shots weighing nearly two hundred pounds. Two engines would drive a single screw propeller. Although her designed speed of 8 knots was the same as the *Merrimack*'s and slow by the measure of first-class warships or even of auxiliary ferryboats, the new *Monitor*, as Ericsson chose to name her, would rely on maneuverability, and she would present almost no target. Shells were supposed to ricochet off her cylindrical turret. With the *Monitor*, for the first time in naval history, a ship's crew would have to live below the water line. This was made possible by forced-air ventilation, itself an innovation.

The singular craft was taking shape in the Rowland works of Brooklyn's Greenpoint section. Her genesis was observed by all who passed, yet it sparked little interest. The *Monitor* did not quit her snug harbor for the cold, murky waters of the East River until January 1862, at about the same time sightings of the *Merrimack* commenced in the Elizabeth River off Craney Point.

Though no one possessed the specifications or even a photograph of the remodeled *Merrimack*, the belief persisted that she would be able to cruise up the coast and lay waste at will cities as far north as Portland, Maine. Charles Ellet, a Philadelphia engineer, was swept up in the fever of the day. He dashed off a pamphlet entitled *Military Incapacity*, which proved much the nautical equivalent of *Uncle Tom's Cabin* as a clarion call. Distributed to Congress, *Military Incapacity* warned: "If the *Merrimac** is permitted to escape from Elizabeth River, she will be almost certain to commit great depredations on our armed and unarmed vessels in Hampton Roads, and may even be expected to pass out under the guns of Fortress Monroe and prey upon our commerce in Chesapeake Bay." Indeed, Ellet was so affected by his trenchant prose that he obtained a colonelcy and bent over the drawing boards to design his own ironclads and rams.

On March 8, the *Merrimack* proceeded to fulfill at least a modicum of the latter-day Jeremiah's predictions. She sank the anchored frigates *Congress* and *Cumberland* in a dubious display of sportsman-

---

*Merrimack was preferred by the navy, though many spelled it without the *k*.

John Ericsson, designer of the *Monitor*.

U.S. Naval Historical Center

ship. After pounding *Cumberland* into splinters, the *Merrimack* smashed bow-on into what was left. Her ram, however, was lost in the process. *Congress* surrendered before being set ablaze. Her captain was dead. The 250 Union officers and men killed represented the navy's heaviest loss of life in any combat to that date.

The Confederates banged off one solid shot at the hard-aground flagship *Minnesota*. The shot tore through a pantry and a cabin, doing little damage other than reducing many shelves of china and glasses to shards. Flag Officer Louis M. Goldsborough of the *Minnesota* remained too distraught to appreciate the lone glimmer of hope in an otherwise disastrous action—the *Merrimack* could steam no closer to the helpless flagship because of the shallows and bars, and her range was thus severely restricted.

As the last shots echoed into silence, the *Monitor* was rounding Cape Charles, the northern sentinel above Cape Henry that watched over Hampton Roads. The strange little vessel had almost foundered on an imperiled passage down the coast. From a distance, her captain, Lieutenant Commander John L. Worden, had seen the telltale puffs of smoke that marked the *Merrimack*'s rampage.

Meanwhile, in nearly impregnable Fort Monroe, Major General John E. Wool, the senior army officer in the area, was preparing an incredibly dire dispatch to the War Department concerning Saturday's disaster. He had to hurry to make the night boat, the old sidewheeler *Adelaide*, since the Signal Corps telegraph line that stretched across Hampton Roads to Virginia's eastern shore and then north was not quite completed.

Secretary of War Edwin M. Stanton was the first cabinet member to learn the news. He happened to be in the signal room of the War Department when it arrived. Short of stature, bearded, irascible, Stanton was a trusted confidant of the president's, though many with whom he conducted affairs of state held decidedly unflattering views of him. The *Merrimack*'s appearance had long been expected, yet the carnage she left still came as a shock. The war secretary was stunned.

In spite of his corpulence and asthma, Stanton raced the short distance to the White House. Lincoln was already at his desk and well into his workday, though it was still early Sunday morning. A frontiersman, the president was accustomed to rising while most slept.

Lincoln's reaction to the catastrophic event was predictable. He sent for his old friend, Senator Orville Browning of Illinois. Browning had been appointed to complete the term of Senator Stephen A. Douglas after Douglas's sudden death the previous July. Both Lincoln and Browning had served in the Illinois legislature, and they had tried cases together and opposed each other during their days as practicing lawyers.

A devout churchman, the clean-shaven, rather severe-faced Browning was dressed and prepared to leave for Sunday worship at the New York Avenue Presbyterian Church, where the Reverend Phineas D. Gurley also counted the president among his flock, if not among the most unquestioning of believers. The president's carriage whisked Senator Browning, his wife, Eliza, and their adopted daughter, Emma,

Chowtime aboard the *Monitor*. The photographer somehow convinced these sailors to remain still during the relatively long exposure of the sensitized plate.

to the White House at a gallop. At 10:00 A.M., Browning joined the president, Secretary Stanton, Secretary of State William H. Seward, and Major General George B. McClellan. As commander of the Army of the Potomac, "Little Mac" McClellan was then assembling a massive force with the aim of taking Richmond via the Peninsula along the James from Norfolk. He was as happy as a child with so many brightly painted lead soldiers.

"There were apprehensions," Browning later recorded in his well-kept diary, "that the *Merrimack* might come here & destroy the Town, but none of the persons present knew her draft of water. It was also apprehended that she might get out to sea and destroy all our transports now on their way to Annapolis with all our accumulations of stores."

There was scant time for prolonged "apprehensions." Lincoln wanted to get down to the navy yard to seek out the opinion of Captain John Dahlgren, eminent ordnance expert, the man for whom the navy's best big guns were named. At about six feet, three inches, Dahlgren was one of the few leaders in Washington who approached the chief executive's lofty height.

Lincoln and Browning left the others and set off at breakneck speed for the navy yard. They arrived "at 10 ½," according to the mathematically meticulous Dahlgren, who postscripted a bit testily, "when I should have been in church."

Dahlgren accompanied the president and Browning to the White House. En route, as Dahlgren later recalled, he offered "but little comfort," while agreeing that a blockade of the Potomac "was about all which could be done at present."

According to Browning, Dahlgren said "there was nothing to prevent the *Merrimac* from coming [to Washington] as she drew only 21 feet of water, and any vessel drawing not more than 22 feet could come here. He also said she could go to New York, lie off the City, and levy contributions at will." Yet the senator did not find Lincoln particularly stunned, but rather "in his usual suggestive mood."

The trio found a burgeoning group in a "private room" (possibly the War Office) of the White House. Joining Stanton, Seward, and McClellan were Secretary of the Navy Gideon Welles, a former lawyer and publisher from Hartford resplendent with his large, gray wig and shaggy beard; Secretary of the Treasury Salmon P. Chase, a dour abolitionist and recent governor of Ohio; Major General Meigs, architect of the half-completed Capitol dome and the Washington aqueduct; Assistant Secretary of War Peter Watson, a Washington attorney; and Lincoln's secretaries, John G. Nicolay and John Hay. Aware that an adequate quorum was present and fearful that archenemies Stanton and Welles might soon be at each other's throats, Browning excused himself, gathered his wife and daughter, and hurried off to church.

Stanton, "the most excited and impressive" of the personalities present, according to Nicolay, was "unable to control his strong emotion." He "walked up and down the room like a caged lion. . . . McClellan was dumbfounded and silent. . . . Lincoln was . . . composed, but eagerly inquisitive . . .

Chase impatient and ready to utter blame . . . Seward and Welles hopeful yet without encouraging reasons to justify their hope. . . . Possibilities . . . were indeed sufficiently portentous to create consternation. What might this new and irresistible leviathan of the deep accomplish?"

"The most frightened man," at least according to the cold appraisal of Welles, "was the Secretary of War . . . at times almost frantic as he walked the room. . . . The *Merrimac*, he said, would destroy every vessel in the service, could lay every city on the east coast under contribution, could take Fortress Monroe; McClellan's mistaken purpose to advance by the Peninsula must be abandoned, and Burnside would inevitably be captured." Major General Ambrose Burnside was carrying on a successful expedition to open up Pamlico Sound and a backdoor route to the cities of North Carolina and Virginia.

According to Welles, Stanton then concluded that "the first movement of the *Merrimac* would be to come up the Potomac and disperse Congress, destroy the Capitol and public buildings; or she might go to New York and Boston and destroy those cities, or levy from them contributions sufficient to carry on the war."

As if such dire prophecies were not enough, Secretary of War Stanton postscripted, according to Nicolay's account, that "a shell or a cannon shot from the *Merrimac* would probably land in the Cabinet room before they separated."

Welles tried to mollify Stanton by pointing out that the draft of the *Merrimack* would not permit her to navigate up the Potomac and that she could not possibly threaten Washington and New York "at the same time." Seward, the former governor of New York, admitted that Welles's revelations gave him "the first moment's relief" he had experienced that Sunday. But not so Stanton, who nervously paced in and out of the room, occasionally sat down to scribble some notes, then was up again as he "swung his arms, scolded and raved," according to Welles.

Several times, the secretary of war went to the window and squinted as though he expected to sight the Confederate menace. Even the president joined in Stanton's pantomime of apprehension. When Secretary of the Navy Welles reported that the *Monitor* should by then have arrived in Hampton Roads and that he was confident she could "resist" if not actually "overcome" her monolithic adversary, Stanton responded with a "mingled look of incredulity and contempt," again according to Welles's account. Stanton himself left no notes to convey his side of this singular meeting of the cabinet.

John Hay observed that the president thought the meeting "a great bore, but blew less than Stanton." Lincoln was in the midst of sad times. He had lost his beloved Willie, age twelve, to typhoid only the previous month, and some felt that he had been distracted since that event.

When the gathering disbanded around noon, Lincoln directed McClellan, Meigs, and Dahlgren to immediately stretch a blockade across the Potomac south of Washington. Stanton then dictated telegrams to the governors of all the coastal states north of Washington warning them of the approach of the *Merrimack* and ordering them to "prepare . . . all possible resources of their own for defence," including rafts of logs at harbor mouths, according to Nicolay.

General McClellan went further, hastening dispatches to commanders of forts along the coast that urged them not only to stand by their cannons but to wheel "temporary batteries" into position to face the Confederate nemesis. Commodore Hiram Paulding, commandant of the New York (or Brooklyn) Navy Yard, was asked to charter the 230-foot *Vanderbilt*, the pride of Commodore Cornelius Vanderbilt's line and, at 3,300 tons, the largest steamship in transatlantic service excepting the *Great Eastern*. It was recommended that the *Vanderbilt*'s bow be filled with timbers and that her sides be iron-plated. She would then sally forth like a mailed knight "at whatever risk" and smash the *Merrimack* into splinters and junk metal.

Cabinet officers crossed jurisdictions willy-nilly, and military leaders trespassed on the prerogatives of others without pausing for breath, much less apologies.

Dahlgren donned an army artilleryman's cap and ordered huge guns and mortars at Giesboro Point, a mile or so south of Washington on the Potomac. It never occurred to the otherwise calculating engineer that in the almost impossible event that the ironclad could steam that far, she would run hard aground and allow riflemen on the banks—perhaps even little boys with rocks—to pick off her sailors at will when they inevitably emerged. Dahlgren thought that the *Merrimack* could make it up the Potomac without grounding, but how could he be sure she could even steam out of Lynnhaven Roads, clearing all the shallows and bars in the area? And what about her gluttony for coal? Where would she replenish her bunkers? Such questions were never even introduced.

General Meigs, switching hats handily to that of naval expert, suggested that boarding parties from "swift steamers" clamber onto the *Merrimack* and "throw cartridges, grenades or shells down her smoke pipes."

For unabashed usurpation, sophomoric imagination, and shameless gall, however, the creation of what Lincoln coined "Stanton's Navy" had to be the lunatic tour de force on the day when Chicken Little ruled the roost. Blandly ignoring the secretary of the navy, Secretary of War Stanton managed to commandeer sixteen canal boats and barges—"if necessary, without consent of owner" were his orders—load them with stone, and arrange for tugs and small steamers to tow them downriver for scuttling. Eight were actually underway by midafternoon. In the hysteria of the moment, no one seemed to take stock of what might prove a literal impasse, and one of Stanton's creation: If the river were obstructed so that the monster could not plow *up* the Potomac, how could a tethered Federal navy steam *down* to offer battle?

With destiny resting in such hands, it was small wonder that Senator William Pitt Fessenden of Maine remembered: "I confess I was so frightened . . . I could not eat my dinner!"

During that morning of trepidation and unrest, the real drama was being enacted in Hampton Roads. *Merrimack*, a bit scarred, minus her ram, appeared about 7:00 A.M. to finish off the USS *Minnesota*. Commodore "Old Buck" Buchanan, the captain of the *Merrimack*, had been wounded by a soldier on shore Saturday and was not aboard. Her executive and ordnance officer, Lieutenant Catesby Jones, had succeeded to command. Jones had recognized the *Monitor* in the illumination cast by the fiercely burning *Congress* the previous evening, yet for reasons known only to him, he did not confide that intelligence to his staff. The *Merrimack*'s four small wooden consorts—three gunboats and a tug—were left in ignorance. Aboard the sidewheeler *Patrick Henry*, Lieutenant James H. Rochelle spotted "an immense shingle floating on the water, with a gigantic cheese box rising from its center; no sails, no wheels, no smokestack, no guns. *What* could it be?"

Apparently, the *Merrimack* and the *Minnesota* opened fire simultaneously as range was closed. While Captain Gershon van Brunt, commander of the *Minnesota*, swung his stern guns into action, his man-o'-war was shaken by a solid ball crashing into her starboard side. "Attack the enemy!" was van Brunt's quite unnecessary order to Lieutenant Commander Worden, whose *Monitor* had lain alongside all night. The time was about 8:00 A.M.

To those on shore, the outcome appeared preordained, a repeat of Saturday's debacle. On the ramparts of Fort Monroe, which served as a kind of grandstand, the correspondent for the *Baltimore American* squinted through a telescope. He concluded that the tiny *Monitor* was "the reverse of formidable." Close beside him, Bill Rogers, a young private with the Tenth New York Regiment, decided even before the opening of hostilities that "this odd little craft [is] no match for the great monster!" And Frederick Curtis, a gunner from the sunken *Congress*, expressed the fears of most of the Union gallery in saying: "We did not have much faith in the *Monitor*; we all expected to see the *Merrimack* destroy her." He was seconded by Dr. Edward Shippen, surgeon from the *Congress*, who offered: "She seemed so small and trifling . . . an additional prey for the leviathan."

The seawise Worden steered the *Monitor* "upstream against the tide" for better control, swung his turret, and got off the first shot. It appeared to hit just where it was aimed, "plump on the waterline." The *Merrimack* replied with a broadside that, according to Paymaster William Keeler of the *Monitor*, "rattled on our iron decks like hailstones."

Aboard the *Merrimack*, Lieutenant Jones, the acting captain, was frustrated on many scores. He had steamed out primarily to engage and destroy the *Minnesota*, and he thought that his pilots were overly wary of sand bars, keeping him "not at any time nearer than a mile" from the Federal flagship. Jones had a great deal of trouble keeping track of the *Monitor*'s guns, since its turret revolved so rapidly. Most distressing of all to Jones was the fact that "it did not appear to us that our shells had any effect upon the *Monitor*," while his adversary's shots "did not often miss."

The handsome steam sloop USS *Minnesota*.

Then the *Merrimack* ran onto a shoal, allowing both the *Monitor* and the *Minnesota* to fire round after round at her.

"We lashed down the safety valves, heaped quick-burning combustibles into the already raging fires, and brought the boilers to a pressure that would have been unsafe under ordinary circumstances," wrote H. Ashton Ramsay, the *Merrimack*'s chief engineer. "The propeller churned the mud and water furiously, but the ship did not stir. We piled on oiled cotton waste, splints of wood, anything that would burn faster than coal. . . . Just as we were beginning to despair, there was a perceptible movement and the *Merrimack* slowly dragged herself off the shoal by main strength."

Jones thought he'd better ram, even though the *Merrimack*'s big iron prow was gone. It consumed the better part of half an hour to maneuver the clumsy craft into position. The reporter for the *Baltimore American* watched the collision from Fort Monroe and observed that the *Monitor* "spun around like a top." After her crew could focus their eyes again, the *Monitor* got off another shot.

The *Merrimack* had sustained no mortal wound from the big missiles, but she was leaking from having gone aground. Jones decided to dispatch boarders in the hope that his men could fight their way inside the otherwise invulnerable turret of the *Monitor* with cutlasses. Worden sensed Jones's intention and dropped astern.

The *Merrimack* again directed her fire at the *Minnesota*, whose officers appeared more concerned with the damage to their china pantry than with the present physical danger. Now they would have to eat off tin plates like their crewmen. A hit started a small fire amidships. Although van Brunt would log some "consternation," the flames were soon extinguished.

The *Monitor* pluckily placed herself once more between the flagship and the *Merrimack* and solidly fielded the next shot. The *Merrimack*'s gunners' line of sight to the *Minnesota* was thus obstructed.

Maneuvering again, the *Monitor* passed so close to the *Merrimack*'s stern that she almost hit her propeller. In the process, Jones discovered the *Monitor*'s weak spot, the low-lying, boxlike pilothouse (or "conning" house) forward. A direct hit dislodged the iron logs sheltering the house and carried away steering gear and signal apparatus. Worden was stunned and blinded. Command of the *Monitor* passed to Lieutenant Samuel Dana Greene, the executive officer.

The *Monitor* had been hit twenty-one times, while firing off some forty-three rounds. Even so, she was not out of ammunition. Neither was the *Merrimack*, which did not log her expenditure of ordnance. The two warships were now commanded by acting captains who were thoroughly exhausted. Both men had had enough. So had their sweat-drenched crews.

"I am going to haul off under the guns of Sewell's Point," Jones reported, "and renew the attack on the rise of the tide." It was noon. The battle had consumed four hours.

Greene maneuvered his little vessel back to the side of the flagship. The *Monitor* deserved full credit for saving the *Minnesota* that day, though the more than five hundred rounds of shot and shells fired at the

Artist's depiction of Rear Admiral John A. Dahlgren before a fleet of monitors. Fort Sumter is also in the background.

Merrimack from the flagship's big guns over the previous twenty-four hours had also been a significant factor in the engagement.

About 4:00 P.M. that Sunday, the final link in the Signal Corps telegraph line was connected. Assistant Secretary of the Navy Gustavus V. Fox, newly arrived in Hampton Roads from Washington, dictated a message to Gideon Welles detailing the day's events. Fox concluded that "the *Monitor* is uninjured and ready at any moment to repel another attack."

Welles received the message shortly after 9:00 P.M., as he was preparing for bed. Moments earlier, he had been informed by Dahlgren that "Stanton's Navy" was in place. Some of the barges were about to be scuttled. Welles dressed and ran excitedly over to the White House. Ushered into Lincoln's study, he blurted out that Washington had been saved and that, in a very literal manner of speaking, "Goliath had met his David."

The president remained worried, however. He issued orders "that the *Monitor* be not too much exposed, and that in no event shall any attempt be made to proceed with her unattended to Norfolk."

Lincoln's concern would prove unwarranted. The *Merrimack* was in bad shape, with bent and broken plates, crushed ribs and beams, and solid-shot indentations everywhere. As before, her machinery was functioning poorly. She would never offer battle again.

Even so, the cities on the East Coast did not feel altogether secure until the *Merrimack* was scuttled by her own crew two months after the epochal battle, when Norfolk was evacuated by the Confederates on May 10 and the big ironclad would have been left at the mercy of Federal artillery.

The *Monitor* did not outlast her opponent by many months. She sank in a gale off Cape Hatteras on New Year's morning 1863, while she was under tow to Pamlico Sound. Her remains, surprisingly well-preserved, were not located and photographed until 1973.

Many questions remain entombed with the *Monitor*, with the wreckage of the *Merrimack* in the mud of the Elizabeth River, and especially in the graves of both ships' officers. What if Worden and Buchanan had faced each other and Worden not been wounded? Might more skillful maneuvering have forced the *Merrimack* onto shoals a second time, where she could have been pounded into surrender? If the old salt Buchanan had been at the helm, might he have rammed the *Monitor* into so much scrap? With both senior commanders directing the battle, might it have ended in a naval donnybrook with both craft sunk or afire?

In 1916, when the British Grand Fleet and the kaiser's High Seas Fleet slugged it out with staggering losses, each side claimed victory. Such was the case after the battle at Hampton Roads. The debate continues.

The Confederacy would launch other ironclads, including the *Virginia II*, the *Albemarle*, and the *Tennessee*, yet none would have the power to evoke such cold, lurking dread as the whispered, chilling warning: "The *Merrimack* is coming!"

The Washington Navy Yard. Note the monitors at anchor on the right and the pyramid of cannon-balls beside the wharf.

The ferry *Westfield* was reincarnated as a shallow-water gunboat. She ran the forts at New Orleans, only to be scuttled in the disaster off Galveston.

Chapter 2

THE FIGHTING FERRYBOATS

"Our country expects every man to do his duty!"

SQUADRONS UPON SQUADRONS OF THE Union's warships were dignified as such by name alone. They were fighting vessels by arbitrary listing. Their magnitude, shape, and general presence inspired neither dread nor awe. If the rebellion were ever to be suppressed, making do had to become a creed both on land and at sea. It was natural that ocean steamers should be mobilized, but ferryboats?

One morning in the spring of 1861, a cluster of New Yorkers ambled down to a familiar pier at the Battery intending to take their regular ferry to Staten Island, either the big *Westfield* or her sister, the *Clifton*. Neither was there. A smaller, wearier boat rested in the slip. The *Westfield* and the *Clifton*, comfortable friends and protectors through fair weather and thick, had paddled off to war.

Farther up the debris-strewn Hudson, the story was repeated. Down the coast, near Wilmington, the venerable *Delaware* was nowhere to be seen. She had been abruptly removed from her longstanding run across the river to Bridgeport, New Jersey.

And so it went that first wartime spring and summer up and down the eastern seaboard from Boston to Baltimore. Like so many overage men summoned to the colors, the well-weathered ferryboats tooted off to help save the Union. The *Westfield*, *Clifton*, and *Delaware* were joined by more than twenty others, some bearing their original christenings, others given new identities by the navy—*Commodore Barney* (once the *Ethan Allen*), six other "*Commodores*" (*Hull*, *Jones*, *McDonough*, *Morris*, *Perry*, and *Read*), *John P. Jackson*, *R. B. Forbes*, *Morse* (formerly *Marion*), *Southfield*, *Whitehall*, *Hunchback*, *Stepping Stones*,

Shohocken, and others. The *Shohocken* had originally been another, smaller *Clifton*, also plying to and from Manhattan and christened in honor of Clifton, New Jersey. The boats were bargains, generally purchased outright. Some went for as little as thirty-five thousand dollars.

The Union's nautical arm was desperate for vessels that could push up bays, rivers, and estuaries, sniffing out the enemy like so many bird dogs plunging into swamps for ducks or geese. Most of the ferries drew only six or seven feet of water. The majority were sidewheelers whose maneuverability compensated for their relatively slow speed. The boats averaged only 7 knots, with the larger ones capable of 12 or 13.

The *Westfield*, at 822 tons, and the *Clifton*, at 892 tons, were easily the "bruisers" of the fleet. The *Westfield* was at least 215 feet long and the *Clifton* 210 feet, some 80 feet longer than many ferryboats. With mixed motives of patriotism and profit, Commodore Cornelius Vanderbilt himself had sold the *Westfield* to the navy for a hundred thousand dollars, making her the most expensive acquisition of her class.

Workhorses designed for heavy cargo, almost any of the ferries could mount several guns, even a big 9-inch cannon. Those with identical bows and sterns carried a cannon on each end. The weakness of the ferries was that they were not oceangoing. They braved the Atlantic at peril of swamping. "Ferryboats, I fear," observed Rear Admiral Goldsborough, who commanded the North Atlantic Blockading Squadron, "are not likely to get along well on our coast, either at this or any other season of the year. They suffer severely from the seas, even when comparatively moderate in force."

But off they gamely waddled. Like the bee, which is held aerodynamically incapable of flight yet flies anyhow, the ferryboats did not understand that they could not go into the open ocean, and they steamed obliviously forth.

If some of their disproportionately large crews—almost a hundred on the *Westfield*, which could operate with about a dozen officers and men in peacetime—were summer sailors or even landlubbers, the same was not true of their officers. The navy dipped into its meager reservoir and endowed the top command of most ferryboats and tugs with Naval Academy graduates like Lieutenants Stephen P. Quackenbush, class of '46, of the *Delaware*; Richard T. Renshaw, '47, of the *Commodore Barney*; and Charles W. Flusser, '53, of the *Commodore Perry*. One exception who might have proved the rule was Commander William B. Renshaw of the *Westfield* (not related to Renshaw of the *Commodore Barney*), who had served as a commercial master.

By late fall and early winter, the ferryboats had been commissioned and were dispatched south one by one. The initial stop was the major anchorage off Fort Monroe in Hampton Roads, no easy journey for a ferry in the wildness of the wintertime North Atlantic.

The ferryboats' first action came in January and February 1862 in General Ambrose Burnside's expedition to seize Albemarle and Pamlico sounds in North Carolina, just south of Norfolk. The sounds

The ferryboat *Commodore Perry* saw action in Pamlico and Albemarle sounds. Note the details in this glass-negative original, especially the larger ships in the background and the supply wagons on the pier.

provided refuge from the storms off Hatteras. Eight rivers emptied into them, providing waterways to the major railheads of New Berne (now New Bern) and Elizabeth City, which were considered vital for the retaking of Norfolk, Raleigh, and Richmond.

Flag Officer Goldsborough was in command. Commodore Stephen C. Rowan, like Goldsborough a veteran of the Mexican War, led six ferryboats. Roanoke Island, one of the earliest settlements in America, fell first. As the attack started, Commodore Rowan issued the Nelsonian proclamation: "Our country expects every man to do his duty!"

Charles Flusser's *Commodore Perry* fought with special gallantry. The rotund, bearded Flusser was a former professor at the Naval Academy. Men sought to be assigned to him because of his ability and his compassion. Flusser exhausted all of his vessel's ammunition—170 shells and 20 shrapnel—at a distance of only eight hundred yards from enemy guns. According to Flusser's account, the *Perry* was "struck eight or nine times by round shot, one shot passing through two empty powder tanks, another between the engine and machinery and through one of our two water tanks. . . . Had the enemy fired shell instead of round shot we must have been destroyed. The only casualty on board was a broken leg, resulting from a large splinter." During the seizure of Elizabeth City, Flusser captured the CSS *Sea Bird*, the flagship of Confederate Commodore W. F. Lynch's so-called mosquitoes. Most of the officers and crew were made prisoners, though Lynch himself escaped.

At Elizabeth City, John Davis, a gunner's mate aboard the large steamer USS *Valley City*, became the war's first Medal of Honor winner in the navy. Davis sat on an open powder keg while others extinguished a magazine fire.

Winton and Plymouth, on the Roanoke River, were in Union hands by the expedition's finale in mid-March, as was New Berne. No ferryboats were lost, though the *Perry, Southfield, Delaware*, and *Hunchback* had acquired many bullet holes and other scars of combat.

The North Carolina sounds had barely been secured when Commander Renshaw of the *Westfield* led a mortar flotilla in Admiral David Glasgow Farragut's assault upon New Orleans. Renshaw's group was composed of twenty old schooners, each mounting a monstrous mortar.

The *Westfield* and the ferry *Jackson* also transported officers and supplies among the large ships of the fleet and even pushed menacing fire rafts out of harm's way. Those ancient weapons of naval warfare were old rafts piled with dry brush, doused with turpentine, and sent ablaze downriver. The largest among them were known as "Hollins Rams." The two ferries fought the fire rafts until April 21, when the fleet passed the twin Forts Jackson and St. Philip, which guarded the Mississippi approaches to New Orleans.

Within two months, the little boats were helping to carry the attack up the Mississippi to Vicksburg, whose high bluffs generously mounted with cannon offered a formidable defense. The luck of the ferries began to change. *Westfield, Jackson*, and *Clifton* were all hit but not disabled. They were moved down the Mississippi again.

They were next called to attack Galveston Island in the gulf, a vital cotton port and the gateway to all of Texas and the Southwest. In October, William Renshaw and the *Westfield* led a group that captured the island. He then established a small garrison.

Renshaw and his men would not hold it for long. General John Bankhead Magruder, McClellan's nemesis before Richmond, launched a counterattack on New Year's Day, employing a tatterdemalion fleet of harbor craft "armored" with bales of cotton. Artillery pieces were rolled onto their rotten decks. Magruder threw the Federals out of Galveston and captured the flagship *Harriet Lane*, formerly of the Revenue Cutter Service, one of the fastest ships in the blockade.

Representing Magruder, Major Leon Smith, a Confederate marine, demanded the surrender of all Union vessels present. Renshaw countered by ordering all the vessels to leave port as soon as possible. Since the *Westfield* had run aground, Renshaw prepared to blow her up.

Something went wrong. As Renshaw prepared to be the last to leave the ship, the *Westfield* exploded prematurely. Thus did Bill Renshaw become the first commander of the fighting ferryboats to give "the last full measure of devotion." Led by the *Clifton*, the surviving Union vessels departed. The Confederates would later charge that Union commanders violated a truce arrangement by steaming out under white flags. Whatever the case, Renshaw and the *Harriet Lane* were irreplaceable losses.

After withdrawing to positions from ten to thirty miles out in the gulf, the Union ships were watched over by the 2,070-ton sloop-of-war *Brooklyn*. Among the battle-scarred little fleet was the ferry *Hatteras*. In her previous modus vivendi as the *St. Mary's*, she had plied the Delaware River between Wilmington and Pennsville, New Jersey, close to the *Delaware*'s route.

In the early afternoon on January 11, the *Hatteras*'s captain, Lieutenant Commander Homer C. Blake, received orders from the flagship *Brooklyn* to investigate a suspicious sail on the horizon. By forcing his engines, Blake was able to overtake the intruder before dusk. She was a big steam sloop of unknown flag and intent. Blake challenged her by light signals: "What ship?"

"His Britannic Majesty's ship *Petrel*!" came the shouted reply.

Blake ordered a boat lowered to check on the "*Petrel*'s" papers. Someone seemed to have forgotten that Victoria was queen. It was *Her* Britannic Majesty. The *Hatteras*'s time had run out.

"Almost simultaneously with the piping away of the boat," Blake would recall, "the strange craft replied, 'we are the Confederate steamer *Alabama*!'" The announcement was accompanied by the unfurling of the Stars and Bars and a crashing broadside from what looked and sounded like every cannon on board. Somehow, the ferryboat withstood the blow and returned fire. The two were so close that their crews began to exchange musket and revolver shots.

"The firing continued with great vigour," according to Blake. "At length a shell entered amidships in the hold, setting fire to it, and at the same instant . . . a shell passed through the sick bay, exploding in an adjoining compartment, producing a fire. Another entered the cylinder, filling the engine room with steam, and depriving me of power."

Remarkably, only two of the *Hatteras*'s crew were killed, with five wounded. There remained no alternative but to hoist a white signal light in token of surrender. It was no contest—a Delaware ferry against a fully armed man-o'-war. The *Alabama*'s crusty but correct commander, Captain Raphael Semmes, accepted Blake's sword and welcomed him aboard. Semmes not only provided his own cabin for Blake, but had set a bottle of fine old Spanish brandy by his bunk as well.

Everything that could *did* go wrong for Major General Nathaniel P. Banks's Department of the Gulf and its small complement of ferryboats. In early September 1863, Banks attempted to "effect a landing" at Sabine Pass, some seventy miles east of Galveston at the mouth of the strategic Sabine River, which leads northward along the Texas-Louisiana border. It seemed a reasonable assumption that four gunboats, seven supply ship–transports, and four thousand soldiers could do the job.

"The attack which was to have been a surprise, and made early at dawn on the 7th," noted Commodore Henry H. Bell, commander of the West Gulf Blockading Squadron, "was not made until 3 P.M. on the 8th after the entire expedition had appeared off Sabine for 48 hours, and a reconnaissance was made on the morning of the 8th."

The day was consumed "in chasing and collecting different divisions of transports," recalled Master Howard Tibbits of the *Arizona*, a transport.

The pilot of the ill-starred *Clifton* was a day late in coming aboard, but her new commanding officer, Lieutenant Frederick Crocker, decided on a reconnaissance anyhow. Crocker steamed into the wrong pass, recognized his error, and steamed out again. The enemy could watch his antics even without long glasses. As a *coup de grâce* to Union plans, an army engineer had defected to the Confederates and presumably told all he knew.

The *Clifton* was hit in the engine room and put out of action. Aground, she was raked by shore batteries until she surrendered. Her consort, *Sachem*, which had not even upped anchor, followed suit. Losing heart, army commanders called the expedition off.

Though they took their lumps, the little ferryboats materially aided some Federal victories while diverting the Confederates' attention in waterways from the Carolinas to the gulf. They maintained the Union's advantage while more modern ships like the monitors were being added to the fleet.

Even in the late spring of 1864, Charles Flusser, by then a lieutenant commander, counted a few of the ferries among his squadron based at Washington, North Carolina. Flusser's flagship was the double-ender *Miami*. He needed all the firepower he could get, since the big Confederate ram *Albemarle* was prowling Pamlico Sound much at will.

Albemarle? What manner of warship was she, and how could the meager ferryboat force play a role in stopping her?

Rumors had commenced early in 1863 that a successor to the *Merrimack* was being built in the cornfields of North Carolina on a tributary of the Roanoke River. She was said to be the brainchild of a veteran naval officer with the auspicious name of Isaac Newton Brown, a man who had resigned his Federal commission almost before hostilities began.

Alarm spread not only through the Union fleet in Pamlico and Albemarle sounds but to the naval base in Norfolk and the mighty army bastion of Fort Monroe. It was as if a monstrous dinosaur had emerged fully preserved from the nearby Dismal Swamp and was on the prowl to destroy and devour everything in sight.

Knowing neither the dimensions nor the name of the supposed juggernaut, the Navy Department was nonetheless so concerned that old schooners and other hulks were sunk in the Roanoke, leaving a channel known only to Union pilots, an expedient designed to protect the town of Plymouth and the fleet from the mighty ram. Then came some information from a spy; the vessel was no figment of the imagination, though nowhere near as large or formidable as the late *Merrimack*. She was almost 160 feet overall, armored with two layers of 2-inch iron plating and a main battery of six cannon, including 8-inchers. Her prow was a solid oak ram covered with 2 inches of iron. Even Isaac Newton Brown and his engineers were unsure of her tonnage.

Finally, on April 17, 1864, word spread through the Union squadron that the *Albemarle* had at last emerged from her cocoon and was on her way to Plymouth along the narrow Roanoke. In command, for lack of someone more experienced with this radical type of craft, was Captain J. W. Cooke, who had earlier participated in the unsuccessful defense of the sounds.

Action commenced on the river and along the shore. During the night of April 18, the ships joined Union troops in forcing back a Confederate attack on two so-called forts, Gray and Williams, protecting Plymouth. Like most secondary or make-do "forts," Gray and Williams featured two or three minor-caliber cannon and soldiers with muskets.

At 12:30 A.M. on April 19, a Tuesday, word arrived: "The ram is coming!" Flusser ordered the ferry *Southfield* chained to his *Miami* to present more concentrated firepower.

"At 3:45 A.M.," William N. Welles, executive officer of the *Miami*, would report, "the gunboat *Ceres* came down, passing near, giving the alarm that the ram was close upon her. . . . Flusser immediately came on deck and ordered both vessels to steam ahead as fast as possible and run the ram down. . . . Our starboard chain was slipped and bells rung to go ahead fast. . . . In less than two minutes from the time she was reported she struck us upon our port bow near the water line."

"Her prow cut through the forward storeroom and into the fireroom," recalled Lieutenant Charles A. French, commanding the *Southfield*. "Our two vessels opened a rapid fire, both of great guns and musketry. When I found the *Southfield* sinking, I ordered her crew to leave in the boats."

On the *Miami*, Welles observed to his dismay that "solid shot from the 100-pounder Parrott rifles and IX-inch Dahlgren guns [made] no perceptible indentations in [the *Albemarle*'s] armor. Commander Flusser fired the first three shots personally, the third being a 10-second Dahlgren shell, IX-inch." The ram continued firing "with her bow pivot gun and kept up a continuous hail of musketry." As the *Miami*'s stern swung in, the crew from the sinking *Southfield* jumped on board. Lieutenant French wanted to report to Captain Flusser. Only then did he learn that the commander had "perished instantly . . . from a fragment of a shell while cheering on and inspiring his men."

Flusser was dead, and almost a dozen of his crew were seriously wounded. The *Southfield* was lost, as was the town of Plymouth. Through brilliant piloting, however, Welles was able to avoid a second charge of the *Albemarle* and save the *Miami*.

Not quite three weeks later, the big ram appeared again, this time with an escort of two lesser ships. Prepared to meet her were six Union double-enders and ferries.

"All eyes were fixed on this second *Merrimac* as, like a floating fortress, she came down the bay," wrote Assistant Surgeon Edgar Holden of the *Sassacus*, a double-ender like the *Miami*. "A puff of smoke from her bow port opened the 'ball,' followed quickly by another."

The battle was as rapid as it was wild. Flanking the Confederate attacker, the well-disciplined Federal gunboats forced one of the *Albemarle*'s escorts, a captured steamer named *Bombshell*, to strike her colors after being hulled time and again by heavy shells. Then came the moment for which the *Sassacus* had planned and practiced. All hopes rested on the strength of the three-ton "bronze beak" that had been fitted onto her prow.

"Lay her course for the junction of the casemate and the hull!" Lieutenant Commander Francis A. Roe shouted to the helmsman. Roe ordered full steam.

"It was a moment of intense strain and anxiety," Assistant Surgeon Holden reported. "The guns ceased firing, the smoke lifted from the ram. . . . Straight as an arrow we shot forward to the designated spot. Then came the order, 'all hands lie down!' and with a crash that shook the ship like an earthquake, we struck full and square on the iron hull, careening it over and tearing away our own bows, ripping and straining timbers at the waterline."

The *Sassacus* "quivered for an instant." The *Albemarle* recovered long enough to bang off one huge ball point-blank that sent Union sailors "whirling around" like tops. Then the two disengaged. The *Albemarle* returned to her anchorage at Plymouth, never again to offer battle (her ultimate fate is the subject of chapter 9), much as the *Merrimack* before her.

Those who perished with their little ferryboats are largely forgotten, save for a plaque here and there and Flusser's grave at the Naval Academy. Only seventeen boats limped back after the war. Left behind in the marshes and estuaries of the East Coast and the gulf were the ribs and the broken, rusting iron of at least five ferryboats. The survivors were sold for whatever they would bring; most were sold as salvage. Few would ever be found in their slips again. A chapter in ferryboat transportation had all but ended, as engineers were learning how to bridge even broad rivers and yawning bays.

In the wake of the fighting ferryboats were wonderful deeds, if imperfectly recorded. Even as they had appeared from obscurity in a time of great need, they disappeared, paddling off into oblivion.

Wartime Nashville, as seen from the Capitol.

National Archives

THE ORDEAL OF CAPTAIN NEWCOMB

"Lt. Col. George Spalding, Provost Marshal,
is hereby directed and without loss of time to
seize and transport to Louisville all pros-
titutes found in this City."

EARLY IN THE WAR, it was the best of times (with no especial apologies to Charles Dickens) in Nashville, the capital of Tennessee, a city of twenty thousand. The more prosperous among the citizens still owned their slaves and held lucrative war contracts with Richmond. The imposing "Rock City" astride the Cumberland River was a modest island of peace and prosperity within a perimeter of battle and want.

Then, in early February 1862, little-known Federal General Ulysses S. Grant stormed Fort Henry on the Ohio River and its companion, Fort Donelson, on the Cumberland. Nashville was abandoned not only by its defender, General Albert Sidney Johnston, but also by Governor Isham Harris. On Monday evening, February 24, Mayor Richard B. Cheatham surrendered his city. One of the very few people who cheered was an old sea captain named William Driver, who had long awaited the moment when he could unfurl the Stars and Stripes above his residence.

All at once, it became the worst of times for the people of Nashville. The city was now a "prisoner of war," according to one sorrowful citizen.

Major General Don Carlos Buell, commander of the Federal Army of the Ohio, ordered Nashville's banks to reopen and its businesses to resume operations. In March, Senator Andrew Johnson, a

Tennessean, was dispatched by President Lincoln to become the military governor. To many inhabitants, Johnson was little more than a traitor. He unlocked the doors of the emptied statehouse and repopulated it with Unionists. While offering amnesty, he simultaneously threatened banishment of those who refused to take the oath of allegiance. Most acceded, though some very halfheartedly. Johnson then commandeered the Southern Methodist and Baptist publishing houses in an effort to keep up with mounting Union paperwork. He closed down the *Nashville Times*, which had thumped for secession, and permitted other papers to print only if their loyalty was impeccable.

Nashville changed radically as it was converted into a military supply depot. The whistles of locomotives and steamboats shrilled well into the night as freight was unloaded for the Union armies. A dozen wood-burning locomotives with their bulbous funnels might be counted at any one time beside the Church Street depot, spewing smoke and sparks skyward. The University of Nashville, the Female Academy, and other schools, along with some hotels and private residences, were remodeled for use as hospitals, making Nashville a center for the wounded and sick. The sprawling Maxwell House (which would give its name to the popular coffee brand) became a vast barracks.

On April 6 and 7, 1862, the second great battle of the war was fought at Shiloh, or Pittsburg Landing, along the Tennessee River about 110 miles southwest of Nashville. That bloody clash took the life of General Johnston and produced a shocking twenty-three thousand casualties, with more than thirty-five hundred killed. The casualty rate represented about 25 percent of those engaged. Most of the Confederate troops had been driven from Tennessee, but at a monumental price. Union General Buell removed his entire army, leaving only a weak garrison—a mere two thousand—to guard Nashville.

Through the spring and early summer, the city was menaced by Confederate cavalry leaders Colonel Nathan Bedford Forrest and General John Hunt Morgan. The remaining Union officers were so concerned over the possibility that the two might join forces that they ordered trees cut down and fences removed to provide corner barricades and a clearer line of sight for the artillery. Andrew Jackson's lovely Hermitage became a strong point in Nashville's defense.

Lawlessness persisted as an internal menace. The streets "swarmed with a host of burglars, brass-knuckles and slingshot ruffians, pickpockets and highwaymen," wrote one resident. A local editor, worried that such a description was not fully inclusive, added "thugs . . . robbers, assassins" to the list, then direly postscripted: "Murder stalks throughout the city almost every night!"

Less menacing to life and limb, if equally depraved, were those who anticipated the genre of black marketeers. Brazen opportunists, they traded to their own usurious advantage in food, clothing, and firearms from the shanty purlieu known as Slabtown. No punishments or threats leveled by the occupation forces at either the "thugs" and "assassins" or the city's shadowy demimonde proved a deterrent. The subculture thrived like poisonous weeds.

Food stocks dwindled, since farmers feared encounters with Forrest's and Morgan's cavalries while driving their wagons into the city. Besides, why feed the Yankees? Shops and even many saloons closed.

Nashville became increasingly dirty. Trash piled into small mountains was burned sporadically. Dead cats and horses decomposed in the open, a fetid lure for swarms of vultures. A correspondent for the *New York Times* wrote that Nashville's streets "even surpass those of New York in accumulated filth, dirt and garbage and, under this tropical sun, steam with odorous exhalations." The rat population thrived as summer temperatures soared to a hundred degrees. One writer mused that the Pied Piper himself would find a challenge beyond belief in Nashville.

In October, Major General William S. Rosecrans moved his fifty-thousand-man Army of the Cumberland into Nashville. This was partly at the behest of Governor Johnson, who had telegraphed Lincoln: "I'll be damned if Nashville shall be surrendered!" The presence of Rosecrans's army put to an end any hope of recapturing the city that the Confederates may have entertained. The soldiers patrolling the streets with fixed bayonets also dulled the edge of violent crime. Yet with the Rock City's population swelling to eighty thousand with the daily influx of refugee blacks, there appeared a new threat: disease.

Although the Union army had proven itself incapable of establishing sanitary conditions in Nashville, it endeavored to provide medical aid to the people. Smallpox was especially prevalent. Vaccination tents were set up for civilians and military personnel. A special camp was established for those already stricken. Local physicians were ordered to report all new cases. Still, the epidemic of the dread fever raged unabated. Army surgeons could only theorize that the citizens were not availing themselves of the free vaccinations. Those who were sick simply took to their beds, where, in most cases, they died. Finally, orders were issued that any residents who could not provide vaccination certificates would be escorted beyond the army's picket lines; they could then attempt to live off the land or struggle south toward Confederate territory. The epidemic ultimately waned, though it was not recorded in the surgeon general's files whether the military efforts deserved credit or whether the bacillus simply burned out.

Many sought an antidote to disease in alcohol. "Nashville whiskey" was as plentiful as the worthless Confederate currency that was still to be found in back alleys or wherever else the wind happened to blow it. Its consumption was having "a very bad effect upon soldiers now in our midst," wrote the *Nashville Dispatch* in bland understatement. Arrests, jail sentences, and even temporary prohibitions did little or nothing to curb intoxication and its attendant excesses, from brawls and property destruction to rape and murder.

Part and parcel of disease and intoxication was another historic camp follower: prostitution.

An impassioned *Nashville Daily Press* correspondent who wrote under the name "Scalpel" described "the foul breathing hole of hell which is belching forth its pestilential breath on those who are so placed as to be without restraining influences." He could have been referring to no place other than Smokey Row, a district spreading upward from the river, so named because of its opium dens. In Smokey Row's seventy or more brothels, hundreds of prostitutes ranging from teenagers to women in their sixties plied the most historic of trades. Some of the older ladies of easy virtue were owners of handsome properties reputed to be valued as high as twenty-five thousand dollars, the price tag of a mansion in 1863. The hustling sisters Rebecca and Eliza Higgins and their friend Martha Reeder were considered the queens of the madams in affluence, volume of business, and overall flair. John Wilkes Booth, who played at the Nashville Theater during the occupation, was rumored to have been a client of the Higginses. It was also whispered, with even less possibility of substantiation, that Andrew Johnson, whose wife was an invalid who lived in Washington, was no stranger to the same sisters. Historians long after the Civil War who thereby tried to establish a Booth-Johnson acquaintanceship went to their graves in unleavened frustration.

Continuing his minor philippic, Scalpel alluded to a soldier killed in that "accursed" place, then quickly conceded the adjective was "too mild a term." He then purported to quote the slain man's sister's lament: "Oh! if he had only died for his country . . . !"

Scalpel wrote that "life after life is lost in the dens around Smokey Row. Hundreds and probably thousands of soldiers are today in hospitals who would have been in the field but for its existence." He suggested that instead of being sent north, the women should "be loaded with whiskey and sent over our lines south where they will do more damage than the same number of smooth-bored five-pounders, especially if a keg of genuine rifled rotgut be sent along as an equivalent for the customary caisson."

Franklin Bailey, a young private stationed in Nashville, wrote his mother that he would need a dictionary "to find words enough, and then I could not find them bad enough to express my hatred of those beings calling themselves women." But he tried anyhow, denouncing the inhabitants of Smokey Row as "abominable, low, vile, mean, lewd, wanton, dissolute, licentious, vicious, immoral and wicked." The shocked Union volunteer of manifestly sheltered upbringing did not identify with the cavalier saying prevalent in those parts: "No man can be a soldier unless he has gone through Smokey Row."

By late spring of 1863, the citizens of Nashville, zealously led by the Bible-thumping clergy, had lashed themselves into a furor over the "Magdalenes" or "Cyprians." The local office of a national temperance and morals society may have spoken for the majority when it assailed the "libidinous women who are making of our fair city a second Gomorrah!"

The Federal commanders, however, were not watchdogs over their troops' morals. They were pragmatic about sin and soul-saving. Their concern was twofold—law and order had to be enforced, with the brawls and stabbings in the red-light district halted once and for all, and disease had to be brought under control. Syphilis and gonorrhea cases overflowed their assigned wards until a former school at the corner of Summer and Lime streets was designated General Hospital 15, for venereal disease patients only. It, too, filled up.

There was ambiguity about the post command at Nashville during June and part of July 1863. Brigadier General Robert S. Granger commanded the Third Division of the Reserve Corps of the Army of the Cumberland, while Brigadier General James D. Morgan commanded the Second Division. Granger assumed Morgan's administrative duties in late May, yet both men exercised authority and signed orders until Morgan took command in Murfreesboro, some twenty miles south of Nashville, about mid-July. In June, Granger complained that the whole odious brew of prostitution and disease had become "an unmitigated source of annoyance" to him. He noted that he was "daily and almost hourly beset by commanders and surgeons of regiments urging [me] to devise some method to rid the city of this class of women, in order to preserve the health and efficiency of [their] troops."

What was the answer?

Threats of punishment had proven no deterrent to the soldiers. Neither had the surgeons' limited bag of medicines been able to repulse the aggressive and durable little microbes. It was Morgan, the outgoing commander, who made the first move. It proved both imaginative and radical. On July 6, he issued "Special Orders No. 29," stating: "Lt. Col. George Spalding, Provost Marshal, is hereby directed and without loss of time to seize and transport to Louisville all prostitutes found in this City or known to be here. . . . The prevalence of a venereal disease at this Post has elicited the notice of the General Commanding who has ordered a peremptory remedy."

If Morgan sounded excessively "peremptory," he was only reflecting the mood of other Union fighters that July. Vicksburg had fallen to General Grant on July 4, inspiring President Lincoln's comment on the long-awaited opening of the Mississippi: "The Father of Waters again goes unvexed to the sea." And Lee's army had been badly mauled at Gettysburg, though the Confederates had conducted a successful retreat across the Potomac into Virginia.

Colonel Spalding faced two challenges: He had to find a means of "transport," and he had to physically round up "all prostitutes."

Accompanied by the assistant quartermaster of the post, Captain J. D. Stubbs, the provost made tracks to the river. Nashville Wharf and most of Front Street, especially the section north of Broad, were teeming with side- and sternwheelers. A number of them were under charter to the United States quartermaster, including a three-month-old vessel, the *Idahoe*. Like most on the western waters, she was over two hundred feet in length and of shallow draft and boasted a flexible capacity for both freight and passengers. Her captain and owner, John M. Newcomb, a bearded, rough-hewn veteran of the Cumberland and Ohio rivers, had in all likelihood raised about fifty thousand dollars to buy or at least take possession of the craft. Spalding did not confide in Captain Stubbs why he selected the *Idahoe* from among the Federal charters. Neither did he confide in Captain Newcomb.

Spalding then turned to his extraordinary roundup. The majority of the wayward were taken by surprise, caught in flying tackles by soldiers as they attempted to jump half-clad from second-story windows or to flee through rear doors. Others were marched kicking, biting, screaming, and swearing into quartermaster wagons at bayonet point.

In such a massive sweep, however, unfortunate errors were inevitable, as was manifested in the apprehension of respectable ladies who happened to be passing near the district of pariahs on their way to market—the fishmongers, for example, hawked their redolent wares on the fringes of Smokey Row. One officer, Lieutenant M. W. Ready, spent some time visiting newspaper offices to deny that he had caused "any decent female to be deported." But although Ready and his fellow officers endeavored to exercise "great prudence," a number of strait-laced Nashville damsels and dowagers were prodded along before the error was conceded.

A few "Magdalenes" attempted the familiar ploy of marrying soldiers. Who had tipped them off to their impending banishment? It may well have been the press. On Tuesday, July 7, the *Nashville Dispatch* was preparing a piece that would appear under the heading "Cyprians" the next morning: "We learn that Gen. Granger has given notice to a large number of women of the town that they must prepare to leave Nashville. It is said they are demoralizing the army, and that their removal is a military necessity. They are to be sent north. . . . If so, a fresh importation may be looked for by the return train."

Aboard his sternwheeler, Captain Newcomb had apparently not read the *Dispatch* that Wednesday morning, July 8, possibly because he was a man of leisurely rising habits when at dock. He was finishing a cup of coffee when a commotion marked by the shrillings of high-pitched voices conveyed to him that something considerably out of the ordinary was taking place. Newcomb was met at the gangplank by a stern-faced Colonel Spalding, who dismissed rudimentary formalities and slapped a written order in his hand:

Capt. Steamer *Idahoe*
Sir

You are hereby directed to Louisville Ky with one hundred (100) passengers put on Board your steamer today, allowing none to leave the Boat before reaching Louisville.

It was signed by the bearer, the provost marshal. Even as Newcomb read the curt directive, the women were being herded aboard, complaining, cursing, and muttering. A few kicked at their guards, who appeared more amused than angry.

The Nashville waterfront. The *Idahoe* resembled the sternwheelers in the foreground, if, indeed, she was not one of them. Note the remarkable stop-action for such a long exposure—the horse drinking, the men talking on the gangplank (perhaps about the carriage halfway in the water), and the dog sniffing behind the barrel.

"I protested against their putting these women on my boat," the rather stunned master would note, "she being a new boat only three months built, her furniture new, and a fine passenger boat. I told them it would forever ruin her reputation as a passenger boat if they were put on her [to make her a] floating whorehouse; and pointed out to them old boats that were in the service at the time, which would have answered the purpose as well as mine; but no: they said I must take them!"

Spalding's only reply was to point silently to the orders the hapless river captain still clutched. The women continued to file aboard, the troops packing them at random into cabins and public saloons.

Newcomb then inquired of Captain Stubbs, who had remained gravely at the provost's side: "How [are] these women . . . to be subsisted? . . . He told me I would have to see Gen. Morgan about that."

The master angrily donned his hat and coat and hurried into the city to confront the general in the state offices. "He told me to subsist them, myself," Newcomb wrote. "I entreated of him to let the Govt. subsist them, that it could do so for much less than I could, his reply was 'you subsist them!' I applied for a guard to be put aboard. Gen. Morgan told me I did not need any but to take charge of [the prostitutes] myself."

A river-steamer captain's pay was no more than two hundred dollars a month. Newcomb's income may have been even less, depending upon the amount of his cargo. He thus maintained that the commanding general was working a hardship of considerable magnitude.

With no food or other supplies, no medicines, and no guards, the *Idahoe* steamed up. That evening, with black smoke and sparks pouring from her twin fifty-foot funnels, located forward, she started upriver toward Ashland City, Clarksville, and destiny.

The next day, Thursday, July 9, the *Dispatch* continued to follow the story. "A large number of women of ill fame were embarked upon three or four steamers and transported northward," it was reported. "The number has been variously estimated at from 1,000 to 1,400—probably five or six hundred would be near the mark. Where they are consigned we are not advised, but suspect the authorities of the city in which they are landed will feel proud of such an acquisition to their population. We hope the commanding officer will issue an order as soon as possible, ordering off all contraband prostitutes—they contribute considerably more toward the demoralization of the army than any equal number of white women, and certainly have no more claims upon our sympathy." "Contrabands" were slaves who escaped into the Union lines. The passenger counts reported by the *Dispatch* cannot be verified.

The following day, the *Daily Press* cynically speculated that the "sudden expatriation of hundreds of vicious white women will only make room for an equal or larger number of Negro strumpets, who have always exerted by far the most deleterious influence." The editor demanded that the "aggravated curse of lechery," referring to the blacks, be "destroyed!"

The *Idahoe* paddled up the river past Cumberland City and Dover and across the Kentucky border to

Linton and Canton, steaming by the smoky glow of the Empire Iron Works during the night. After Eddyville, she at last entered the Ohio River near Smithland, Kentucky, more than a hundred miles from Nashville, and headed along the southern borders of Illinois and Indiana for Louisville.

On July 14, the *Idahoe* anchored off Louisville. The *Louisville Daily Democrat* noted that she had "on board one hundred and fifty women of ill repute." Newcomb's count was 111, but the way his unwelcome passengers milled around—oblivious to even the most rudimentary discipline, belaboring him all the while—made it impossible to ascertain just how many *were* aboard the *Idahoe*. The paper also reported: "Two more boats are expected in a day or two."

The journey had been pure hell. When not harassing the hapless master or cursing, the women had vented their frustrations by smashing their fists against the bulkheads and tearing off the veneer. The more muscular among them picked up chairs and shattered them against stanchions. "I had to buy meat and vegetables at enormous high prices from storeboats along the river," Newcomb lamented, "and in addition at many places, to buy ice and medicines, these women being diseased and more than one half of them sick in bed.

"I applied to the Commissary's . . . along the route, for . . . stores, to feed these women, but at each place was refused by the officers in charge, and the Civil as well as Military authorities would not allow my boat to land, and put guards along the shore to prevent me from doing so."

Supplies were only part of the captain's vexation. The women waved to men on shore and sometimes lowered their dresses over their shoulders. Even the dullest dolt could catch the message; bills were waved aloft in acknowledgment. "Having no guard," Newcomb wrote, "I could not keep men along the route from coming on board to these women, when at anchor and being angered because I strove to drive them away, both themselves and these bad women destroyed and damaged my boat, and her furniture to a great extent."

The master was forbidden to disembark his burden in Louisville, but Brigadier General Jeremiah T. Boyle, Kentucky's military governor, evinced a small measure of solicitude. As Newcomb reported, "He gave me a guard and ordered me to proceed to Cincinnati to await further orders there."

Meanwhile, the strait-laced Nashville journalists were expressing unleavened satisfaction. Under the headline "Better State of Things," the *Daily Press* wrote: "Since the decampment of the 'wayward daughters,' a decided improvement in the manners of our town is visible. The shameless behavior of these women upon our thoroughfares had long blighted the gentility of society, and now that we are rid of their presence, the young ladies and matrons of our city can resume their pleasure walks and shopping pilgrimages without being insulted."

On July 16, the *Idahoe* hove to at Newport, Kentucky, across the river from Cincinnati. For the guards placed aboard at Louisville, it had been a grand and satisfying trip. The women had not even charged them. The *Cincinnati Daily Gazette* noted: "The *Glide* came up yesterday, from Nashville, bringing a very fair cargo of freight, while the *Idahoe* also came up bringing a cargo of one hundred and fifty of the frail sisterhood of Nashville, who had been sent North under military orders. There does not seem to be much desire on the part of our authorities to welcome such a large addition to the already overflowing numbers engaged in their peculiar profession and . . . the poor girls are still kept on board."

"Much desire" was an understatement. Armed members of the Cincinnati constabulary were posted on the docks to prevent any attempt at landing the "frail sisterhood." On board, the protests, the debauchery, and the damage continued. The guards from Louisville had already been effectively seduced and were in no position to preserve even a modicum of order or to stop the women from hustling the *Idahoe*'s crew or "visitors" from shore. Men in rough work jackets kept rowing alongside under cover of darkness, clutching greenbacks with shaky anticipation.

Days later, the *Daily Gazette* chronicled: "The *Idahoe* still lies at Newport with its living cargo still on board, the municipal authorities of the cities of Cincinnati, Covington and Newport continuing to be too sternly virtuous to allow them to land."

In an act of desperation, Captain Newcomb managed to persuade the army's signal office to telegraph Secretary of War Stanton in Washington to advise him of the *Idahoe*'s plight.

Stanton was an experienced decision-maker accustomed to working out high-level gambits involving military operations, domestic challenges related to the war effort, and espionage, which he often feared to be lurking in his own office, but he was wholly unprepared to deal with a bunch of prostitutes on a river steamer off Cincinnati. *Why* did General Boyle and Andy Johnson, whom Stanton regarded with contemptuous indifference at best, bother him with such chaff? In mounting anger, the secretary of war dictated orders to send the *Idahoe* back to Nashville, where General Granger, under pain of reassignment to some remote field command, would *have* to receive the women.

After thirteen days that Captain Newcomb would never forget, the steamer sounded a blast on her whistle and headed westward for Rock City. On August 3, the "frail sisterhood" was industriously at work once more in Nashville, and river traffic on the Ohio and the Cumberland had reverted to its primary function, that of transporting Union troops.

While the return to Nashville marked the end of an incredible voyage, it did not complete the story. The chastened Granger, aware that his ploy to rid Nashville of prostitutes had been about as successful as General Lee's plan to invade the North through Gettysburg and Harrisburg, settled upon a more pragmatic expedient. He legalized prostitution.

Colonel Spalding, the provost, established the procedures. Every "public woman" had to be licensed for a fee of five dollars, providing she passed a physical examination. Under penalty of arrest and imprisonment, she then had to report every ten days for a checkup at a cost of one dollar per visit. Examinations were conducted in a remote part of Nashville in an old brick building that was converted toward the end of August into a hospital "for the reception of valetudinarian females from the unhealthy purlieus of Smokey."

For once in its checkered history, the army seemed to have satisfied everyone. The people of Nashville perceived an opportunity to redeem their fallen daughters. The latter were everlastingly thankful for the medical help rendered at reasonable cost. Some sixty were treated in the first weeks.

The surgeons grew fascinated with the sociology of prostitution. They prepared detailed "biographies" of 126 of the hundreds who passed through their unusual clinic, asking the women what circumstances had led them, young and old alike, into "this deplorable expedient."

There were many answers, or purported reasons. The subjects had been victimized by the "cruelties of their friends." Orphaned, they had been ill-treated by guardians whose indifference "drove them into the streets," or they had been "mistreated by husbands." The more outspoken confessed prostitution to be "an easy way to make money," while others were yet more unabashed in admitting they "just liked" what they were doing. These were summarily categorized as nymphomaniacs by the solemn physicians. (Indeed, many of the practitioners, in the tradition of St. Luke, could claim some experience of their own with such insatiable females.) Eleven women promised to lead "virtuous unmarried lives" thenceforth, while three times that number said they were ready to succumb to the conformity of marriage.

It was at this juncture that the commanding officers found out about the dubious research. The government, they maintained, cared not a whit about the ladies' morals or lack of them, or even their future, if any. The program was meant "solely for the purpose of preserving the health of the Army!"

That goal would be realized in a relatively few months. Surgeons from other occupied cities traveled to Nashville to study the plan. The number of soldiers reporting to the old brick building for treatment of venereal disease dwindled to negligible proportions.

Thanks in some small part to the personal sacrifice of Captain Newcomb, the military "health" of the Union army was proven in subsequent action in Tennessee. Major General George H. Thomas, commanding a hastily assembled army including the Nashville post, furiously fought back two assaults by Lieutenant General John B. Hood's Army of Tennessee—first at Franklin, fifteen miles south of Nashville, at the end of November 1864, and two weeks later in front of the city itself. (Hood had led his army out of Atlanta before the onrushing legions of Major General William T. Sherman.) Thomas then commanded the Army of the Cumberland. The Confederates' stinging defeat in Tennessee by the "Rock of Chickamauga" would be regarded by some historians as a death knell of the rebellion.

The twin victories ended the need for a large occupation force, but they did not put to rest the saga of the *Idahoe*. Captain Newcomb had been dunning the quartermaster for expenses and damages since August 3, 1863, only to be met with outright refusals or frustrating silence. Newcomb envisioned lower-grade clerks in the quartermaster's office tossing one after another of his plaintive communications into the trash.

In August 1865, some four months after Appomattox, a tired and harassed riverboat captain mopped his brow in the Washington humidity as he sat before the office of the secretary of war. In his pocket was a lengthy, handwritten chronicle of an abortive voyage to Louisville. John Newcomb's epistle concluded: "I wish to say to your honor that I was compelled to subsist these women, that it cost me all that I have made a charge for, to do so, that this claim is merely a reimbursement of my money which I had to expend while complying with the orders of the Officers of the United States Government. . . . I had to leave my business and travel from Cincinnati to [Washington] to see if I could collect it, it being over two years due me. I am here now one week going from one office to another, to see to get my papers, and to effect a settlement, which I have not yet done, nor a likelihood to have done, unless your honor will please to direct payment of this account so justly due me, and for so long a time."

Again, the unhappy master of the *Idahoe* received no satisfaction. Secretary Stanton was out of town. It was rumored that he was resting and fending off a potential nervous breakdown that threatened to arise from a burgeoning sense of guilt. There was good reason. That July, Stanton had played a key role in sending Mary Surratt, one of the four so-called Lincoln conspirators, to the gallows. A court-martial's recommendation for commutation in her case had been carefully kept from President Johnson, and certain editors had already denounced her execution as legalized murder.

Newcomb waited in vain through August, September, and most of October. Then, in the last week of the month, a letter was brought aboard the *Idahoe* at Cincinnati. Dated October 19, it was from the Third Auditor's Office of the Treasury Department, and it tendered payment "for damages to the State-rooms, furniture & bedding, cabin furniture, tableware, etc., on the Steamboat '*IDAHOE*,' by prostitutes transported by order of Gen. Morgan from Nashville, Tenn., to Louisville, Ky., . . . for subsistence and medicines furnished to 111 prostitutes . . . at the rate of $1.50 a day." Enclosed was a check for exactly $5316.04. It was about what Newcomb had initially requested. Now he could close the books on the disastrous summer of 1863.

Or could he?

As the *Idahoe* creaked and tooted her way through the rivers, even as far south as New Orleans, Newcomb was made aware that his original fears had been horribly realized. Little children along the banks jumped up and down at his passing and chanted: "Here comes the whorehouse!"

In bars, he was introduced as "the captain of the floating whorehouse." He tried to ignore it, but the passage of time did not seem to lessen the smart.

Finally, under another master, the *Idahoe* was sunk in 1869 in the Ouachita, or Washita, River, which flows through southwest Arkansas and Louisiana. The cause was not announced, though some river folk quipped that she had destroyed herself in shame.

John Newcomb sailed on with other stern- and sidewheelers. Years later, as the war receded into the limbo of semireality and he neared retirement, he chanced upon an allusion in a newspaper to the "faerie boat of love." The image brought back a flood of memories, not all of them pleasant.

Could it just possibly be referring to . . . ?

Drawing of the USS *Indianola*.

U.S. Naval Historical Center

Chapter 4

THE HOAX THAT CAME TO STAY

"An American flag was raised aft, and a
banner emblazoned with skull and crossbones
ornamented the bow."

LIGHT-YEARS DISSIMILAR from the *Idahoe* and Master Newcomb, the *Indianola* and Admiral Porter performed their own unique roles in putting down the rebellion.

Men and their ships have always acted upon each other to alter their respective destinies. The relationships were especially personal and dramatic in the Civil War. Even admirals accustomed to manipulating entire fleets were often diverted by the challenges and the needs of particular vessels. The *Indianola* was not Porter's flagship, but her fate was for a time intertwined with the admiral's fortunes.

Named for a city in Iowa south of Des Moines, *Indianola* was a 511-ton gunboat built at Cincinnati by the Joseph Brown works. Cincinnati contributed heavily to Union manufacturing, particularly with its shipbuilding facilities and ironworks. The larger sister of the *Tuscumbia* and *Chillicothe*, *Indianola* was armored with 3-inch iron plate, and she was powered by four engines that drove both sidewheels and a screw propeller. Yet even with all that propulsion, she could wheeze and strain only up to a maximum of 6 knots. Her avoirdupois was augmented by two heavy 11-inch and two 9-inch Dahlgren cannon. Since she drew a mere five feet of water, *Indianola* was created for river warfare and nothing else.

The price was considerable—exactly $183,662.56. When inquisitive reporters asked Joseph Brown how he figured the 56 cents, they were told bluntly to mind their own business. Indeed, the ironclad's specifications—especially her armament, armor, and engines—were considered so secret that the War Department joined the navy in forbidding newsmen from coming on board.

A late bloomer, the juggernaut of the western waters did not go into commission until October 1862. She rated the highest ranking officer in the area, Lieutenant Commander George Brown, commander of the naval forces of the Department of the Ohio. The twenty-seven-year-old from Rushville, Indiana, had graduated from Annapolis in 1855, and he had seen action with the blockading fleets off New Orleans and Mobile.

Although his clumsy vessel was imperfectly tested, she was urgently needed in the "Father of Waters." After his success at New Orleans, Farragut thought he could steam his fleet up the Mississippi and capture Vicksburg. It was not to be. The bluffs guarding the strategic river port provided a natural defense. Cannon mounted on them could score hits on attacking fleets as easily as shooting fish in a barrel. An ambitious attempt to bypass Vicksburg altogether by digging a canal across the mile-wide De Soto Peninsula, just south of the city where the river turned back on itself, was abandoned. Though the project was sound in concept, engineers did not possess sufficient equipment or manpower.

The Mississippi seemed indeed the South's own river. The Confederates navigated its waters in the vicinity of Vicksburg much at will. On July 15, 1862, the ram CSS *Arkansas*, under the protection of shore batteries, defiantly steamed through the entire Union fleet. Damaged by Union fire, she nonetheless found refuge.

That same month, the discouraged Farragut withdrew to New Orleans and waited for General Grant to coordinate plans for a land assault on Vicksburg. He appointed to the temporary rank of admiral a fifty-year-old officer named David Dixon Porter, a gaunt man with a full beard who had started the war as a mere lieutenant. Farragut created the Mississippi Squadron for Porter.

Immediately beset by problems of materiel and logistics, Porter could at least point to a salty lineage. His grandfather had been a merchant captain during the Revolutionary War. His father was David Porter, who was aboard *Constellation* during the naval war with France and the *Philadelphia* during the Tripolitan War; he had been taken prisoner by the pirates after the ship was captured. As a teenager, David Dixon Porter served for three years—from 1826 to 1829—with his father, who then commanded the Mexican navy. During that time, the younger Porter was captured and imprisoned by the Spanish. Released, he entered the United States Navy in 1829, before the Naval Academy was established. He again served south of the border, though this time on the United States side in the war with Mexico.

Despite his experience, David Dixon Porter was ill-prepared to conquer the formidable impasse that was Vicksburg, the Sebastopol of the Civil War. Except for that bastion, the Union could boast control of the Mississippi. The Father of Waters was the key to Middle America. Like his army counterparts,

Admiral Porter (bearded, center), here pictured with staff aboard the USS *Malvern* in Hampton Roads in December 1864. William Barker Cushing (see chapter 9) is at the extreme left, his coat over his arm.

Library of Congress

Porter planned to outflank Vicksburg. He would steam his fleet through the several tributaries of the Mississippi. The Yazoo, snaking in from the northeast, proved the most entangling of quagmires. Cottonwoods, cypresses, and oaks stretched their branches over the narrow channel of the river, dangling vines that actually ensnarled the riggings of passing ships. Snipers hidden in the thick underbrush lining the shore picked off unwary sailors. It was difficult to fight back with either cannon or rifles.

Underscoring the heartbreak and apparent futility of the whole gambit, the new ironclad *Cairo* struck a "torpedo" (mine) in the murky Yazoo on December 11, 1862, and sank within minutes. In command was Lieutenant Commander Thomas O. Selfridge, who had survived the destruction of the *Cumberland* by the *Merrimack*. Earlier, the ram *Lancaster* had been sunk by cannon fire, with her sister, the USS *Switzerland*, severely damaged.

Admiral Porter needed all the help he could obtain, especially the big, tough ironclads, which could absorb the "minie" balls lobbed by sharpshooters and some of the shells of small caliber. In mid-December, he looked at his confidential shipbuilding progress sheets from the Navy Department. Among the vessels under construction was the *Indianola*, languishing in Cincinnati. Footnotes on the charts hinted that she was experiencing "trouble" with her four engines and her steering gear. Porter snorted—weren't *all* ships beset by the same sort of imponderables? The villain was often the wrong coal, due to difficulty in obtaining high-quality fuel, or proper lubrication for the pistons and gears, especially the reduction gears. Reciprocating engines, Porter had long held, were just too complex and cranky for steamships. Ho for the days of sail!

Still, he would have to make do with the new warships. Porter scribbled off orders to Cincinnati. Commander George Brown received them on the raw, wet morning of January 3, 1863. He was instructed to get underway for Louisville, Kentucky, immediately. Brown filled out his crew, took aboard stores and ammunition, and bunkered coal from barges along the route.

February was at hand when *Indianola* put her last stop—Cairo, Illinois—astern and tied up in the vicinity of Vicksburg. There, new orders awaited Brown. He was to escort and protect two vessels attached to the Mississippi Marine Ram Brigade, an army squadron commanded by Brigadier General Alfred W. Ellet, the brother of Colonel Charles Ellet, author of the *Military Incapacity* pamphlet and the man who conceived the river-ram fleet. Charles had been killed before Memphis on June 6, 1862, in an otherwise victorious river battle that secured the strategic city. In a way, he had proven a victim of his own design, since it had been at his recommendation that the rams were left largely unarmed except for their prows. Some quipped that this army brigade within the navy was a family affair. The ram *Queen of the West*, bearing scars from the Memphis action, was commanded by nineteen-year-old Colonel Charles Rivers Ellet,* son of the late engineer. He was a steely eyed youth with a narrow moustache.

*A colonel at nineteen! George Custer was a general at twenty-four. The Confederacy was just as free with rank. Regardless of ability, such inexperience would take its toll.

The USS *Cairo*, sunk in the Yazoo River by a "torpedo" in December 1862.

U.S. Army Military Historical Institute

Protected only by her crew's rifles and muskets, the *Queen of the West* steamed off on a new mission. Her consort that February was a rusting old sidewheeler, the *DeSoto*, whose engineers had reason to speculate that termites and carpenter ants would get her before the enemy did.

Porter's orders for Brown and the *Indianola* were highly specific. Brown was to put two coal barges "somewhat lightened of coal" alongside as shields and "select dark and rainy nights for running the blockade." Should he capture a Confederate steamer, he was to "daub over her white paint with mud and protect her decks with cotton bales." He was to requisition the needed cotton at "Jeff Davis' plantation." The brothers Joseph and Jefferson Davis shared the ownership of the eight-hundred-acre Brierfield, and it was there that the president of the Confederacy had lost his wife of three months, Sarah, who was the daughter of Zachary Taylor. He subsequently married Varina Howell. The plantation continued to operate under the daily threat of Union takeover. Admiral Porter made use of Brierfield's assets, especially the slave force, but he did not have enough men to seize and occupy it. Thus, Commander Brown was also ordered to "gather up the best single male Negroes."

On the prowl at that time was the glowering ram CSS *William Webb*, 656 tons, 195 feet long, a converted towboat and, with a reputed top speed of nearly 20 knots, perhaps the fastest vessel on the river. If attacked by her, the commander of the *Indianola* was to "fire shrapnel" should the *Webb*'s decks be protected with cotton bales. Admiral Porter found shrapnel "good incendiary shell."

Obediently, Brown cast off "at 10:15 P.M. on the 13th instant [February]. The weather was all I could desire," he reported. "At 11:10 P.M. I was abreast of the upper batteries which did not open fire. But in the space of 19 minutes," eighteen guns from the batteries on the Vicksburg bluffs barked into life. Not one shell found its target. Brown could only marvel at the poor aim. He was clear. Not quite two hours later, at 1:00 A.M. on February 14, *Indianola* anchored "about 4 miles below Warrenton," just south of the port city on the Mississippi, because of a fog.

In the meantime, Colonel Charles Rivers Ellet and the *Queen of the West* had been both busy and successful. He had captured a steamboat with the unlikely name *Era No. 5*, loaded with the welcome cargo of forty-five hundred bushels of corn. He repeatedly rammed the steamer *Vicksburg* at her wharf, though he did not sink her. Fire from the sentries ignited the *Queen*'s protective cotton bales, but her crew was able to throw them overboard before serious damage was caused.

Ellet's daring and rather novel foray next took him up the Atchafalaya and Red rivers. When he saw enemy wagon trains ashore, he stopped his "fleet," which now numbered three vessels, and sent raiders to destroy them. But his luck ran out on the fourteenth, when he grounded in the Red River beneath a forty-gun battery. It was target practice, since Ellet mounted no cannon. The *Queen*'s boiler and at least one steampipe were soon ruptured. Ellet abandoned ship, transferring his men to the *Era No. 5*. Then he set fire to the *DeSoto*, fearful that she, too, would ground and be captured. Although some of his crew were taken prisoner, the colonel was able to escape with his remaining men and steam for the Mississippi, about fifty miles to the east.

Two days later, on the morning of the sixteenth, Ellet rendezvoused ten miles below Natchez with Commander Brown, who had made "but slow progress . . . owing to dense fog." In the afternoon of the same day, Brown cranked up his engines, with the *Era No. 5* leading.

"At 5:10, a steamer was seen abreast of Ellis Cliff," Brown reported, "which I at once recognized as being the rebel gunboat *Webb*. . . . I cleared for action, and was going ahead at full speed, when the *Webb* turned and started down. I fired two 11-inch shot at her, both of which were good line shots; one struck within at least 50 yards of her. . . . The *Webb* at this time was making most excellent speed, and soon disappeared."

During the next two days, the captain of the *Indianola* learned that the Confederates had repaired the *Queen* in record time and that she and the *Webb* were undoubtedly coming after him. More ominous yet, Union spies believed that boarding parties were being assembled on both ships. Brown began to procure cotton for the purpose of filling "the space between the casemates and wheelhouses," and he instructed his crew in the defense against boarders. He remained at anchor, however, off Grand Gulf, about twenty miles below Vicksburg on the snakelike river and a good ten miles south of the nearest protecting Federal batteries.

The unwelcome news was quite true. On February 23, a flotilla of four diverse steamers—the *Webb*; the hastily repaired *Queen*, under the command of Major J. L. Brent; a gunboat, the *Dr. Beatty*; and the tender *Grand Era*—was underway from Natchez and other anchorages. Lieutenant Colonel Frederick B. Brand aboard the *Dr. Beatty* and Major Brent each believed that he was in command of the little expedition, but the conflict of impressions or, indeed, the confusing similarity of the Confederate officers' names did not impair the operation.

"The moon was partially obscured by a veil of white clouds," wrote Brent on the twenty-fourth, "and gave and permitted just sufficient obscurity to render uncertain the aim of the formidable artillery of the enemy. We first discovered [the *Indianola*] about 1,000 yards distant, hugging the eastern bank of the Mississippi, with his head quartering across and down the river. Not an indication of life was given as we dashed on toward him—no light, no perceptible motion of his machinery was discernible."

Brown, putting the time at 9:30 P.M., was not in agreement. In spite of the fact that the night was "very dark," he spotted the four Confederate vessels coming "three miles below, and stood down the river to meet them. . . . The *Queen of the West* was the first to strike us, which she did after passing through the coal barge lashed to our port side, doing us no serious damage."

Brent, on board the *Queen*, was not so sanguine, noting: "So tremendous had been the momentum of the attack that for nearly five minutes we could not disengage ourselves, but remained stuck fast. In this position our sharpshooters opened fire on every light and crevice that could be seen, but no living men were to be seen on the enemy's decks."

At that point, the *Webb* smashed into the *Indianola*'s bow "with terrific force," penetrating for a distance of about eight feet. The *Indianola*'s coal barges drifted away and sank, leaving a clear line of sight for Brown's gunners. The 9-inch Dahlgrens opened fire with their characteristic deep roar—and missed. It wasn't easy to take accurate aim in the darkness and overriding confusion of the melee, though the captain of the Union vessel tried his utmost.

Brown "exposed himself everywhere," H. M. Mixer, the acting assistant surgeon of the *Indianola*, would report. "He stood upon the hurricane deck, swept by volleys of musketry, grape and canister shot, looking out for the rams, giving orders to his pilots, and with his revolver firing upon the pilots of the enemy. He stood on his knees on the grating on the main deck to see to it that the engineer correctly understood the orders from the pilots." Brown could not use the pilothouse because poor nautical design and an overabundance of cotton bales had reduced visibility from its sanctuary to nil.

The *Queen* finally backed off and, using the force of the current, rammed the *Indianola* two more times, losing two of her complement to fire from the Union vessel and sustaining four wounded.

"The [next] blow we received was from the *William H. Webb*," according to Brown, "which crushed in the starboard [paddle] wheel, disabled the starboard rudder, and started a number of leaks abaft the shaft." The following blow further damaged the rudder. Torrents of water poured into the holds.

At that juncture, as Brown was preparing to run his half-awash command ashore, the *Dr. Beatty* appeared alongside. The shouted command from Colonel Brand was plainly heard on both ships: "Prepare to board!" Brown called to his adversary that he was "in a sinking condition!" Ordering a momentary halt, Brand inquired if the *Indianola* was being surrendered. Brown replied that she was, offering his sword. Brand was not hesitant in accepting it.

The unequal battle had lasted an hour and a half. Only one of the *Indianola*'s crew had been killed, with two wounded. Some seven were "missing," probably having managed to escape ashore. Before surrendering, Brown had only enough time to throw his signal books overboard and cut the steam lines.

The victors were jubilant. The *Indianola* was "one of the most formidable ironclads in their Navy," Brand exulted, "protected in every manner possible, with thick heavy timber and heavy iron plates." *Webb* and *Beatty* took their big prize in tow, only to see her grounded on a sand bar off Palmyra Island.

Even as the Confederates started for Vicksburg with their prisoners, there was mounting rage in the Union camps and in Washington. Apprised of the loss by telegram, Secretary Welles vented his wrath on Porter, the admiral commanding the Mississippi Squadron, demanding "a sufficient number of ironclads to destroy [the *Indianola*] or ascertain her fate. . . . She is too formidable to be left at large!" If Stanton, Welles's bête noire, did not seem to be making much progress in capturing Vicksburg with his big army, that was his problem, but the testy navy chief was certain his sailors should be making a far better showing.

Porter was mad at just about everybody. His "calculations" had, as he figured it, been "disarranged." As for Ellet, what in thunder was an army officer doing as captain of a ship, even a riverboat? The *Queen* had "grounded under the guns of a battery which she had foolishly engaged." Had Ellet "waited patiently," Porter ventured, "he would have been joined in less than 24 hours by the *Indianola* [which was] detained 18 hours by fog at the mouth of the Yazoo." As for Brown's blunder in losing *Indianola*, it was "the most humiliating affair that has occurred during the rebellion. . . . It almost disheartens me," Porter lamented to Secretary Welles in reply. Further, it appeared to him that the ironclad was "indifferently fought. . . . She gave up too soon. . . . She would have gained victory if properly managed!"

Since he lacked "sufficient" ironclads, Porter had to do something fast—like perform a miracle.

As Confederate engineers and "ordinary laborers" (slaves) poured from the Davises' plantation onto Palmyra Island in a frantic attempt to raise the *Indianola*, Porter's handymen were bending to their own project—a "cheap expedient," by the admiral's assessment—at an even more furious pace. All that Tuesday night and into the early minutes of Wednesday morning, February 25, the Union men toiled to a strange nocturnal symphony of hammers, saws, and rasping crowbars as they coaxed heavy logs unwillingly into place.

"I set the whole squadron at work," Porter reported, "and made a raft of logs three hundred feet long, with sides to it, two huge wheelhouses and a formidable log casemate, from the portholes of which appeared sundry wooden guns." Some observers believed that Porter's men were adding superstructure to an existing barge rather than creating a raft. "Two old boats hung from davits fitted to the 'ironclad,'" the admiral continued, "and two smokestacks made of hogsheads completed the illusion; and on her wheelhouse was painted the following:

"'DELUDED REBELS, CAVE IN!'

"An American flag was raised aft, and a banner emblazoned with skull and crossbones ornamented the bow.

"When the craft was completed, she resembled at a little distance the ram *Lafayette*, which had just arrived from St. Louis. The mock ram was furnished with a big iron pot inside each smokestack, in which was tar and oakum to raise a black smoke."

It seemed incredible, but by Porter's own testimony, corroborated by enemy observers, the decoy warship was finished and ready to be "towed at midnight," at which time she was cast adrift "close to the water batteries of Vicksburg." It didn't take "the Vicksburg sentinels long to discover the formidable monster," and the cannon "opened on her with vigor."

A dual purpose was thus served, since the admiral had long been seeking a secure method of pinpointing the exact location of the principal opposing batteries. Porter was quite incredulous that his ploy had garnered such instant fruits.

Second Lieutenant S. Hassler of the Thirty-seventh Ohio Infantry, downriver at Young's Point, logged the "firing from the rebel batteries near the city, at 12 P.M., occasioned by a boat which is now lying below the mouth of the canal."

The alarm spread instantly through the Confederate camps. According to Colonel Wirt Adams, who commanded a Mississippi cavalry regiment, the *Queen of the West*, bearing her many battle scars, arrived at Vicksburg "in great haste, reporting a gunboat of the enemy approaching. All the vessels at once got underway in a panic, and proceeded down the river, abandoning without a word the working party and fieldpieces [on the wreck of the *Indianola*]. The Federal vessel did not approach nearer than 2½ miles, and appeared very apprehensive of attack."

What was especially baffling to the enemy, Porter would observe, "was [seeing] this huge ironclad pass the batteries, apparently unharmed, and not even taking the trouble to fire a gun!

"Some of our soldiers had gone down to the point just below Vicksburg to see the fun, and just before reaching Warrenton, the mock monitor caught the eddy and turned toward the bank where these men were gathered.

"The soldiers spent several hours in trying to shove the dummy off into the stream."

Though abandoned by the *Queen* and the *Webb*, the salvagers on board the *Indianola* learned of the new menace from couriers sent from the Davises' plantation. When they stared, they could just barely make out her silhouette; she was still aground. According to nineteenth-century historian James Russell Soley, "The lieutenant in command of the working party . . . after watching the monitor for several hours, lying in her stationary position . . . allowed his apprehensions to get the better of him, and on the night of the 26th* determined to abandon the vessel.

"The two 9-inch guns of the *Indianola* were thrown overboard and the two 11-inch were loaded with shot, placed muzzle to muzzle, and so fired. The fieldpieces were also thrown overboard, and an attempt was made to blow up the ship, which resulted in wrecking the casemate and sinking the hull in the shoal water off the bank. This destruction completed, the whole party fled to the shore."

As Colonel Wirt Adams continued in his dismal (at least in the estimation of his superiors) report, "Many of them wandered about Palmyra Island, . . . and about 25 are supposed to have been captured by the crew of the last Federal gunboat. . . . With the exception of the wine and liquor stores of the

---

*Discrepancies exist in contemporary documents as to whether the date in question was Wednesday the twenty-fifth or Thursday the twenty-sixth. Indeed, the entire time frame of the construction of the bogus warship and its unique "cruise" is in some doubt.

Indianola, nothing was saved. The valuable armament, the large supplies of powder, shot, and shell are all lost."

When Porter's mock ironclad was finally pushed back into the river, she drifted close to the *Queen of the West*, apparently retreating southward "almost as fast as the *Queen*," the admiral noted. "But at length the latter left her formidable pursuer far behind."

The *Queen* would never fight again. She was soon recaptured and destroyed, since there were no adequate yards nearby to repair her. The *Webb* had been so badly damaged in her fight with the *Indianola* that she was sent to Shreveport, where she would remain. Wirt Adams could not bring himself to believe that *he*, of all people, had been hoodwinked. He struggled to comprehend why the *Queen* and the *Webb* had fled, when they might "possibly have captured the other gunboat of the enemy" and made the scuttling of the *Indianola* unnecessary, should they have remained.

The editor of the *Vicksburg Whig* deplored the recent "piece of folly." Too late, he had identified the nemesis as a "Yankee barge." He noted that "the authorities, thinking that this monster would retake the *Indianola*, immediately issued an order to blow her up. . . . A few hours afterwards another order was sent down countermanding the first . . . but before it reached the *Indianola* she had been blown to atoms; not even a gun was saved. Who is to blame . . . ?"

Who indeed, except perhaps the wily Admiral Porter.

Historian Soley postscripted that "the results accomplished . . . were of vital importance. [The mock ironclad] prevented one of the most powerful vessels of the squadron with all her equipment from falling practically uninjured into the enemy's hands. That portion of the stores of the *Indianola* of which alone the enemy retained possession did not greatly benefit him in the operations of the war.

"It was a long time before the Confederate authorities could rid themselves of the idea that the National forces had another ironclad below Vicksburg." The syndrome that afflicted the Confederates after the incident recalled the state of panic that had haunted East Coast cities at the appearance of the *Merrimack*.

Word of this several-days-in-February gambit was slow and garbled in reaching Admiral Farragut in New Orleans. When fragments finally trickled onto his beautiful flagship, *Hartford*, the impetuous officer came to believe that the *Indianola* was indeed manned by the enemy, that she was a much more formidable man-of-war than had actually been the case, and that she was veritably running amuck. Farragut immediately steamed up the Mississippi. Not only did he encounter stiff fire from Port Hudson, but he lost the comfortable old frigate *Mississippi* after she wandered aground. The reckless admiral had to set her afire, and, according to Porter's description, she "blew up with an awful sound that carried joy to the hearts of the Confederates."

In four months, Vicksburg would fall to General Grant. The victor was immensely aided by Porter's fleet, which swelled to almost sixty vessels by July 4, 1863, the date of surrender. Many poured mortar shells night and day into the besieged, strategic river town. The role of the dummy gunboat, as Sir Winston might have phrased it in the next century, was not inconsiderable. It freed the Mississippi of the powerful *Webb* and the captured *Queen*. As Soley concluded, the Confederates developed a phobia about "a toothless monster" and a fleet infinitely more powerful than the one Porter possessed at the time.

At the very least, it was a hoax that came to stay.

Artist's depiction of the explosion of the *Caleb Cushing* off Portland, Maine.

Collections of the Maine Historical Society

Chapter 5

THE "INVASION" OF PORTLAND, MAINE

*"What a row there was! Every man jack in
Portland rolled up his sleeves and started for
that dock armed with everything from ancient blunderbusses to cutlasses."*

THE WAR WAS WAGED in the South, in the Midwest, and on their various waterways. The broad
Mississippi, the "Father of Waters," was certainly an actively contested theater of action. But could the
rebellion be exported to the peaceful, remote shores of Down East?

It was a bright, beautiful morning in Portland, Maine, on Saturday, June 27, 1863, the sort of
sparkling early summer weather unique to New England's seacoast. Visitors arriving on the train or the
night boat from Boston pronounced the weather heavenly. Most of Portland's inhabitants were well
into their daily routines. Grizzled old Jedediah Jewett, collector of customs at this, the largest port north
of Boston, had breakfasted and was about to leave his house for John Todd's barbershop a few minutes
after 8:00 A.M.

The aging, tar-reeking wharves were a study of noise and activity. The sidewheeler *Forest City*, the
night boat from Boston, had just warped in and was unloading. The propeller-driven *Chesapeake*, of the
New York Line, was readying to put into Casco Bay and on down the coast. Both advertised fine
accommodations, though many people considered the fares a bit steep—to Boston, it was $1.50, and to
New York, a whopping $5.00.

The several military posts in the area had long since sounded reveille and were into their morning orders. At Camp Lincoln, the Seventh Maine Volunteers' band was practicing for its Sunday concert. It was the only large musical unit remaining in the city, the well-known Poppenberg Band having been mobilized only the previous day amidst much tooting, booming of drums, and crashing of cymbals; the band's many admirers had gone to the railroad station to wave little flags and handkerchiefs. Across the bay, at Fort Preble, the Seventeenth Infantry was going through gun and quarters inspection. The post chaplain sat in his study preparing a memorial service for Lieutenant George S. Kimball, killed fighting with the First Maine Cavalry. His body had just been brought home.

Kimball had been no exceptional case. Many of Maine's youngest and best were far from home, in action throughout the troubled, contested South. Those in Brigadier General Neal Dow's brigade were participating in the final assaults upon Vicksburg. And the Twentieth Maine, already bloodied from the fighting at Fredericksburg and Antietam, was under forced march over the steamy Maryland cornfields towards Frederick. The alarm was out. General Lee's forces were pouring into Gettysburg.

Like the chaplain at Fort Preble, Jedediah Jewett had a funeral to contemplate. The captain of his revenue cutter, a medium-sized schooner, the *Caleb Cushing* (named for a contemporary New England statesman who had been President Franklin Pierce's attorney general), had dropped dead of a heart attack early Friday morning. Jewett had not even known that Bill Clark was ill.

As the customs collector was stepping from his front door, one of his clerks appeared, out of breath and manifestly distraught. The *Caleb Cushing*, he reported, had been seized and was at that moment about to sail out of Casco Bay toward the open Atlantic.

Curiously enough, Jewett mistakenly assumed that the *Caleb Cushing*'s first lieutenant and acting master, Dudley Davenport, was "the party who had run off with [the ship]." His suspicions revolved around Davenport's Southern ancestry. Jewett reflected. Phlegmatic, a creature of habit, he resolved to continue with his plans for his morning shave at Todd's barbershop before taking action.

En route, another possibility occurred to him. Could those Confederate raiders he had been reading about just possibly have . . . ?

Some eight weeks past, in early May, a twenty-three-year-old recent Annapolis graduate, Second Lieutenant (or Ensign) Charles Williams Read, had embarked on a fruitful career of raiding along the East Coast. Having finished at the bottom of his class, Read could not understand why he had been graduated at all. The moustached, rather ragged young man from Yazoo, Mississippi, was nicknamed "Savez," about the only romance-language tidbit he had gleaned from his coursework.

Read had served under wily blockade-runner John Maffitt while the latter captained the *Florida* before moving on to the *Lilian*. With a crew of twenty-two and some dummy, or "Quaker," guns to compensate for a lack of armament, Read had then taken his first command, the prize brig *Clarence,* into Atlantic coastal waters. He quickly transferred his operation to the larger, captured *Tacony.* A firebrand among secessionists, Read had learned well from Maffitt. By Wednesday, June 24, 1863, he had burned twelve sailing ships, including a handsome clipper and six fishing schooners, and he had bonded five others "payable to the President of the Confederate States 30 days after the ratification of a treaty of peace between the Confederate States and the United States." It had the ring of supreme optimism.

That same Wednesday night, by the light of a whale-oil lamp, Read confided to his private diary how he had acquired yet another "flagship" earlier that day: "The latest news from Yankeedom tells us that there are over 20 gunboats in search of us. They have the description of the *Tacony* and overhaul every vessel that resembles her. During the night we transferred all our things on board the schooner *Archer* [out of Southport, Maine]. At 2 A.M. set fire to the *Tacony* and stood west. The schooner *Archer* is a fishing vessel of 90 tons, sails well, and is easily handled. No Yankee gunboat would even dream of suspecting us. I therefore think we will dodge our pursuers for a short time. It is my intention to go along the coast with a view of burning the shipping in some exposed harbor [and] of cutting out a steamer."

On Friday, the *Archer* raised Portland Light. In midafternoon, Read overtook two Falmouth dory fishermen, "who taking us for a pleasure party, willingly consented to pilot us into Portland." From the fishermen, identified as Albert J. Bibber and Elbridge Titcomb, the Confederate "learned that the revenue cutter *Caleb Cushing* was in the harbor . . . and the passenger steamer to New York, a staunch propeller, would remain in Portland during the night. I at once determined to enter the harbor, and at night to quietly seize the cutter and steamer."

Read sailed into Casco Bay at sunset, then "anchored in full view of the shipping." He outlined his revised plan to his officers—they would seize the New York steamer and put to sea. His engineer, Eugene Brown, shook his head, expressing doubts as to his ability to raise steam single-handedly on such a large vessel. In the unlikely event that he could, daylight would overtake them, the nights being "very short."

The events of the hour seemed to favor the raiders. On nearby Cushings Island, a large party was in progress at the fashionable Ottawa House. At times, the sounds of raucous laughter and breaking glass drowned out all other nocturnal noises.

By midnight, Read had made his final decision. He would seize the cutter *Cushing* rather than the steamer.

He carried out his plan at 1:30 A.M. on Saturday. Most of the *Cushing*'s crew were asleep in their hammocks. They could not have been more surprised.

"Keep quiet and we will not harm you!" Read commanded, leveling a revolver at a lieutenant. "You are a prisoner of the Confederate States of America!" Even as Read was finishing his rather theatric pronunciamento, he recognized his captive as Dud Davenport of Georgia, a classmate at the Naval Academy. It was Read, not Davenport, who delivered a tirade on patriotism. "Why, you ought to be ashamed of yourself," he deplored, "deserting the South!" He continued in that vein for some minutes, until he realized it was time to get on with his work. After putting Davenport and the rest of the *Cushing*'s crew in irons (by the "rules of war," officers were supposed to remain free on "gentleman's honor"), Read's boarding party attempted to let go the anchor chain. It would not slip, so the Confederates had to laboriously haul in the anchor inch by inch.

There was no wind. Read signaled his men on the *Archer* to come with two dories and help row the cumbersome *Caleb Cushing* out of the bay. It was a bright night, and the *Cushing*, her lights still burning, could be seen from the Portland wharves. In fact, Reuben Chandler, the baggagemaster for the *Forest City*, waiting for the Boston night boat, saw the revenue cutter being towed past Diamond Island through Hussey's Sound, a northern, undefended passage into Portland Harbor. Chandler waved his hand at the disappearing shape reflexively, though none on board could have noticed his friendly gesture. The baggagemaster had never before seen the *Cushing* rowed out at that hour. Nonetheless, he "thought nothing of it." The fact that there was no wind seemed to explain everything. Chandler filled his pipe and continued to await the arrival of the *Forest City*. He was soon joined by the *Cushing*'s prospective new commander, Lieutenant James H. Merryman. Preoccupied with the challenge of keeping his pipe stoked, Chandler neglected to inform the lieutenant that his proud and sturdy cutter was heading for a destination quite unknown.

The *Forest City* docked ahead of schedule at about 4:00 A.M. Her captain had passed the *Cushing* on the way in and politely signaled a greeting. It had seemed like a routine meeting in the bay.

Another officer, a boatswain, a gunner, and fourteen seamen attached to the *Cushing* returned to the wharf from their night on the town in various stages of insobriety as dawn hinted rosily in the east. Some had participated in the big party at the Ottawa House on Cushings Island. They knew that their ship was not at anchor where it should have been, but they showed little inclination to learn the reason. Many, perhaps most, were simply too drunk to care.

From then on, there was confusion over who issued the alarm, when it was given, and what the rationale was leading to it.

"I at once came to the conclusion that this was an exigency when I ought not to wait for orders," Jedediah Jewett would write to his superior, Secretary of the Treasury Salmon P. Chase. Yet John Todd, the barber, swore earnestly that Jewett had relaxed in his chair and insisted upon finishing his shave before he did *anything*. On the surface, it appeared a textbook example of savoir-faire.

Not to be upstaged, Portland Mayor Jacob McClellan reported that it was *he* who set the wheels in motion by commandeering the *Forest City*, a direct contradiction of part of Jewett's statement. Lieuten-

Artist's depiction of the burning of the *Tacony*.

Collections of the Maine Historical Society

ant Merryman and the phlegmatic Reuben Chandler simply assumed that history would label *them* latter-day Paul Reveres.

Whatever the source, word soon reached Fort Preble and Camp Lincoln, where, respectively, preparations for obsequies and a band concert came to a clattering halt.

Captain Nathaniel Prime moved out of Fort Preble with twenty-eight armed soldiers of the Seventeenth Infantry, a 6-pounder field piece, a 12-pounder howitzer, and forty extra muskets for expected citizen volunteers.

Colonel Edwin C. Mason ordered all of the Seventh Volunteers at Camp Lincoln within sight or hearing to fall in, garnering a force greater than Captain Prime's. Some were clad only in partial uniforms, minus tunics that warm morning, though they did carry their muskets. (The newer, faster, vastly more accurate rifled guns were too scarce for garrison issue.) The order to march was given, and the Seventh Maine was off. The spectacle of sudden action after months of dull camp duty was infuriating to the bandsmen. They waved their trombones and bugles and shouted in protest. *What* was a band for if not to hearten the troops for battle, even though in this case the army seemed to be mixed up in the navy's business? Colonel Mason relented. He passed word for the band to come along. Those who managed to play their instruments as they ran tried a somewhat breathless "We'll hang Jeff Davis . . . !"

Portland had already gone wild.

"The bells were rung and men, women and children soon filled the streets and were rushing hither and thither in aimless fright," Major George L. Andrews, post commander at Fort Preble, wrote. He was seconded by Reuben Chandler: "What a row there was! Every man jack in Portland rolled up his sleeves and started for the dock armed with everything from ancient blunderbusses to cutlasses. Fishermen and storekeepers, stevedores and bakers, undertakers and teamsters, doctors and one college professor all speaking at once and raring to go. By cracky, they were mad as hornets!"

So many were storming aboard the *Forest City* that Captain John Liscomb had to turn the fire hose on those still crowding up the gangplank, lest the ship capsize. At least two hundred had piled on, and some of them were already on the top decks taking potshots at debris in the water. Having finished his shave, Jedediah Jewett was by then aboard. He had just dispatched the small tug *Casco* to Fort Preble to carry the troops to the larger steamer.

The New York night boat *Chesapeake* was still making an heroic effort at raising steam. Firemen, bare to the waist, were furiously stoking the furnaces. Topsides, the scene from the *Forest City* was repeated, with one added element—since it was obvious there remained a little time before embarkation, the *Chesapeake*'s impromptu voyagers had hit upon the idea of a picnic. Not only rifles and ammunition were toted aboard in ever-mounting profusion, but provisions as well—bread, slabs of bacon and salt fish, pickles, beer, wine, and whiskey, in ample quantity for a polar expedition.

Finally, listing to one side and then the other, the *Forest City* threw off her lines and churned away from the dock. Those left behind either cheered her on or cursed Captain Liscomb for hosing them away. Outside the wheelhouse, Captain John Coyle, agent for the steamship line, kept his eye to the telescope, "for all the world like John Paul Jones," it appeared to the bemused Liscomb. The only touches lacking were period costume and the *Bonhomme Richard*.

"I arranged with each boat," Jewett would report, "a series of signals to be given from the Marine Observatory on Munjoy Hill, to point out the course for each steamer. The *Forest City* and tug went out first."

Lieutenant Merryman, the *Caleb Cushing*'s commander-to-be, almost missed the departure in the overwhelming confusion. He had been knocked off his feet twice by the fire hose. Not to be thwarted, he "jumped on board . . . as she was leaving the wharf," he reported, "and finding the deputy collector, Mr. Bird, on board offered my service. I also found Lieutenant Richardson, with the boatswain, gunner, and 14 seamen of the *Cushing* and, assuming command of the party, proceeded to make my dispositions for the recapture of the cutter."

By then, the determined Merryman was one of four or five hundred making their "dispositions" for returning the stolen ship to Union hands. Furthermore, since Merryman was capless and coatless and without insignia of rank or even of service, the crew of the *Cushing* had no idea who he was. He grabbed one of the extra muskets, an action that tended to identify him with the citizen mob. The sailors humored Merryman and let him think he really *was* the new captain of the *Caleb Cushing*, snickering among themselves as they did so. Merryman did not recognize the charade.

The situation was far more disturbing to the army officers. Captain Prime, for one, would complain: "The steamer was filled with citizens without any knowledge of the responsibilities of the situation, and who apparently had left the harbor for a pleasure trip." This was war. It made Prime's military blood boil.

The Seventh Maine band had been playing almost continuously since sailing—from the stirring "Battle Hymn of the Republic" to the wistful, sentimental favorite of Union and Confederate soldiers alike, "Lorena." The music, too, contributed to the jaunty atmosphere.

Thus, the *Forest City* paddled forth with "every plank in her groaning under the strain," or so it sounded to Reuben Chandler, at least.

Meanwhile, Lieutenant Read was having his own troubles. The wind had picked up slightly, but even so he was barely clear of the bay. And the Confederates could not find guns or ammunition. When Read asked a captive crewman, Robertson Williams, the latter returned: "Go find it yourself!"

The magazine was finally located. It contained nearly a hundred rounds of powder and shot for the cutter's 32-pound and 12-pound guns, but it was locked and buttressed with thick timbers. Neither could the key be found nor the lock broken. In the ready boxes on deck were no more than half a dozen rounds. But no matter. The hotheaded Read would go down fighting. "Clear for action. . . . Prepare to fire!" were his orders.

According to Merryman, "We ran within two miles of [the *Cushing*] by 11.20 A.M., when she commenced firing her pivot gun, throwing well-directed line shots to within 70 yards of us. As we approached her, she fired five shots in rapid succession, the last one falling within 30 feet of us." Or, as Reuben Chandler reported the opening of hostilities: "We saw a big puff of smoke burst out at the stern—then heard a report—and a fountain of water shot up about 20 feet off our port bow."*

To the critical Captain Prime, however, it was a very disorganized way to pursue a war. "The accumulated advice and disjointed comments of these [citizens on board] bewildered the captain, who stopped his boat and awaited the arrival of the propeller *Chesapeake*, some 2 miles astern of us," he would write. In fact, the captain of the Seventeenth Infantry was so disgusted that he neglected to order his subordinate, Lieutenant Edward Collins, to return fire with the two guns that had been toted aboard.

The *Chesapeake* soon hove to nearby. After her officers and those of the *Forest City* "held a short consultation," the two ships "together started for the *Cushing*," according to Merryman. They were greeted by "three shots, the last a stand of grape, and all ineffectual."

They were "rounds of junk," Reuben Chandler believed, including some rocks used for ballast. Chandler joined the soldiers and citizens who were tumbling into the *Forest City*'s boats, clutching their assorted rifles and muskets. They started rowing, or attempted to do so. Since the great majority were not sailors, the procedure was attended by the utmost confusion and smashing of oars against oars. The "mother" ships began to pull ahead of the little boats.

From the Confederates' perspective, however, it appeared that a boarding party was indeed en route. "I was mortified to find that all projectiles . . . were expended," Read recalled. "From the movements of the enemy's steamers it was evident that they intended to attack us simultaneously on each side . . . and therefore I directed the cutter to be set on fire and the crew to take to the boats."

Not surprisingly, Chandler and the others "hadn't gone far" in the dory when they "saw the Confederates going over the side in boats, and smoke pouring out of the *Cushing*."

Dud Davenport and some twenty of his crew, still wearing handcuffs and leg irons, were placed in one boat. When they protested, Read ordered the keys thrown down to them. The released *Cushing* captives began rowing, and the *Chesapeake* started for them.

"A few moments later," according to Merryman, "two more boats left [the *Cushing*] and instantly smoke and flames were seen bursting from her wardroom and cabin companionways. By the aid of my

*It is most unlikely that the *Cushing*'s light cannon could have carried two miles—certainly not with any accuracy.

glasses, I perceived that her decks were deserted and that the *Cushing* was doomed to destruction. Expecting every moment to see her blown to atoms, for I had learned that her magazine contained 500 pounds of powder, I advised Captain Liscomb to bear away for the boats containing the pirates and run them down.

"As we neared them, however, they frantically displayed white handkerchiefs and masonic signs, and the steamer was therefore steered clear of them and stopped. They were ordered on board, and as they came up the side were seized by the soldiers and tied. The commander . . . declaring himself a lieutenant in the Confederate Navy, handed me his sidearms and claimed to be a prisoner of war." Merryman questioned Read "a few minutes," then turned him over to Captain Prime.

At that juncture, the day's only fatality occurred. Daniel Gould, one of the civilians on the *Forest City*, picked up a rifle surrendered by the Confederate crew and examined it, peering down the muzzle. "I wonder if it is loaded?" he asked rhetorically in the hearing of a friend.

It was. Gould dropped to the deck, a bullet through his forehead.

Silence descended over the steamer. The band stopped playing. An officer who said he was a surgeon with the Seventeenth Infantry, knelt, shook his head, and stood. "Take him below," someone ordered, as the *Forest City* got underway.

"Giving up all hope of saving the cutter," Merryman continued, "we steamed to the eastward looking for the schooner *Archer*, in which we had learned from the prisoners, they had reached Portland Harbor, after destroying the *Tacony*. At 1:48 P.M. the cutter [*Cushing*] blew up with a fearful explosion and disappeared from our view. At 2 P.M. we overhauled the *Archer* and, firing a shot across her bows, hove her to."

Merryman had just lost his new command. A boarding party from the *Forest City*, a mixed group of soldiers and civilians, seized the *Archer*'s unresisting crew and once more raised the United States flag.

Read proved rather uncommunicative, but not so his men. Jedediah Jewett learned that "it was their intention, after firing the gunboats here, to have proceeded to Bath, burn the shipping there, and so run across the coast of Maine."

The victorious fleet, led by the hard-paddling *Forest City*, thumped back to Portland. The wharves were lined with loudly cheering men, women, and children. Church bells were rung once more.

Yet even before disembarking, there arose the question of jurisdiction over the captive Confederates. Were they the prisoners of the Seventeenth Infantry, the Seventh Volunteers, or the collector of customs? Jewett, as often happened, won out. Flanked by soldiers, the little band of raiders was marched through shouting lanes of people to the city lockup, despite the protests of the Fort Preble commandant, Major Andrews, who did not think it safe. Denied the honor of overseeing the charges, Andrews nonetheless ringed the jail with a disproportionately large guard carrying bayoneted rifles.

His fears were not wholly warranted. Curious natives passed by the place of confinement. Whatever they may have expected to see or hear, it was singing that greeted them—ballads far more familiar south of the Mason-Dixon line, such as "Way Down in Alabama" and "The Bonnie Blue Flag," and, of course, the familiar "Lorena." All conveyed a strangely provocative message to a New England city that had already contributed a great deal to the prosecution of the rebellion.

As the military command had sought, the prisoners were moved in a few days to established camps, including the infamous prison at Elmira, New York. As an officer, Read was permitted to join other Confederates of rank in Fort Warren, in Boston Harbor. There, he wrote Confederate Naval Secretary Mallory a brief letter describing his misadventures, concluding with a plaintive request: "As all of our clothing was distributed as relics to the people of Portland, I beg that you will, if possible, remit to Assistant Paymaster Nixon a sufficient sum of money to purchase my men a change of clothing."

The young lieutenant would be exchanged before the end of the war. Those fishermen he had "bonded" could tear up their "payable to the President of the Confederate States" certificates.

Naval warfare was not entirely new to the Portland area. In September 1813, Captain William Burrows and the United States brig *Enterprise* had battled Captain Samuel Blyth and the British brig *Boxer* within sound of Portland. It was His Majesty's warship that had surrendered. Both commanders had perished, to be buried atop Eastern Promenade.

The excitement of Charles Read's invasion of June 1863 was not destined to be repeated in the Spanish-American War, though Fort Preble again awaited the enemy. And neither in World War I, when the fort was equipped with guns capable of hurling tons of projectiles many miles out to sea, nor in World War II did the Germans violate the security of the Down East seaport as had a bearded, rather unkempt lieutenant during the War Between the States.

Upon reflection, some in Portland would profess to find the postrebellion peace just a touch humiliating. Was their snug vineyard astride Casco Bay no longer so desirable?

Drawing of the CSS *Hunley*.

U.S. Naval Historical Center

Chapter 6

THE HOMICIDAL *HUNLEY*

U.S.S. New Ironsides
Off Morris Island,
February 18, 1864

Sir: I dispatch the Paul Jones *with information of the loss of*
the U.S.S. Housatonic, *which was sunk by a "David" tor-*
pedo last night about 9:30 o'clock.

S. C. Rowan
Captain and Senior Officer
Off Charleston

Rear Admiral Jno. A. Dahlgren
Commanding South Atlantic Blockading Squadron

NEW IRONSIDES WAS SO spectacular that some said she had statues in the park clapping their hands in wonder. She was the largest, newest, most powerful, and most heavily armed man-o'-war in the navy. At 232 feet and 4,120 tons, she was at least the size of most transatlantic steamships, and she bristled with ten guns on either side, including a main battery of the latest 11-inch Dahlgrens. Her 4½-inch armor plating against a 27-inch oak backing underwater made her virtually invulnerable to anything an enemy could hurl at her, as her name suggested. Assaulting the giant was said to be like attacking the Great Wall of China with hammer and chisel.

She was ordered to patrol the contested channels into Charleston, a city that had been a highly desirable prize in Union eyes since the firing on Fort Sumter on April 12, 1861, had signaled the opening of the rebellion. The ship was under the command of Captain Stephen Rowan, who had distinguished himself in Pamlico Sound. *New Ironsides* at once became the kingpin of the blockading fleet. Her presence was sorely needed, since the port area of the beautiful old Southern city was a haven for runners. Washington placed the highest priority on thwarting them.

In riposte, the South bent every effort to blowing the accursed Union fleet out of the water. One foggy night in the summer of 1863, an ingenious mine, or "torpedo," hooked by wires to electric batteries on shore was placed in the customary anchorage of *New Ironsides* off Morris Island, which was soon to be captured by the Union. For several evenings, Captain Rowan turned in, oblivious to the menace a few fathoms beneath his pillow. The device never detonated, but the South persisted.

On October 5 of the same year, *New Ironsides* had been secured for the night. Ensign C. W. Howard, on watch, had scanned the horizon with his long glass and concluded that no runners were churning in or departing that evening. Then, detecting a moving shadow scarcely the size or silhouette of an oncoming ship, he sang out: "Boat ahoy!"

Immediately, a round of musketry from the approaching visitor rattled through the rigging of the big warship. Ensign Howard was mortally wounded before sailors tumbled out of their bunks and began returning fire. The attacker, as Captain Rowan would report, was "a very peculiar looking steamer.

"Almost at the same time" Rowan continued, "the steamer struck us near No. 6 port Starbd. side, exploding a large Torpedo, shaking the vessel and throwing up an immense column of water, part of which fell on our decks. The steamer then dropped astern. Continued firing at her with Musketry as long as she was in sight, also fired two Guns from Starbd. broadside, dispatched 2d and 3d Cutters in pursuit of steamer. Monitors *Weehawken* and *Catskill* also got underway in pursuit. The explosion of the Torpedo knocked down armory bulkhead and storerooms in wake of the explosion."

In addition to Howard, there were other, lesser casualties. One sailor suffered a broken leg, another "severe contusions." Yet the *New Ironsides* had survived a blast that might have sunk a lesser vessel.

The next day, as carpenters grabbed hammers and saws to repair the damage, two crewmen from the attacking vessel who had been plucked out of the water were questioned. One was the commanding officer, Lieutenant William T. Glassell, formerly of the United States Navy and only recently released from Fort Warren for refusing to take an oath of allegiance. Glassell was under no obligation to explain himself or provide details of his erstwhile command or mission. Papers, however, were found in his coat, and they were hurried to Captain Rowan.

The papers described a cigar-shaped "submarine" fifty feet long and six in diameter, carrying a spar torpedo charged with sixty pounds of powder and projecting about ten feet from the bow. The vessel's name was *David*.

The bearded, rather corpulent Rowan was neither impetuous nor emotional, yet *David* instantly fascinated him. The concept, he declared in a note to Assistant Secretary of the Navy Gustavus V. Fox, should be emulated as soon as possible by the Federal navy, but the resultant craft should be armed with torpedoes "containing ten times the amount of powder" as the Confederate prototype. "By all means," Rowan postscripted, "let us have a quantity of these torpedoes, and thus turn them against the enemy. We can make them faster than they can!" It was only then that it occurred to him that he and the *New Ironsides* had played the role of the mighty Goliath in the Confederate scenario, with the submarine *David* as the pygmy opponent. Rowan chuckled at his discovery.

The Davids had evolved to fill the need for serving up the Confederacy's "torpedoes" (more correctly, mines). They appeared the economical answer to the South's desperation for countering the North's naval supremacy. Confederate ordnance engineers became masters in the art almost overnight, filling rivers and harbors with the deadly devices as though sowing oyster beds. Mines were so plentiful by August 1864, when Farragut forced the forts of Mobile Bay (see chapter 8), that they were the inspiration for his immortal "Damn the torpedoes! Full speed ahead!"

There were several types. The pronged torpedo was anchored on the bottom and detonated by cannon primers that were connected by a tripwire at keel level. The frame torpedo was designed to explode when ships' propellers fouled trigger lines. There were even beer-barrel torpedoes, packed with more than a hundred pounds of powder, and raft torpedoes; both were fired by friction fuses. The buoyant torpedo, moored just below the water's surface and studded with sensitive explosive caps, was certainly the granddaddy of the infamous horned mines of World Wars I and II.

The first success had come in December 1862 with the destruction of the *Cairo* on the Yazoo. Her nemesis had been a crude type of frame torpedo activated not by a battery but by a tripwire controlled from the dense thickets along the river.

That victory lent impetus to torpedo development, insuring the continued existence of the newly established Naval Submarine Battery Service in Richmond. Prior to the destruction of the *Cairo*, the project had been considered so revolutionary that bureaucrats had not a whit of interest in funding it. Celebrated astronomer, hydrographer, and navigator Commander Matthew Fontaine Maury had organized the Richmond office before his departure for England.

Yet it remained for a young engineer on duty in Charleston, Captain Francis D. Lee, to create something that resembled a true torpedo rather than a floating box or barrel. He called it the "spar torpedo," and its initial purpose was to at least harass, if not sink, the blockading fleet.

As with most men with radical ideas, Lee met opposition. Commodore Duncan Ingraham, former head of the Office of Ordnance and Hydrography in Richmond, now flag officer at Charleston, scoffed at the "newfangled notion" in the junior engineering officer's head. The spar torpedo could neither float nor be moored. It had to be delivered by another ship, which sounded to Ingraham like pure nonsense.

It looked like the spar torpedo would go the way of the great reptiles and the dodo, but Captain Lee persisted. Lieutenant Glassell eventually heard about the invention, and he in turn interested George Trenholm, wealthy Charleston exporter, industrialist, and supplier of many necessities to the Confederacy, a man who would later become treasury secretary in Richmond. Trenholm provided Glassell and Lee small boats for practicing with the novel torpedoes.

The two officers actually attempted an assault on the blockading fleet before Glassell came to the conclusion that steam, not oars, was the "only reliable motive power." At that juncture, Theodore Stoney, another wealthy resident, joined Glassell and Lee in their enthusiasm. He agreed to finance the building of the first *David*, a steam-propelled vessel designed to be totally submerged except for the smokestack and a hatch by which the captain could navigate and direct the fight. It was ready by the fall of 1863, and Glassell lost no time in putting it to work, recalling that on the evening of his triumph, "a light north wind was blowing, and the night was slightly hazy, but starlight [sic], and the water was smooth."

Glassell was on his way to "pay [*New Ironsides*] the highest compliment"—that is, to destroy her in history's first submarine attack. Accompanying him were Assistant Engineer James H. Tomb, Pilot J. Walker Cannon, and James Sullivan, the fireman, who had to keep the small steam engine pounding. The little *David* wallowed awash toward the target at 6 knots before it was challenged by the unlucky Ensign Howard. The firing commenced. Glassell wrote of the explosion: "My little boat plunged violently, and a large body of water which had been thrown up descended upon her deck, and down the smokestack and hatchway.

"I immediately gave orders to reverse the engine and back off. Mr. Tomb informed me then that the fires were put out, and something had become jammed in the machinery."

Since the enemy appeared to be "in no amiable mood," directing "a hailstorm of rifle and pistol shots" at its assailant, Glassell ordered his small crew to take to the water. Fireman Sullivan was picked up by a Federal ship. Tomb and Cannon returned to the *David*, fired up the boiler, and limped to Charleston. Lieutenant Glassell was afloat for more than an hour before a Federal transport schooner rescued him. He found himself en route back to the damp cells and soggier foods of Fort Warren. Perhaps because of the personal prejudice of Navy Secretary Welles, the navy placed little weight on resignations like Glassell's. They still pointed to his Naval Academy oath to defend the Union. Yet Glassell and other sincere Southern patriots, defending what they considered states' rights, believed their first loyalty was to their home states. Such was the dilemma of all Southern officers and enlisted men.

Submarine development had to proceed minus Glassell's inspiration and loving dedication. *David*, however, did not appear quite the answer to underwater engagements. She was, in a manner of speaking, as remote from a true submersible as the gibbon is from Homo sapiens.

During this time, another Southerner of inventive proclivities, the little-known Captain Horace L. Hunley, had been in New Orleans bending over blueprints of quite a different submersible, a stubby affair named *Pioneer*. He had abandoned it in April 1862 after preliminary trials in Lake Pontchartrain, when New Orleans fell to the Federal army.

Hunley, a shy, nondescript individual, moved to Mobile and obtained modest governmental assistance. Although Secretary of the Navy Mallory's interest in Hunley's radical marine design was diffident at best, General Pierre G. T. Beauregard, commander of the defenses of the Carolina and Georgia coasts and the man who had ordered the firing upon Fort Sumter, was supportive. He needed all the aid he could muster to keep the glowering Union fleet at bay.

Hunley joined forces with James McClintock (another naval captain) and Baxter Watson to create a new iron-hulled vessel in the machine shop of Parks and Lyons in Mobile. It sank during its first trials, without loss of life. Beauregard had to decide whether to abandon the project altogether or let the inventors try one more time. He gave the go-ahead.

A third vessel, the *Hunley*, was fashioned out of an iron boiler about twenty-five feet long and five feet in diameter. Submerging and rising were controlled through several devices: water ballast tanks fore and aft were fitted with both seacocks and pumps; "flat castings" bolted to the keel could be jettisoned to lighten the craft; and two five-foot fins were worked by levers. An "ordinary propeller" was designed to be turned by eight crewmen, and a conventional rudder and helm were supposed to keep *Hunley* on course. Two hatches with glass windows facing the bow afforded some visibility. The craft was also equipped with a compass and a depth gauge, a simple mercury tube.

There was a signal omission—how was the crew to be supplied with oxygen?

The craft was to be armed with a copper cylinder torpedo containing ninety pounds of powder "with percussion and friction primer mechanism set off by . . . triggers." The original plan involved dragging the torpedo about two hundred feet behind the *Hunley*, but experiments employing other boats showed that the torpedo kept catching up with the mother ship. It was thus decided to use a spar, after the example of the *David*—a twenty-two-foot-long pine boom would be hooked to the bow in a special socket.

In the winter of 1863–64, *Hunley* was shipped by rail to Charleston on a flatcar. Awaiting her was an eager volunteer from the Confederate navy—Lieutenant John Payne—and eight seamen.

William A. Alexander, a mechanical engineer formerly with the Twenty-first Alabama Regiment who had been "detailed" to work on the building of the submersible and who would soon follow it to Charleston, later recalled: "All hands aboard and ready, they would fasten the hatch covers down tight, light a candle, then let the water in from the sea into the ballast tanks until the top of the shell was about three inches underwater. . . . Seacocks were then closed and the boat put under way.

"The captain would then lower the lever and depress the forward end of the fins very slightly, noting on the mercury gauge the depth of the boat . . . then bring the fins to a level; the boat would remain and travel at that depth. To rise to a higher level in the water, he would raise the lever and elevate the forward end of the fins. . . . If the boat was not under way, in order to rise to the surface it was necessary to start the pumps and lighten the boat by ejecting the water from the tanks."

Lieutenant Payne, an officer imbued with more daring than common sense, resolved to attack the blockading fleet on his very first cruise. Torpedo in place, Payne mustered his crew with the exhortation: "Sink the Yankees!"

Alexander pronounced the obituary: "Eight men had gotten aboard when a swell [perhaps from a passing ship] swamped the boat, drowning the eight men."

Miraculously, Payne struggled to the surface. The five-foot "overhead" and the propeller shaft running the length of the vessel made it all but impossible to extricate oneself from the *Hunley* in an emergency. Men of even average height had to stoop very low.

The boat was raised from its shallow grave and cleaned out, and the victims were buried with full military honors. A regimental band played a muted "Dixie."

Payne remained undaunted and unabashed. This time, he'd *really* "sink the Yankees!" Again, eight men volunteered. *Hunley* did not even clear the wharf at Fort Sumter, however; she foundered with a sickening gurgle. Payne and two others fought their way up. The brash young officer had had enough. He had pushed his luck too far. He requested reassignment to a more mundane, time-tested ship, like a supply barge.

Fourteen men had perished in a couple of weeks. It was small wonder that *Hunley* was being referred to around the Charleston waterfront, and especially in the saloons, as the "peripatetic coffin." General Beauregard was appalled. He had approved the suicidal project, and it was therefore *his* fault. Rather than scrap the whole business, though, he decided to bring in the first team. He summoned Alexander, Hunley, and Lieutenant George E. Dixon from Mobile. Dixon, a friend of Alexander's from the same Alabama regiment, was also a mechanical engineer. He had assisted materially in the boat's genesis. Machine-shop proprietor Thomas Parks, acknowledged as one of the best in this specialized field of marine construction, proceeded to Charleston accompanied by several of his mechanics. The assembled force was thence referred to as the "Hunley and Parks" crew.

The men teamed up like surgeons poring over a patient *in extremis*. In a surprisingly few days, *Hunley* was pronounced fit to brave her natural (or unnatural) habitat for the third time.

Alexander, slated to go, relinquished his place to Parks, who pleaded for the dubious honor. Alexander was lucky. The boat plummeted to the harbor bottom again, taking the lives of its inventor—Horace Hunley—Parks, and every other soul on board, nine altogether.

"Enough!" cried Beauregard. "Let her lie in the mud. She will kill no more!" A total of twenty-three men had been drowned in less than a month. There was something almost demoniac about the craft. It was as though the *Hunley* were possessed by a sentient, willful urge to kill. She was homicidal.

Alexander and Lieutenant Dixon were of a different mind, however, and they managed to convince

Beauregard that the submersible should at least be raised and an effort made to determine the cause of the repeated malfunctioning. Alexander would write that *Hunley* "was lying on the bottom at an angle of about 35 degrees, the bow deep in the mud. The holding-down bolts of each cover had been removed. When the hatch covers were lifted, considerable air and gas escaped. Captain Hunley's body was forward with his head in the forward hatchway, his right hand on top of his head (he had been trying it would seem, to raise the hatch cover). In his left hand was a candle that had never been lighted, the seacock on the forward end, on *Hunley*'s ballast tank, was wide open, the cockwrench not on the plug, but lying on the bottom of the boat.

"Mr. Parks' body was found with his head in the after hatchway, his right hand above his head. He also had been trying to raise the hatch cover, but the pressure was too great."

Alexander's general postmortem was that Captain Hunley, unaware that the angle of the fins was allowing the vessel to dive quickly enough, had let in too much water ballast, and the craft had embedded itself deep in the mud. Hunley had apparently been attempting to pump out the forward tank, but he had not closed the seacock. In addition, the keel ballast was still fastened, although the retaining nut had been loosened.

Engineer Tomb was still on duty in Charleston. He had given *Hunley* a tow from time to time with his *David* (now used primarily as a tugboat), and he had developed a decided antipathy toward the former. He noted that "she was very slow in turning, but would sink at a moment's notice and at times without it. . . . She was a veritable coffin." He knew of what he spoke. The next time he had given *Hunley* a tow, the torpedo "got foul of us and came near blowing up both boats."

A short time after the third disaster, Tomb was standing on a wharf with Lieutenant Dixon watching the vessel dive under the Confederate receiving ship *Indian Chief*. "She did not rise again," Tomb reported.

When *Hunley* was raised the fourth time, seven dead men were removed. The toll was now thirty in an incredibly brief period. She was proving as certain an instrument of execution as a gallows or a firing squad.

Nonetheless, the confidence of Alexander and Dixon remained sturdy. Both men, in fact, settled down to a generally happy winter of trials off Sullivan's Island, with comfortable quarters in the small, picturesque village of Mount Pleasant overlooking Fort Sumter, about a mile and a half south across what was then known as "Rebellion Road" ("Treason Trough" to the Federals). Just to the east were sand bars tagged—of all things—"Drunken Dick Breakers."

Chain booms had recently been employed to girdle *New Ironsides* and the monitors in the harbor. Alexander and Dixon planned to attack the frigate USS *Wabash*—Admiral DuPont's flagship in the Port Royal Expedition—twelve miles outside the harbor, in the open sea.

Alexander described his daily routine: "Leave Mt. Pleasant about 1 P.M., walk seven miles to Battery

Marshall [the anchorage on the northern tip of Sullivan's Island] on the beach (this exposed us to fire, but it was the best walking), take the boat out and practice the crew for two hours. . . . Dixon and myself would then stretch out on the beach with the compass between us and get the bearings of the nearest vessel as she took position for the night; ship up the torpedo on the boom, and, when dark, go out, steering for the vessel [*Wabash*], proceed until the condition of the men, sea, tide, wind, moon, and daylight compelled our return to the dock; unship the torpedo, put it under guard at Battery Marshall, walk back to quarters at Mt. Pleasant and cook breakfast."

Because of the great expenditure of effort in propelling the *Hunley* by manpower—even as the galleys of old—Alexander and Dixon failed to come close enough to loose their torpedo. Six or seven miles proved the outer limit of endurance, at least navigating close to the surface. It seemed time for an extended submergence test.

"Dixon and myself and several of the crew compared watches, noted the time and sank," Alexander wrote. "In 25 minutes after I had closed the after manhole and excluded the outer air the candle would not burn. . . . [We] turned on the propeller cranks as hard as we could. . . . Each man had determined that he would not be the first to say 'up!'"

There was silence except for an occasional "How is it?" broken by a gasping chorus of "Up!" Pumps were started, but they did not help. Then it was discovered that one pump was choked by seaweed. It was cleared.

"Darkness prevailed," Alexander continued. "All hands had already endured what they thought was the utmost limit. Some . . . almost lost control of themselves. It was a terrible few minutes."

But they wrestled *Hunley* to the surface. "Fresh air! What an experience! Well, the sun was shining when we went down, the beach lined with soldiers. It was now quite dark, with one solitary soldier gazing on the spot where he had seen the boat going down for the last time. He did not see the boat until he saw me standing on the hatch combing, calling on him to stand by to take the line. We had been on the bottom two hours and thirty-five minutes!" The mark was certainly a record.

Alexander did not realize that the "solitary soldier" had already informed General Beauregard that the submarine was lost. For the "fifth time," the latter had stormed—surely this was too much! What would Jefferson Davis or General Lee say to Beauregard's squandering lives like that? Lee was preoccupied with Grant's massive military buildup in northern Virginia. Grant was obviously poised for a great new campaign south. The situation in Charleston was bad enough, with Federal troops on the outer islands and their ships forming an almost unbroken barrier along the horizon. They were starving out the city. Soap was six dollars a bar, brown sugar nearly four dollars a pound when it could be found, and an ordinary field hand (slave) six thousand dollars!

When Alexander and Dixon reported to Beauregard, the general's considerable surprise was leavened by incredulity that the craft could have been underwater so long. He did not believe them at first. The harassed general finally ordered that *Hunley* must not make like a submarine anymore. No diving! Some of her superstructure had to be above water at all times.

Alexander conducted further tests until February 5, 1864, when he received orders back to Mobile "to build a breechloading repeating gun." It was a "terrible blow" to Alexander. A few days after his departure, he received a letter from Lieutenant Dixon noting that the wind was still howling from an unfavorable direction but that he had a full crew—five navy men and at least one man from a local battery known as the "German Artillery." Another note followed stating that Dixon hoped to get underway any night.

Dixon had by then resolved upon a target, the 1,240-ton propeller sloop-of-war *Housatonic*. Only two years old, she mounted thirteen guns and carried a crew of 160. On the morning of February 17, Dixon mustered his men and gave them the news: "Tonight, we sink the *Housatonic!*"

It was a mild, clear day. Citizens of the besieged city read in Wednesday's *Charleston Daily Courier*: "We have no new movements to record. The enemy continues to keep up a slow fire upon the city. Eleven shells were fired on Tuesday, with about the usual effect. The enemy were working upon their batteries at Cummings' Point. A very heavy blow prevailed all day yesterday, causing most of the fleet to retire to Lighthouse Inlet."

In the gloom of evening, at about 7:00 P.M., the soldiers at Battery Marshall waved their lanterns in Godspeed as the *Hunley* moved away from the island awash but not fully submerged, in conformity with orders. She was soon swallowed by the darkness, the wavelets lapping the shoreline in her wake.

On board the *Housatonic*, Lieutenant Francis W. Higginson was standing watch. The young officer had participated the past September in a daring reconnaissance on Fort Sumter. Captain C. W. Pickering had presumably turned in. The moon was in its first quarter, as logged, and the stars dazzled out of a deep blue sky. After the cold winter winds, it was a welcome night, the kind that the merchant sailors, in their own description, had "signed on for."

At 8:45 P.M., another sailor on watch, Acting Master J. K. Crosby, "discovered something in the water about 100 yards from and moving toward the ship." He thought it had "the appearance of a plank moving in the water."

A plank it was not. As Higginson would report, "It came directly toward the ship, the time from which it was first seen till it was close alongside being about two minutes.

"During this time the chain was slipped, engine backed and all hands called to quarters." The men tried in vain to bring the aft pivot gun to bear, the only one that could be depressed for a target so close. It was "pivoted to port," yet the object was coming in from the starboard, presumably at *Hunley*'s usual 3 or 4 knots. "The torpedo struck the ship forward of the mizzenmast, on the starboard side in a line with the magazine."

There was a blinding flash of light and a concussion that shook every ship in the fleet. Even in

Artist's depiction of the USS *Housatonic*.

OFFICIAL RECORDS OF THE UNION AND CONFEDERATE NAVIES

Charleston, house windows and cupboard plates were rattled. Within a minute, the *Housatonic* sank, stern first, "heeling to port."

The submarine era had dawned in an apocalypse of fire and thunder.

Some of the crew saved themselves by climbing into the rigging, which projected above the surface. Others started swimming toward the nearby *Canandaigua* and the numerous ships of the blockading fleet that were steaming to the *Housatonic*'s aid. Captain Pickering was seriously injured by the magazine explosion, but only five lost their lives.

Nothing was seen of the *Hunley*. The seven or eight who had manned her pyramided the submersible's attrition to nearly forty. Lieutenant Dixon, Hunley, Thomas Parks—three of the pioneers in the South's submarine effort were gone, sacrificed to an implacable underwater denizen.

"A glorious success!" exulted the *Daily Courier*, but Richmond saw it quite differently. The waste of lives could ill be afforded. All those human beings and all that expenditure of time, money, and effort had garnered one medium-sized enemy vessel that could be replaced immediately. There would be no more *Hunley*s or *David*s. The experiment was finished, completed, forever closed.

When Alexander heard the news in Mobile, he "cried out with disappointment that [he] was not there," but he soon "noted that there was no mention of the whereabouts of the torpedo boat." Perhaps it had been carried out to sea, or Dixon had been picked up by a passing ship. He could not bring himself to believe that he would never again see his friend and colleague.

The Federal government was disturbed for a different reason. The Union navy had quietly been working on a pair of its own submarines, one in the Georgetown Navy Yard outside Washington and the other in Brooklyn. But since the monitors, closely akin to the submersibles, had proven eminently successful, was there a real need for a more radical vessel so patently dangerous?

The *Intelligent Whale*, constructed in Brooklyn, proved to be quite stupid. It was put permanently in dry dock after almost drowning its builder, O. S. Halstead, who was firmly denied recompense. Any member of the navy so ill-advised as to attempt to sneak the clumsy Gargantua out to sea was threatened with court-martial.

The designer of the other, unnamed craft had collected ten thousand dollars in advance and prudently left the country. Angry naval architects dubbed his tour de force a "medieval leftover." A circus owner wryly offered to buy it for his traveling sideshow before officers demolished the curiosity with axes and sledgehammers. Even the name of the hapless inventor was expunged from departmental files—he had become, in bureaucratic nomenclature, a nonperson.

Most who perished with the *Hunley* would also remain anonymous, largely because of the Confederacy's poor recordkeeping. While *Hunley*'s crews must have possessed a lack of imagination, their bravery in the face of insurmountable odds was at least comparable to that of cavalry leaders such as Jeb Stuart and Stonewall Jackson or, on the Union side, Phil Sheridan and George Custer.

The primary problem was that the pioneers on the *Hunley* possessed neither experience nor proper tools. Their efforts anticipated the development of the true submarine by only a few years.

In the next decade, Robert Whitehead, an Englishman, invented the self-propelled torpedo. Its principle would endure. A miniature submarine in itself, the torpedo was driven by twin propellers operated by an ingenious 40-horsepower compressed-air engine. A gyroscope was soon added to keep the torpedo on course, while its speed was increased to at least 16 knots. Since dynamite was introduced in the United States immediately after the Civil War, the Whitehead torpedo quickly became a deadly weapon.

In the 1880s and 1890s, new practical applications of the long-known principles of the internal combustion engine and the development of the lead battery and the electric motor made it possible for an Irish emigrant in the United States, John P. Holland, to build the first authentic, workable submarines. He was closely followed by the undersea boats of Simon Lake.

Though it lacked needed technology in its efforts at developing submersibles, the Confederacy nonetheless scored with its "torpedoes," or mines. Of forty Federal vessels—steamers, transports, and warships, including the *Housatonic* and *New Ironsides*—that came into contact with the new weapon, only nine survived.

Thus, the trusting young men of the *Hunley* did not die wholly in vain.

The river steamer *Black Hawk*, a sidewheeler that saw heavy fire from Confederate troops on shore while lashed to the *Osage* during the Red River venture.

Chapter 7

THE MAN WHO SAVED THE SHIPS

Public Resolution No. 34

Resolved by the Senate and the House of Representatives of the United States of America in Congress assembled, That the thanks of Congress be, and they are hereby tendered to Lieut. Col. Joseph Bailey, of the Fourth Regiment Wisconsin Volunteers, acting engineer of the Nineteenth Army Corps, for distinguished services in the recent campaign on the Red River, by which the gunboat flotilla under Rear Admiral David D. Porter was rescued from imminent peril.

Approved June 11, 1864

JOSEPH I. BAILEY WAS ONE of those rarities of the human species whose talents seemed to coincide with his nation's challenge for survival and its critical need for special people.

A chunky, rather short individual who would later be distinguished by a full and formidable beard, Joe Bailey grew up in Ohio and Illinois. There are blank pages in the record of his boyhood and teen years, and little is known of his parents and the locales his family called home. It is known that he studied civil engineering. By the age of twenty-one, he was sufficiently qualified to offer his services professionally.

Two years later, in 1849, Joe Bailey learned of what sounded like a good thing—the building of the Milwaukee and La Crosse Railroad, which was to traverse the lower part of Wisconsin to La Crosse, on the Minnesota border. The line's success as a much-needed carrier of grain and lumber seemed preordained. Bailey did not envision his role merely as that of civil engineer, but of land speculator as well.

Late that year, the twenty-three-year-old bachelor arrived with a partner, Jonathan Bowman, at a picturesque area on the Wisconsin River just below the present site of Dells, some fifty miles northwest of Madison. There, the two men claimed at least four hundred acres of land in Columbia County and commenced development of the village of Newport.

The location was not selected by chance. It was generally understood that because of terrain and other factors, the railroad would cross the river there. With the building of a bridge would arrive a cornucopia—a station, sidings, hotels, stores, banks, and all the good things to be expected along a right of way, even saloons and bawdyhouses. Just upstream, where Dell Creek passed through a deep, narrow gorge and joined the Wisconsin River, a dam was projected that would make the river navigable for Mississippi steamboats.

After the Wisconsin legislature approved the dam, wharves, mills, and warehouses were blueprinted. Thus, by the mid-1850s, the fortunes of Newport and Joseph Bailey were soaring. Places of business had sprung up, and schools, churches, and even a small model of the celebrated Mary Lyon Female Seminary of Holyoke, Massachusetts, had opened their doors.

Then the bubble burst. In 1856, it was announced that the railroad would transit the river at the adjacent and even newer Kilbourn City. Work on the dam would be indefinitely delayed. Whether they were the victims of fraud or just the fortunes of land speculation, Newport became a ghost town and Joe Bailey started looking for a new occupation. He turned to logging, as did many in Wisconsin. Not much interested in felling trees, he applied his engineering acumen to floating logs downriver and developed skills in building rough dams to increase water levels when the logjams became impassable.

It was fitting, then, that with the outbreak of the war early in 1861 Bailey should organize a company of lumbermen. He was commissioned a captain in the Fourth Wisconsin Infantry (later the Fourth Cavalry). As an engineer, he supervised the construction of barracks, hospitals, and other buildings, as well as canals and levees.

The versatile Bailey was frequently detached from his regiment to serve with other commands. Promoted to major in 1863, he played a significant role in erecting the siege works before Port Hudson, twenty-five miles north of Baton Rouge on the Mississippi. The investment of Port Hudson in the late spring and early summer of 1863 was nearly simultaneous with that of Vicksburg to the north. The major river port fell to the forces of General Grant on July 4, Port Hudson three days later.

During that campaign, the Southern steamers *Starlight* and *Red Chief* were captured—by Union cavalry, singularly enough—then left dry and stranded in Thompson's Creek, near Port Hudson. For

Bailey, refloating the vessels was as simple a matter as breaking a logjam. He obtained permission and sufficient manpower to construct wing dams, which were rather crude but effective obstructions of logs and stones that raised the water level while leaving a narrow channel for floating ships. His plan worked. The steamers were salvaged.

Obviously pleased, the army promoted him to lieutenant colonel that summer. For a frustrated Wisconsin land speculator, Joe Bailey was doing quite well. He had served in the most active of duties for more than two and a half years, but the war showed no signs of letting up for him. As at Newport, fate had more in store, though this time the impetus commenced far away, in an unlikely place—Paris.

Late in 1863, the adventurer Napoleon III was arranging for Archduke Ferdinand Maximilian of Austria to become emperor of Mexico, where French troops controlled certain vital areas. Should Napoleon's plan be accomplished, the United States would have unfriendly forces facing its southern border, and the French might seek to absorb Texas into Mexico once more; it had been annexed as a state only in 1845. Lincoln was further vexed by the hostile Confederates on the Texas side of the border. In short, Old Glory *had* to be restored over Texas.

The Union's performance in Texas had been poor, what with the debacles at Galveston and Sabine Pass. Brownsville had been occupied briefly, but insufficient troops had made withdrawal necessary. The War Department figured it was time to try coming in through the back door, via Louisiana and the Red River. The plan was to capture Alexandria and Shreveport on the way for use as bases.

General Nathaniel P. Banks, with an almost uninterrupted record of failures, would be in command. Wily Admiral Porter, with a much better track record, would support him with a fleet spearheaded by ironclads. Major General William T. Sherman was called upon to lend troops to augment Banks's strength of ten thousand. He did so most grudgingly, and for good reason. Late that winter and during the spring of 1864, "Old Tecumseh" was in Chattanooga readying for a major push south. His glittering prize was Atlanta, industrial center and vital rail hub.

Even before Banks's expedition could get started, Porter lost one of his ironclads, the *Conestoga*. On March 8, 1864, it collided with the steamer *General Price* on the Mississippi near Vicksburg. It was the third time the *Conestoga*'s captain, Lieutenant Commander Thomas O. Selfridge, had been sunk—he had been aboard the *Cumberland* and the *Cairo*, as previously noted.

Union fortunes then took an upturn. The fleet that Porter described as "the most formidable . . . ever . . . in western waters" steamed proudly down the Mississippi into the Red River—thirteen ironclads, four so-called tinclads (lightly armored, shallow-draft gunboats), and six transports, which also filled certain supply and hospital functions.

On March 14, Federal troops under Major General A. J. Smith took Fort de Russy as Confederate General Richard Taylor withdrew. On the sixteenth, Smith's soldiers were billeted in Alexandria.

Arriving there the same day, Admiral Porter hurried off an exultant letter to Secretary Welles in which he remarked, "It is not the intention of these rebels to fight. The men are tired of the war."

During the ensuing week, reinforcements poured into the little Louisiana town. Union forces kept advancing aboard the ships and by land until they reached Natchitoches, fifty miles above Alexandria, on April 2. Shreveport, the wartime capital of Louisiana and the greater goal, was but seventy miles above Natchitoches, though Banks's forces would never see it.

Confederate General Taylor, seemingly demoralized, kept falling back, but he regrouped at a crossroads some forty-five miles northwest of Natchitoches and soundly trounced his adversaries on April 8. The next day, Smith's corps routed the Confederates. The scene of the battle, which like so many others in the war bore a paradoxically bland name, was Pleasant Hill. Banks's enemy appeared to be weary of continuous fighting and unable to afford losses.

Yet as the spring days passed and growing clouds of mosquitoes attested to ever-warmer weather over swamp country, it became obvious that the expedition should be abandoned. There were several compelling reasons. Smith's corps had to rejoin an increasingly impatient Sherman in Chattanooga. The spring freshets, unlike the insects, had not materialized; the river was falling instead of rising. Small squads of enemy infantry and cavalry were never far from the banks. Snipers appeared from nowhere and were gone. The big naval guns were ineffective against such small, mobile targets. And worst of all from the standpoint of unity, Banks and Porter were blaming each other for the deteriorating campaign. They wrote letters to the War and Navy departments and to others in authority who might present a sympathetic audience. "I cannot express to you my entire disappointment with this department," Porter confided to his friend Sherman. "You know my opinion of political generals [Banks]. It is a crying sin to put the lives of thousands in the hands of such men. . . . This army is almost in a state of mutiny and not fit to go into a fight."

In April, Banks ordered the advance halted and the fleet brought back down the river to Alexandria. The Confederates were waiting. On April 12, they struck at a landing above Alexandria known as Blair's Plantation. Their first target was the *Osage*, an Eads-class single-turret monitor built for river operations. The 532-ton ship mounted two 11-inch Dahlgrens and could, if pressed, steam up to 12 knots. Her commander, none other than Tom Selfridge, had lashed *Osage* to the transport *Black Hawk*. While at low ebb, the river was less than swift, and Selfridge needed more tonnage for control. In spite of his precautions, the pair went aground anyhow.

"We had been for some time vainly trying to get the *Osage* afloat," Selfridge would write, "when the pilot of the *Black Hawk* who, from his elevated position, could see over the bank, reported a large force issuing from the woods, some two miles back. I ascended the pilot house, and from their being dressed in Federal overcoats, thought they were our troops; but soon their movements—dismounting and picketing their horses—convinced me they were enemies. . . . Then commenced one of the most curious fights of the war, 2,500 infantry [an obvious exaggeration] against a gunboat aground.

"The battery unlimbered some hundred yards below and abreast of the *Lexington* [another gunboat], which opened upon it with her port broadside, while I sent a few raking shells from the *Osage* in the same direction. Compelled to plant their guns close to the edge of the bank in order to reach us, on account of the low state of the river, they could not long maintain the situation, and soon retired with the loss of one gun dismounted."

Next, the Confederate infantry advanced across the fields column after column. "One regiment would come up, deliver its fire, then fall back under cover and another advance," Selfridge noted. "It was necessary carefully to reserve our fire until the rebels were about to fire, or our shots would have gone over them to the rear. . . . The fire of 2,500 rifles at point-blank range, mingled with the slow, sullen roar of our two great guns was something indescribable. The few soldiers on the *Black Hawk* sought refuge on the *Osage*, while the frightened crew of the steamer stowed themselves in her hold.

"During the three-quarters of an hour that this singular combat lasted, I had expended every round of grape and canister, and was using shrapnel with fuzes cut to one second when the firing suddenly ceased and the enemy drew off."

Before the withdrawal, Selfridge had spotted "an officer on a white horse" through his long glass. War was war. He ordered his gunners to take aim. Thus died Brigadier General Thomas Green, mourned by the Confederates as an "irreparable" loss.

There were no fewer than sixty bullet holes through the *Osage*'s pilothouse. Even so, only seven Union soldiers and sailors were wounded, and none died.

The next incident in the Red River campaign began on April 15, when the 700-ton *Eastport*, formerly a Confederate vessel, struck a "torpedo" (mine). Unlike many of the crude devices, this one actually exploded. The *Eastport* settled slowly into the muddy river bottom just off Grand Ecore, four miles south of Natchitoches. Her decks were awash. The largest of the ironclads, the *Eastport* was a valuable ship, especially with her 9-inch Dahlgrens.

For the next eleven days, it was a case of refloating and grounding for some fifty miles below Grand Ecore. On the twenty-sixth, Lieutenant S. Ledyard Phelps, the *Eastport*'s captain, despaired of salvaging her and made the terminal decision to scuttle. *Eastport* did not die willingly or easily. Eight barrels of gunpowder and several fuse trains were finally expended. On the final attempt, Phelps barely had time to jump ashore after applying the torch to the train. The hapless riverboat was blown to bits in a display reminiscent of the eruption of Mount Vesuvius.

The Confederates' harassment of the ships was almost continuous. The 178-ton sternwheeler *Cricket* was rushed by more than a thousand riflemen. Moored to a small wharf, *Cricket* was for the moment

The little sternwheeler *Cricket*, temporarily Admiral Porter's flagship, engaged Confederate forces on shore in a fierce battle. Note the gunports and armor.

Admiral Porter's flagship. Only a broadside of grape and canister from the little craft's cannon and the loosing of her lines saved her from being boarded.

About three hours later, however, and twenty miles downriver, near the entrance to the Little Cane River, *Cricket* was rounding a bend when eighteen enemy cannon concealed in the cane and high grass opened up.

"The after gun was struck with a shell and disabled," Porter would recall. "Every man at the gun [was] killed or wounded. . . . The crew from the forward gun was swept away by a shell exploding, and the men were wounded in the fireroom. . . . I made up a gun's crew from the contrabands [runaway slaves]."

Porter no longer heard the comforting thump of the engines. He hurried below. The chief engineer lay sprawled on the greasy grating, a red gash in his head. The admiral ordered one of the oilers, "a terrified young man," to open up the throttles and get the ship underway. Returning to the wheelhouse, Porter found the pilot wounded. He took over the helm himself to complete, with his crippled crew, the run past the Confederate battery.

Cricket had been struck at least thirty-eight times, with half her crew of fifty killed or wounded. Then she ran aground. Those who were still able turned to fighting a smoldering fire in an ammunition locker.

During that time, a sister sternwheeler, the *Juliet*, was also hit and disabled, some fifteen of her crew killed or wounded. The greatest casualties, however, were sustained by a pump boat, *Champion 3*, which took a hit in her boiler room. Scalding steam killed all but fifteen of her crew, who were logged as four engineers and nearly two hundred freed slaves. (The number is disproportionate to the size of the vessel. Either naval figures are in error or most of the former slaves were passengers.) She was lost along with another of her class, the *Champion 5*, which was set afire.

Miraculously, Porter backed the *Cricket* out of the mud and, before it was completely night, steamed to the protective sides of the *Osage* and *Lexington*, which had themselves engaged in a furious, day-long barrage. In the morning, the riddled, helpless *Juliet* arrived, in tow by the ironclad *Fort Hindman*. The latter, also badly shot up, carried thirteen dead or wounded.

The navy's casualties—reportedly upwards of three hundred—were the worst for a single day's action since the *Merrimack*'s first foray into Hampton Roads. Yet aside from the scuttling of the *Eastport* and the loss of the two pump boats, all the other ships of the fleet had been saved. Ahead, however, were the dreaded falls of Alexandria. Instead of the needed seven feet of water, there were but three feet and a few inches that spring, the shallowest level in twenty years.

The falls were really a series of wild rapids a mile in length. They were studded with rocks, many just below the surface. The river measured 758 feet at its widest point; where it narrowed, the current could be as rapid as ten miles an hour, making navigation perilous at any time of the year.

The troops could fight their way east to Vicksburg or south to New Orleans. But if the ships could not pass the falls, Admiral Porter could lose his entire fleet. Marooned, they could be picked off one by one by the furious assaults of the enemy. The crews would be killed or taken prisoner, or they could abandon their vessels and join their chances with the army's.

The navy command was not alone in its concern for the ships. Joseph Bailey, now on the staff of Major General William B. Franklin, who commanded the Nineteenth Corps and was himself an engineer, had "become assured" earlier in the month "that by the time the fleet could reach Alexandria there would not be sufficient water to float gunboats over the falls."

According to Bailey, "It was evident . . . that they were in imminent danger" and that "their capture or destruction would involve the destruction of our army, the blockade of the Mississippi and even greater disasters to our cause."

On the very morning of the battle of Pleasant Hill, Bailey had proposed to Major General Franklin that the engineers "increase the depth of water by means of a dam." It had seemed to Bailey that the commanding officer "expressed a favorable opinion" of the proposal. Franklin, however, was wounded in the fighting at Pleasant Hill. Feverish and overdue for sick leave, he did not act at once. From April 9 to April 17, the Wisconsin engineer heard no more from his superior. Then, concerned about the repeated grounding of the *Eastport* (which was not to be destroyed until the twenty-sixth), Franklin gave Bailey a letter of introduction to Admiral Porter "and directed me to do all in my power to assist in the raising of the *Eastport*, and to communicate to the admiral my plan of constructing a dam to relieve the fleet," according to Bailey's account. It was also considered "advisable" that Porter confer with Banks "and urge him to make the necessary preparations, send for tools, etc."

Bailey traveled the Red River and its banks, inspiring his conclusion: "The entire country is a swamp." He met with Porter and Major General "Black" David Hunter, a tough, moustached, sixty-two-year-old cavalryman who had incurred especial Confederate wrath by integrating many blacks into his forces. Hunter was then acting as emissary for General Grant, who recommended termination of the Red River venture. It was one he had never endorsed.

Confronting these senior officers, Bailey came to the point very quickly, urging that engineers should "increase the depth of water by means of a dam." With mounting enthusiasm, he concluded, "I wish I was as sure of heaven as I am that I can save the fleet!"

Hunter did not melt easily. The formidable cavalry commander growled that he did not harbor "the slightest confidence" in the "feasibility" of the proposition. Porter quickly seconded: "If damming would get the fleet over, it would have been afloat long ago." Less restrained yet, the admiral would write to Secretary Welles, "This . . . [looks] like madness!"

On the other hand, both Hunter and Porter respected General Franklin. They were also pragmatists, and they wanted to cover their tracks against abysmal failure. Brigadier General James Grant Wilson, aide-de-camp to Banks, would later reveal that Hunter told Banks that "the experiment had better be tried inasmuch as General Franklin recommended it."

Banks was desperate. He had to salvage what he could of his troops and transports. He *had* to believe in a miracle. He also had the word of an engineer on his own staff, Captain J. C. Palfrey, that the dam was "entirely feasible." The time involved was the "only question." Thus, on the morning of April 30, Banks signed an order offering the full support of his command. He confided to Wilson that he held "perfect confidence in [the project's] practicability."

Though Bailey would report that "during the first few days I had difficulty procuring details," he soon "gained confidence" in the contingent. It was impressive in size and, shortly, in enthusiasm as well. Banks ordered several of his staff officers and nearly three thousand men, drawn chiefly from western-states regiments, to work on the massive undertaking.

"There were also employed," recalled General Wilson, "some 200 army wagons and about 1,000 horses, mules, and oxen. Several hundred hardy lumbermen, belonging to a regiment from Maine were employed on the right, or north bank in felling trees, while an equal number were engaged in hauling them to the river bank.

"Flat boats were constructed on which stone was brought from above, after being quarried and the work was begun at the foot of the falls by running out a tree dam made from the heavy timber and stone, crosstied with the trunks of other large trees, and strengthened every way which Yankee ingenuity could devise. This dam extended out into the river a distance of above 300 feet. Four large Navy coal barges were then filled with stone and brick, and sunk at the end of the dam."

Bailey's "Yankee ingenuity" was amply illustrated in his manner of coping with the left, or south, bank, which was strangely treeless. There, Wilson reported, "a series of heavy cribs were constructed from material obtained by demolishing some old mills and barns, while the brick, iron and stone required to sink them and hold them in their place were procured by tearing down two large sugar houses, and by taking up a quantity of railroad iron, buried in the vicinity of Alexandria." The task, Wilson was pleased to add, was carried on night and day "without cessation, the men working willingly and cheerfully, although many were compelled to stand up to their waist in water during the damp and chilly nights, and under a burning sun by day, and notwithstanding very many had no faith in the success of the great undertaking."

The general was seconded by Admiral Porter, who observed, "Every man seemed to be working with a vigor I have seldom seen equalled, while perhaps not one in fifty believed in the success of the undertaking."

Oak, elm, and pine trees, some dating back to the days of De Soto, General Wilson thought, were toppled by the loggers from Maine and Wisconsin. "Mules and oxen," he reported, "were dragging the trees, denuded of their branches, to the river's bank; wagons, heavily loaded, were moving in every direction; flat boats carrying stone were floating with the current, while others were being drawn up the stream in the manner of canal boats."

All the while, hundreds of soldiers and those few sailors who could be spared from the trapped ships were at work on the dam. Wilson noted that they were occupied in "moving heavy logs to the outer end of the tree dam, throwing in brushwood and branches of trees to make it right, wheeling brick out to the cribs, carrying bars of railway iron to the barges . . . [and] contributing to the completion of the work, while on each bank of the river were to be seen thousands of spectators, consisting of officers of both services, groups of sailors, soldiers, camp followers and citizens of Alexandria, all eagerly watching and discussing the chances of success."

It was not quite a Roman holiday, but the residents of sleepy little Alexandria had certainly never seen such a spectacle. They were both curious and cynical, some of them growing so bold as to inquire, "Well, Yank, how's the dam?"

Frequent skirmishing resulted in its customary net of prisoners on both sides. It was readily established from the captured Confederates that Richard Taylor and the officer who relieved him, General Edmund Kirby-Smith, were fully confident that they would capture the Union ships *in toto* and that Banks's entire army would be en route to Andersonville prison following the capitulation.

At the very least, the novel project was "an endless subject of mirth," as was obvious to Wilson. "Numberless were the witticisms to which it gave birth."

That first week of May, Wilson reported, the thousands of "swarthy figures at work on land and water, passing to and fro; the campfires of the army which surrounded us on every side; the loud commands of the officers' [sic] superintending the work; the noisy shouts of the teamsters; the sound of falling trees, and the roaring of rushing waters—formed in its *tout ensemble* one of the most impressive scenes we ever witnessed.

"Mingled with those sounds we often heard, as we passed on our rounds among the men, the sweet strains of 'Annie Laurie,' or the martial notes of 'The Battle Cry of Freedom' while at the other end of the dam, among the dusky members . . . the popular refrain of 'John Brown's Body' and some of those peculiar and plaintive plantation melodies of the South."

Since the construction had been conceived by an army officer and endorsed by a general, it was to be expected that many among the army contingent should be confident in the eventual success of the project—about 50 percent, by Wilson's informal calculations. Not so among navy personnel—Wilson judged that, at best, a mere 10 percent had "the slightest faith in our saving their fleet." In fact, he could name only one navy officer "who from the inauguration of the work believed it would be the means of saving the squadron." That man was Lieutenant A. R. Langthorne, commander of the ironclad *Mound City*. By General Banks's appraisal, Langthorne "was always ready to answer the call of the officers charged with the construction of the work." Otherwise, Banks was critical of the "little aid or encouragement . . . rendered by officers of the Navy." Another apparent exception to the general lack of confidence among navy personnel was Admiral Porter, who had initially branded the project "madness." Now, as the dam neared completion, Porter wrote, "There seems to have been an especial Providence looking out for us, in providing a man equal to the emergency."

Joe Bailey was a practical man who did not indulge in flights of fancy. He entertained scant interest in posterity or history. He did not maintain a diary, merely noting that "the work progressed rapidly, without accident or interruption." Wilson found that the stoic engineer "paid no attention to . . . jeers or jokes, nor did he ever for a moment lose heart or hope, but worked on manfully."

Regardless of Banks's ingrained sense of rivalry where his sister service was concerned, the navy was not idle. Crews were toiling to remove as much armor plating from the fleet as possible, dumping it in a freak spot in the river known as the "five-fathom [thirty-foot] hole." There, the shifting sands swallowed the commodity that was so precious to the enemy. Most of the fleet's guns, ammunition, chain cables, anchors, and even provisions were laboriously loaded on wagons and hauled below the falls. Eleven old 32-pound cannon were spiked, burst, and then tossed overboard.

By the morning of Sunday, May 8, after eight days of work, the water had risen sufficiently at the upper falls to allow three of the ships to steam down to within a short distance of the dam. They were the *Fort Hindman*, still carrying her battle scars, Selfridge's *Osage*, and the *Neosho*, an ironclad. It was hoped that in another day, the rest of the fleet, with slightly deeper drafts, would have sufficient water to pass the upper falls. About 5:00 A.M. on Monday, however, the pressure was so great that the water swept away two of the coal barges that were an integral component of the dam.

"Seeing this unfortunate accident," Porter wrote, "I jumped on a horse and rode up to where the upper vessels were anchored, and ordered the *Lexington* to pass the upper falls if possible, and immediately attempt to go through the dam. I thought I might be able to save the four vessels below, not knowing whether the persons employed on the work would ever have the heart to renew their enterprise.

"The *Lexington* succeeded in getting over the upper falls just in time, the water rapidly falling as she was passing over. She then steered directly for the opening in the dam [a sixty-six-foot channel], through which the water was rushing so furiously that it seemed as if nothing but destruction awaited her.

"Thousands of beating hearts looked on anxious for the result; the silence was so great . . . a pin might almost be heard to fall."

In General Wilson's view, the gunboat might just as well have been approaching the brink of Niagara Falls. "She entered the gap," he wrote, "with a full head of steam . . . passed down the roaring, rushing torrent; made several spasmodic rolls; hung for a moment, with a harsh, grating sound, on the rocks below; was then swept into deep water, and rounded to by the bank of the river.

"Such a cheer arose from that vast multitude of sailors and soldiers, when the noble vessel was seen in safety below the falls, as we had never heard before."

And Porter postscripted, "Joy seemed to pervade the face of every man present."

Next, *Neosho*, which had already come down from the upper falls, steered for the opening. Losing his nerve, her pilot ordered the engines stopped. This was in direct violation of Porter's orders to plow full speed ahead. Momentarily, *Neosho* disappeared.

The admiral and the rest of the spectators were wholly convinced that the worthy ironclad was gone. Then "she rose, swept along over the rocks with the current," Porter reported. Her only damage was a hole in her keel.

Osage, with the war-tested Selfridge at the helm, "came through beautifully without touching a thing."

Porter noted with some surprise that "instead of disheartening Colonel Bailey," the accident involving the two coal barges only served to goad him to further exertions, while the men "cheerfully went to work to repair damages, being confident now that all the gunboats would be finally brought over.

"These men had been working for eight days and nights up to their necks in water in the broiling sun, cutting trees and wheeling bricks, and nothing but good humor prevailed amongst them."

As it turned out, the two barges had grounded against sharp rocks beside the dam, thus acting like the fenders of a ferry slip for vessels going through the channel.

Inspiring the workers to even greater efforts, Bailey constructed wing dams about a mile upstream at the upper falls. They would have the effect of slowing the rapid current and making the ships' passage through the main dam less violent. The task was accomplished in the remarkably short time of three days. The water was now rising four inches every twelve hours.

"On the 11th," Porter continued, "the *Mound City, Carondelet* and *Pittsburg* came over the upper falls, a good deal of labor having been expended in hauling them through, the channel being very crooked, scarcely wide enough for them." The admiral was by then suffering from an attack of rheumatism. He was unable to ride a horse, which thus kept him aboard his flagship, *Black Hawk*. He turned many of his prerogatives temporarily over to Commander Selfridge.

On the twelfth, the sidewheeler *Chillicothe*, the *Louisville*, and the *Ozark* were assisted over the upper falls by two tugs. A few hours later, their hatches battened down, the three made it through the main dam under a full head of steam. By all accounts, it was a most beautiful sight. Again, those on the banks cheered.

By the end of the next day, all of the imprisoned ships were over the falls. They awaited only coaling and the replacement of their guns, ammunition, and stores. Just one man was lost in the hazardous operation, a seaman who was swept off one of the tugs. On the fourteenth, the fleet was on its way to the relative safety of the Mississippi. Two small, light-draft gunboats—the *Signal* and the *Covington*—were ambushed thirty miles below Alexandria, however, and destroyed with heavy loss of life.

From his cabin, Porter, still "severely indisposed," wrote Secretary Welles: "Words are inadequate to express the admiration I feel for the abilities of Lieutenant Colonel Bailey. This is without doubt the best engineering feat ever performed. . . . He has saved to the Union a valuable fleet, worth nearly $2 million; more, he has deprived the enemy of a triumph which would have emboldened them to carry on this war a year or two longer. . . . The highest honors the Government can bestow on Colonel Bailey can never repay him for the service he rendered his country."

Bailey's job was not quite finished. As the ships steamed back variously to New Orleans and to Vicksburg, he was called upon to assist Banks's wagon trains over the six-hundred-yard-wide Atchafalaya River. He improvised a pontoon span by using two old steamers.

His rewards were not slow in coming. In addition to a formal thanks from Congress, Bailey was presented with an elegant sword and a purse of three thousand dollars. These were frosted with a brevetted promotion to brigadier general.

After commanding the Engineer Brigade in the historic assault on Mobile Bay in August, Bailey was promoted to major general for his "gallant and meritorious service." Returning to more familiar territory, he led the Second Brigade, Second Cavalry Division, of the Military Division of the West Mississippi until June 1865, two months after the surrender. There were straggling groups of diehard Confederates to flush out and "persuade" to surrender.

Apparently still a bachelor, Joe Bailey tried to wind down from his uncommonly vigorous war years as a farmer in Newton County, Missouri, on the Kansas border. In 1866, unable to enjoy his secure and relatively uneventful life, he ran for county sheriff and was easily elected. There were plentiful challenges for him in that wild, desolate land of bushwhackers, cattle thieves, and desperadoes of every origin, size, and inclination. In marked contrast to other sections of the West and Northwest, Indians presented no problems in Newton County.

As with every project he undertook, Bailey immersed himself fully and furiously in his new and highly needed profession. An accomplished rider, he galloped the length and breadth of his county in pursuit of the lawless. After only a few months of wearing his badge, he became a well-respected legend. "There goes Sheriff Bailey!" was a familiar cry in the little towns of Newton County, many scantly larger than whistle stops. The average resident knew Bailey only as the local sheriff, not as an engineer who had rescued a Union fleet.

On March 21, 1867, devotion to duty carried Bailey north to Vernon County and the town of Nevada. He was hot after a pair of outlaw brothers named Pixley who were the scourge of western Missouri. Unlike a Saturday-matinee western, however, right did not win out over wrong, the white hat over the black. One of the Pixleys got the draw on Sheriff Bailey.

Thus, in a pinpoint frontier town, died the hero of the Red River, the man who saved the ships.

The *Hartford*. Farragut was lashed to the rigging as he made good his order to "Damn the torpe-does!" Since his pilots knew where most of the devices were sunk, his act was neither as bold nor as brave as legend would make it.

Chapter 8

DAMN THE TORPEDOES!

"Can you say 'for God's sake' by signal?"

THE UNION'S ARMIES WERE engaged on two major fronts that spring and summer of 1864. Sherman was tearing away at Atlanta in fulfillment of his promise to "make Georgia howl!" Grant was marching south for Richmond, barreling onward in spite of fearful casualties. He was rich with reserve forces. He could squander them—and he did so, especially at bloody Cold Harbor on June 3, when seven thousand Union troops died or were wounded in one frightful hour.

New Orleans, Vicksburg, Nashville, and Norfolk were in Northern hands. The port of Charleston was bottled up. Other centers in the South besides Atlanta and Richmond were threatened. There was one city, however, a major haven for blockade-runners, that remained open, as if to taunt the Federal army.

Compared with the massive forces of Grant and Sherman, there was little manpower in the vicinity of Mobile, Alabama—only portions of the Trans-Mississippi Department of Major General Edward R. S. Canby. In fact, the army counted exactly eighteen hundred effectives in the environs of Mobile in late July. That relative handful was under the command of Major General Gordon Granger. He was apparently no relative of General Robert Granger in Nashville, but the challenge faced in Mobile by the stocky, balding, and bearded officer appeared equally insuperable.

The charming old Alabama gulf city was protected by more than fifty forts and redoubts in concentric circles, with two glowering kingpins at the mouth of Mobile Bay—Fort Morgan on the east and Fort

Gaines on the west, on Dauphin Island, where Granger had established a beachhead. Between them, they mounted more than a hundred guns. General Joseph E. Johnston had pronounced Mobile's defenses "the strongest in the Confederacy."

Granger, however, was not alone. Admiral Farragut had been spoiling, ever since his triumph at New Orleans and, more recently, Porter's debacle in the Red River, to seize Mobile Bay, if not the city itself. With the army's or, surely, the Navy Department's support, so much the better. If not, the impetuous Davy was determined to storm ahead on his own.

A Southerner by birth, Farragut had remained fiercely loyal to the Union. When beckoned to join secession, his reply had been: "Mind what I tell you. You fellows will catch the devil before you get through with this business."

He already considered the challenge of the lower Mississippi the apogee of his long career, noting: "I have now attained what I have been looking for all my life—a flag—and having attained it, all that is necessary to complete the scene is a victory. If I die in the attempt, it will only be what every officer has to expect. He who dies in doing his duty to his country and at peace with his God, has played out the drama of life to best advantage."

A meticulous flag officer, Davy Farragut wanted no detail left to chance. "You must be prepared to execute all those duties to which you have been so long trained in the Navy," the admiral wrote, "without having the opportunity of practising. I expect every vessel's crew to be well exercised at their guns. . . . I shall expect the most prompt attention to signals; and verbal orders, either from myself or the captain of the fleet."

By the first of August, Farragut had amassed an impressive fleet of eighteen fighting ships off Pelican Bay, leading into Mobile Bay and the twin forts. The fleet included eight screw sloops—"ships of the line"—led by the flagship *Hartford*, with four monitors, three double-enders, and three supporting, smaller men-o'-war.

Opposing the Union navy was, effectively, but one Confederate vessel, the new ram *Tennessee*, 209 feet in length, with a battery of 7- and 6.4-inch rifled guns. Her iron plating was backed by 23 inches of yellow pine and white oak. Though formidable, she was not as large as the *Merrimack* and did not possess as much firepower. It was scarcely a coincidence that the *Merrimack*'s commander, Franklin "Old Buck" Buchanan, now an admiral, captained the *Tennessee*. Three old sidewheeler gunboats were her sole consorts.

This was the stage, then, and these the protagonists. The ensuing action took place in the three-mile mouth between Forts Morgan and Gaines, planted with nearly two hundred torpedoes. It will be narrated in the words of Admiral Farragut and four officers: Dr. Daniel B. Conrad, fleet surgeon of the Confederate navy, aboard the CSS *Tennessee*; Dr. William F. Hutchinson, assistant surgeon of the big sloop USS *Lackawanna*; Commander James D. Johnston, captain of the *Tennessee*; and Lieutenant John C. Kinney, army signal officer attached to the USS *Hartford*.

———————

FARRAGUT   On the 8th of July, I had an interview [with Generals Canby and Granger] on board the *Hartford* on the subject of an attack upon Forts Morgan and Gaines, at which it was agreed that General Canby would send all the troops he could spare to cooperate with the fleet. Circumstances soon obliged General Canby to inform me that he could not dispatch a sufficient number to invest both forts. . . . On the 1st instant [August] General Granger visited me again on the *Hartford*. In the meantime, the [monitor] *Tecumseh* had arrived at Pensacola and Captain [Tunis A. M.] Craven had informed me that he would be ready in four days for any service. We therefore fixed upon the 4th of August as the day for landing of the troops and my entrance into the bay.

CONRAD   We had been lying idly in Mobile Bay for many months, on board the ironclad ram *Tennessee*, whose fighting deck differed materially from that of the Federal monitors. It resembled the inside of the hip-roof of a house, rather than the "cheese-box" of Ericsson's *Monitor*. On the 1st of August we saw a decided increase in the Federal fleet, which was then listlessly at anchor outside of Fort Morgan, in the Gulf of Mexico. . . . They appeared like "prize fighters" ready for the "ring." Then we knew that trouble was ahead. . . . On the 3d of August we noticed another accretion to the already formidable fleet; this was four strange looking, long, black monsters—the new ironclads. . . .

   We had been very uncomfortable for weeks in our berths on board the *Tennessee*, in consequence of the prevailing heavy rains wetting the decks, and the terrible moist, hot atmosphere, simulating that oppressiveness which precedes a tornado. It was, therefore, impossible to sleep inside; besides, from the want of properly cooked food, and the continuous wetting of the decks at night, the officers and the men were rendered desperate. We knew that the impending action would soon be determined one way or the other, and every one looked forward to it with a positive feeling of relief.

HUTCHINSON   The morning of August 4, 1864 dawned beautifully clear, and the blue waters of the Mexican Gulf stretched away southward a thousand miles to the Venezuelan shore, while to the north its waves splashed lazily in a tropical sun against the white sand of Dauphin Island and Mobile Point, between which curved the winding channel of entrance to the bay. . . . It was evident that something was brewing, and when, an hour later, the signal displayed from the *Hartford* read, "Commanding

Admiral Farragut (right) with Captain Percival Drayton aboard the *Hartford* off Mobile.

officers repair on board the flagship"—all hands were on the alert, knowing the signal meant a war council.

. . . At noon on the 4th of August, the order of battle was sent on board the ships which were to participate. . . . Then we knew that before 24 hours passed, we should either be inside Mobile Bay, conquerors of the stronghold and captors of the rebel fleet, or be ourselves quietly at rest beneath its muddy waters. [That evening] we clinked glasses merrily with our stay-behind comrades, and they bade us good night with envious faces, cursing their luck—each one wishing that something might happen to one of the attacking fleet, so that his own ship could have a chance in the fray.

JOHNSTON   On the evening of the 4th of August, it was plainly to be seen that the blockading fleet . . . was making preparations to attempt the passage of Forts Morgan and Gaines. . . . Similar preparations were made by our vessels, which had been anchored just within the bay for nearly three months, in daily expectation of impending disaster. During the night, a blockade runner entered the bay [quite a feat considering the presence of the Union ships] and was boarded by the executive officer of the *Tennessee*.

HUTCHINSON   Morning came at last, after so busy a night that only an hour could be given to sleep. At eight bells, or four o'clock, all hands were turned out, and our [the *Lackawanna*'s] consort, the *Seminole*, steamed alongside and was made fast to us on the port side. The vessels were double-banked in this manner, in order that the farthest from the fort and protected from its fire might carry the other through, should she either be disabled by shot or have her propeller entangled in any of the numerous floating ropes with which the rebels had filled the channel, for that express purpose.

The morning was beautifully clear, and the battlements of Forts Morgan and Gaines, with the few gaunt pines on Mobile Point, stood out in clear relief against the blazing eastern sky, all giving promise of a fine day. . . . The *Brooklyn*, with the *Octorara*, steamed into position at the head of the line, and the other vessels fell in as soon as possible, at intervals of 50 yards. The flagship did not lead, because the *Brooklyn* was fitted with an ingenious contrivance to catch torpedoes, called a devil, composed of a number of long iron hooks attached to a spar, which was slung from the bowsprit and sunk even with the ship's keel, and for the further reason that her commander, Captain [James] Alden, knew the channel thoroughly, as he had been chief of the coast survey in antebellum days, and author of the official charts of the harbor.

At twenty minutes to six, the line was formed, and we commenced to steam in slowly, the Admiral's order being to carry the lowest possible pressure, so as to avoid as much as possible the fearful scalding effect of the steam, should the boilers be pierced. The ships were dressed from stem to stern in flags, as if for a gala day, and every man sprang to his station with a will when the long roll called all hands to general quarters.

KINNEY   It was a weird sight as the big ships "balanced to partners," the dim outlines slowly emerging like phantoms in the fog. [This ancient practice of doubling up ships was to be abandoned even by the Spanish-American War.]

CONRAD   I had been sleeping on the deck of the admiral's [Buchanan's] cabin for two or three nights, when at daybreak, on the 5th of August the old quartermaster came down the ladder, rousing us with his gruff voice, saying, "the officer of the deck bids me report that the enemy's fleet is under way." Jumping up, still half asleep, we came on deck, and sure enough, there was the enemy heading for the "passage" past the fort. The grand old admiral of 60 years, with his countenance rigid and stern, showing a determination for battle in every line, then gave his only order: "Get under way, Captain Johnston. Head for the leading vessel of the enemy, and fight each one as they pass us."

JOHNSTON   All the light spars had been sent down, leaving only the lower and top masts standing, while the boats had been hauled upon the beach at Sand Island just within the bar, on the morning previous.
   All hands were immediately called on board the Confederate vessels, and after hurriedly taking coffee, the crew were set to work to slip the cable and buoy the anchor.

FARRAGUT   The attacking fleet steamed steadily up the Main Ship Channel, the *Tecumseh* firing the first shot at 6:47. At 7:6, the fort opened upon us and was replied to by a gun from the *Brooklyn*, and immediately after the action became general.
   It was soon apparent that there was some difficulty ahead. The *Brooklyn*, for some cause which I did not then clearly understand . . . arrested the advance of the whole fleet, while at the same time the guns of the fort were playing with great effect upon that vessel and the *Hartford*.
   [It was, presumably, at this time that the *Brooklyn* signaled the flagship to be wary of torpedoes, and Farragut made his oft-quoted reply, "Damn the torpedoes!" supposedly within the hearing of the *Hartford*'s captain, Percival Drayton, a South Carolinian who had remained loyal to the Union. The statement may or may not have been followed by "Full speed ahead!" or "Full steam ahead!" Like many sayings that have become part of our national lore, Admiral Farragut's version of bushido may have been apocryphal in whole or part.]

HUTCHINSON   It is a curious sight to watch a single shot from so heavy a piece of ordnance [as that of the forts]. First, you see the puff of white smoke upon the distant ramparts and then you see the shot coming, looking exactly as if some gigantic hand had thrown in play a ball toward you. By the time it is half way, you get the boom of the report, and then the howl of the missile, which apparently grows so rapidly in size that every green hand on board who can see it, is certain that it will hit him between the eyes. Then, as it goes past with a shriek like a thousand devils, the inclination to do reverence is so strong that it is almost impossible to resist it. . . .

The battle was a fair one, ships against brick walls and earthworks, each side doing its level best. As the fleet came into action, however, the broadsides came too fast and heavy for any mortal beings to stand, and the rebel soldiers fled from the parapet in dismay.

[Brigadier General R. L. Page, commanding Fort Morgan, held a different viewpoint, asserting that "most of the projectiles" passed "over our heads" and that "the spirit displayed by the garrison was fine. The guns were well served, and all did their duty nobly."]

Shell, grape and canister from the great cannon went hissing through the air, until it seemed as if hell itself had broken loose, and smoke was so dense on the decks and water that both fort and vessels were completely hidden and we both fired at the flashes of the guns alone.

[In order to see better, Farragut climbed up the rigging ratline by ratline. Since he held his spyglass in one hand and the *Hartford* was maneuvering sharply, his perch was precarious at best. Worried, Captain Drayton ordered his veteran chief quartermaster, the heavily bearded John H. Knowles, up with "a piece of lead line." Assisted by the admiral himself, who initially endorsed the wisdom of the expedient, Knowles made the rope "fast to one of the forward shrouds, and then took it around the admiral to the after shroud, making it fast there," according to Drayton's account. Nonetheless, Farragut did not long benefit from the captain's solicitude. Undoing the lashing himself, he climbed higher still.]

The rebels now opened from the guns of the water batteries, 8-inch guns and Armstrong rifles, which being on a level with the ships, did fearful execution. The [sloop] *Monongahela* was struck many times, and Lieutenant Roderick Prentiss, her executive officer, had his right leg torn off by a whole shell, and Captain J. R. M. Mullany, of the *Oneida* [also a big steam sloop] lost an arm in the same way. The latter vessel was struck by a heavy shell which, having penetrated completely through the chain armor and side of the vessel, exploded in her starboard boiler, instantly filling her engine and firerooms with steam. Every one of the fireroom gang was disabled, many being instantly killed by inhaling the vapor. . . . The vessel was disabled and was towed in by her consort, the [large ironclad] *Galena*, nevertheless keeping her guns going steadily. . . .

The ram *Tennessee* started out from behind the fort just before the head of the line was abreast of it, intending to attack the fleet; but, receiving two or three broadsides, changed her course and ran back

Artist's depiction of the Federal fleet entering Mobile Bay. The Confederate ram *Tennessee* is passing in front of Fort Morgan to meet the enemy. The Union monitor *Tecumseh* is foundering after having struck a mine.

again closely followed by the *Tecumseh*. . . . The latter neared the fort, pounding away at the ram with 15-inch solid shot.

CONRAD   We observed that one of the monitors [the *Tecumseh*] was apparently at a standstill; she "laid to" for a moment, seemed to reel, then slowly disappear into the gulf. Immediately, immense bubbles of steam, as large as cauldrons, rose to the surface of the water, and only eight human beings could be seen in the turmoil.

[The *Tecumseh* had struck a floating cask torpedo. Johnston pronounced the amen: "The event was the most startling and tragic loss of the day." There would seem to be scant dispute that this was the last major war whose combatants evinced any compassion for each other.]

HUTCHINSON   Captain Craven was already partly out, when the pilot [John Collins] grasped him by the leg and cried, "let me get out first, captain, for God's sake; I have five little children!" The captain drew back, saying "go on, sir," gave him his place, and went down with his ship, while the pilot was saved.

[Collins himself would be quoted as asserting that Craven had drawn back, saying, "After you, pilot." Collins maintained, "There was nothing after me. When I reached the upmost round of the ladder, the vessel seemed to drop from under me." Officers of the Confederate navy, generously enough, confirmed this exchange. The escape hatch, near the pilothouse, was the Achilles heel of the monitors, wide enough to allow only a single man out at a time. The turret of the *Tecumseh* was a sealed tomb, although two or three gunners miraculously squeezed through its narrow ports. Boats put out from the fleet and, chivalrously, from Fort Morgan, but only 21 of the 114 officers and men aboard the monitor survived the sinking, which occurred in less than two minutes.]

CONRAD   There was a dead silence on board the *Tennessee*. The men peered through the portholes at the awful catastrophe, and spoke to each other in low whispers, for they knew that the same fate was, probably, awaiting us. We were then directly over the torpedo bed, and, shut up tightly as we were in our iron capsule, in another moment it might prove our coffin.

FARRAGUT   I determined at once, as I had originally intended, to take the lead, and after ordering the *Metacomet* to send a boat to save, if possible, any of the perishing crew, I dashed ahead with the *Hartford*, and the ships followed on, their officers believing that they were [going to a noble death] with their commander-in-chief.

I steamed through the buoys where the torpedoes were supposed to have been sunk. [Conrad was informed by Union officers afterwards that they "could hear the torpedoes snapping under the bottoms of their ships, and that they expected every moment to be blown sky high."] These buoys had been previously examined by my flag-lieutenant, J. Crittenden Watson, in several nightly reconnaissances. Though he had not been able to discover the sunken torpedoes, yet we had been assured by refugees, deserters, and others of their existence, but believing that from their having been some time in the water, they were probably innocuous, I determined to take the chance of their explosion.

HUTCHINSON By this time the fleet was nearly past the forts, and the head of the line about crossing the middle ground, the ram [*Tennessee*] still lying quietly under the guns of the fort. Cheer after cheer rent the air from hundreds of lusty throats, as the ships came, two by two, inside the bay, the goal we had been longing for so eagerly for three long years.

Comrades shook hands, congratulated each other and hurrahed until hoarse. The wounded were brought up from below and comfortably stowed away in cots.

[Out of range of the forts' big guns, the fleet dropped anchor. It was a little before 8:00 A.M., time for "chow down"—breakfast. During a lull in battle, there was nothing precedent-shattering about this. Historically, when naval commanders have been in doubt about their next order, they have turned to "chow," "sweepers," polishing the brass, or swabbing the guns. As a matter of fact, Buchanan reacted in the very same way aboard the *Tennessee*.]

CONRAD The order was given, "go to breakfast!" For us on the *Tennessee* to eat below was simply impossible, on account of the heat and humidity. The heat below was terrific; intense thirst universally prevailed. The men rushed to the scuttle-butts, or watertanks, and drank greedily. Soon, hard tack and coffee were furnished, the men all eating standing, creeping out of the ports on the after deck to get a little fresh air, the officers going to the upper deck.

Admiral Buchanan, grim, silent and rigid with prospective fighting, was "stumping" up and down the deck, lame from a wound received in his first engagement in the *Merrimack*. In about 15 minutes we observed that instead of heading for the safe lee of the fort, our iron prow was pointed for the enemy's fleet. Suppressed exclamations were beginning to be heard from the officers and crew: "the old admiral has not had the fight out yet; he is heading for that big fleet; he will get his fill of it up there!"

Slowly and gradually this fact became apparent to us, and I, being on his staff and in close association with him, ventured to ask him: "are you going into that fleet, admiral?" "I am, sir!" was his reply. Without intending to be heard by him, I said to an officer standing near me: "well, we'll never come out of there whole!" But Buchanan had heard my remark, and turning around said sharply: "that's my lookout, sir!"

[Thus, it would prove a short breakfast aboard the ships of both fleets. Buchanan was the personification of aggression. On the other hand, he was impelled by a number of factors that day, not the least of which was excessively low coal in his bunkers. In a short time, he would not be able to get up steam at all. The diminishing supply of coal was plaguing the entire Confederate navy. Locomotives could effectively burn wood. Ships could not.]

FARRAGUT   I perceived the ram *Tennessee* standing up for this ship . . . at 8:45. I was not long in comprehending his intention to be the destruction of the flagship. The monitors and such of the wooden vessels as I thought best adapted for the purpose were immediately ordered to attack the ram, not only with their guns, but bows on at full speed, and then began one of the fiercest naval combats on record.

HUTCHINSON   On she came, steadily and fast, paying no more attention to the terrible fire that was concentrated upon her from the entire fleet than to so many hailstones, and attempted to ram several of the large ships. . . . Soon the monitors came up, and solid 11- and 15-inch shot struck her a dozen a minute* from a range of less than 100 yards without the slightest effect, she blazing away with her battery of 7-inch Brookes rifles. Never was ship more gallantly fought against more fearful odds.

Finding what small impression our fire was making upon her, the admiral now signalled the *Lackawanna*, *Monongahela*, and *Ossipee*, "run down rebel ram!" Four bells—"go ahead, full speed!" rang from the bridge, the captain's post, and we went at her.

CONRAD   As we approached the enemy's fleet one after another of Farragut's wooden frigates swept out in a wide circle, and by the time we reached the point where the monitors were, a huge leading frigate was coming at the rate of 10 miles an hour, a column of white foam formed of the dead water piled in front of its bows many feet high. Heavy cannonading from the monitors was going on at this time, when the leading wooden vessel came rapidly bearing down on us. . . .

Captain Johnston in the pilot house gave the word to officers and men: "steady yourselves when she strikes. Stand by and be ready!" Not a word was heard on deck.

FARRAGUT   The *Monongahela*, Commander J. H. Strong, was the first vessel that struck her, and in doing so carried away his own iron prow . . . without apparently doing her adversary much injury.

*The three remaining monitors could not possibly have fired a dozen rounds in sixty seconds, since each could loose only about twelve shots an hour.

HUTCHINSON   The *Lackawanna* was more fortunate and delivered a fair blow, going at the tremendous speed of 14 knots, just where the iron house joined the main deck, with a shock that prostrated every man on deck and tore to atoms her solid oak bow for six feet as if it had been paper. No more damage was done the ram by this tremendous blow than if a lady had laid her finger upon the iron sheathing. . . . The *Lackawanna* backed clear of the *Tennessee*, when the latter swung around on our port beam and delivered her broadside into us at three feet distance. . . . Her shell, 98-pounder percussion, all exploded on the berth deck, just as they entered the ship, entirely destroying the powder division. . . . The surgeon's steward and one nurse were torn into such small pieces that no part of either of them was ever identified.

The scene on the berth deck was dismal enough. So full of smoke that where a moment before was a crowd of busy men, nothing was visible except the red glare of the blazing woodwork which had taken fire from the exploding shell, with no sound beside the groans of the wounded and dying and thunder of cannon overhead, a new element of horror was added by the news that the magazine was on fire!

In that chamber were stored 17 tons of gunpowder, and if the flames reached that, out shrift were short indeed. In the magazine of a man-of-war, the powder is put up in cartridges of red flannel, of various sizes, and these are stored for greater safety in copper canisters, each containing about 100 pounds.

In passing up the cartridges to the boys whose duty it was to carry them to the guns, and who are called powder monkeys, the gunner had shaken out on the floor of the magazine passage a small quantity of powder which lay in little heaps along the passage, a long narrow way leading from the berth deck to the main chamber. From one of these little heaps to another, and around the prostrate form of the gunner, who had been stunned by the concussion, flame was flashing toward the deadly mass, when the ship's armorer, George Taylor, came at a leap down from the spar deck, and seeing at a glance the deadly peril, sprang down into the passage and extinguished the fire with his naked hands, burning them to the bone.

FARRAGUT   The *Hartford* was the third vessel which struck her, but as the *Tennessee* quickly shifted her helm, the blow was a glancing one, and as she rasped along our side we poured our whole port broadside of IX-inch solid shot within 10 feet of her casemate.

[The admiral was once again lashed to the rigging, "a position from which he might have jumped to the deck of the ram as she passed," according to Signal Officer Kinney.]

JOHNSTON   Early in the action, the pilot of the *Tennessee* had been wounded by having the trap door on top of the pilot house knocked down upon his head by a shot from one of the enemy's ships. . . . Therefore, I remained in the pilot house, for the purpose of directing the movements of the ram.

The *Tennessee*, here pictured after she had been speedily repaired and put into service under the Stars and Stripes.

KINNEY The *Tennessee* now became the target for the whole fleet, all the vessels of which were making toward her, pounding her with shot, and trying to run her down. As the *Hartford* turned to make for her again, we ran in front of the *Lackawanna*, which had already turned and was moving under full headway with the same object. She struck us on our starboard side, amidships, crushing halfway through, knocking two portholes into one, upsetting one of the Dahlgren guns, and creating general consternation.

For a time it was thought that we must sink, and the cry rang out over the deck: "Save the admiral!" The port boats were ordered lowered, and in their haste some of the sailors cut the falls, and two of the cutters dropped into the water wrong side up, and floated astern. But the admiral sprang into the starboard mizzen-rigging, looked over the side of the ship, and, finding there were still a few inches to spare above the water's edge, instantly ordered the ship ahead again at full speed, after the ram.

The unfortunate *Lackawanna*, which had struck the ram a second blow, was making for her once more and, singularly enough, again came up on our starboard side, and another collision seemed imminent. And now the admiral seemed a trifle excited. He had no idea of whipping the rebels to be himself sunk by a friend, nor did he realize at the moment that the *Hartford* was as much to blame as the *Lackawanna*. Turning to [me], he inquired:

"Can you say 'for God's sake' by signal?"

"Yes sir."

"Then say to the *Lackawanna*, 'for God's sake get out of our way and anchor!'"

In my haste to send the message, I brought the end of my signal staff down with considerable violence upon the head of the admiral, who was standing nearer than I thought, causing him to wince perceptibly.

FARRAGUT We soon got clear again, however, and were fast approaching our adversary. . . . She was at this time sore beset. The *Chickasaw* was pounding away at her stern, the *Ossipee* was approaching her at full speed, and the *Monongahela, Lackawanna* and this ship were bearing down upon her, determined upon her destruction. Her smokestack had been shot away, her steering chains were gone, compelling a resort to her relieving tackles, and several of her port shutters were jammed.

JOHNSTON The monitors kept up a constant firing at short range. . . . One of these [11-inch] missiles struck the iron cover of the stern port and jammed it against the shield so that it became impossible to run the gun out for firing. . . .

[While machinists and carpenters were being summoned on the double in the hope of repairing the extensive damage, a solid shot from one of the monitors tore one crewman to pieces and shattered a metal shield. Jagged splinters killed one seaman and broke Admiral Buchanan's left leg below the knee.]

The admiral sent for me, and as I approached he quietly remarked, "well, Johnston, they've got me. You'll have to look out for her now. This is your fight, you know." While returning to the pilot house I felt the vessel careen so suddenly as nearly to throw me off my feet. I discovered that the *Hartford* had run into the ram amidships, and that while thus in contact with her the Federal crew were using their small arms by firing through the open ports.

. . . Realizing the impossibility of directing the firing of the guns without the use of the rudder, and that the ship had been rendered utterly helpless, I went to the lower deck and informed the admiral of her condition, and that I had not been able to bring a gun to bear upon any of our antagonists for nearly half an hour, to which he replied:

"Well, Johnston, if you cannot do them any further damage you had better surrender."

I concluded that no good object could be accomplished by sacrificing the lives of the officers and men in such a one-sided contest, and therefore proceeded to the top of the shield and took down the ensign. . . . While in the act, several shots passed close to me, and when I went below to order the engines to be stopped the firing of the enemy was continued.

I then decided, although with an almost bursting heart, to hoist the white flag.

HUTCHINSON The ram now stood away for the fort, followed by the whole fleet and almost covered with shot. . . . At 10 o'clock precisely she hauled down her colors, and ran up the white flag, amidst thundering cheers from all hands of us, and feelings of indescribable exultation.

[Captain William E. Le Roy of the sloop *Ossipee* had already gathered speed to ram when he saw the white flag. The end of the wild contest had come with unexpected suddenness. Too late, he gave orders to reverse engines and cease fire. The big warship hit the *Tennessee*'s starboard quarter, but without doing significant damage.]

JOHNSTON Her commander hailed, saying "this is the United States steamer *Ossipee*. Hello, Johnston, how are you? Le Roy—don't you know me? I'll send a boat alongside for you." When I reached the deck of his ship, he remarked, "I am glad to see you, Johnston. Here's some icewater for you, I know you're dry; but I have something better than that for you, down below."

CONRAD We immediately carried all our wounded upon the roof into the fresh air, which they so much needed. From that elevated place I witnessed the rush of the petty officers and men of the monitor, which was nearest to us, to board the captured ship.

After some confusion as to who should convey Admiral Buchanan's sword to the victorious Farragut, Captain Le Roy designated an officer to carry it, with dignity, to the flagship. The Union admiral was not hesitant about accepting the token of submission.

Thus ended an historic engagement of one ship pitted against an entire fleet. The Union lost heavily, with 172 killed and 170 wounded; the Confederates suffered 12 killed, 20 wounded, and 243 captured.

In the terse amen of Captain Drayton of the *Hartford*, it was "a pretty sharp skrimmage!"

The ram *Albemarle*, here pictured in the Norfolk Navy Yard after being salvaged. Note the female observers on the foredeck.

U.S. Naval Historical Center

Chapter 9

FIGHTING MAN OF THE NORTH CAROLINA SOUNDS

USS *Monticello*
Hampton Roads, Virginia, July 9, 1864

Confidential

SIR: Deeming the capture or destruction of the rebel ram Albemarle
*feasible, I beg leave to state that I am acquainted with the waters held by
her, and am willing to undertake the task.*

*If furnished with three low-pressure tugs, one or more fitted with tor-
pedoes, and all armed with light howitzers, it might be effected, or if rubber
boats were on hand to transport across the swamp to a point immediately
abreast of Plymouth. If detailed for this work, I would like to superintend
the outfit of the boats.*

I am, sir, very respectfully, your obedient servant,

W. B. Cushing
Lieutenant, Commanding

Acting Rear-Admiral S. P. Lee
Comdg. North Atlantic Blockading Squadron,
Hampton Roads

HEROES COME IN ALL SIZES AND TYPES, fully equipped to hammer out their contributions to history. None is a die stamp of any other—try, for example, comparing Joe Bailey and Davy Farragut— yet all possess a common denominator, a measure of courage far more generous than that accorded the average man or woman. They tend to be innovative, and they tend to be obsessed by a desire to succeed. They are sublimely confident of overcoming challenges considered overwhelming by the average person.

A very special case in point was William Barker Cushing.

"Will," as most of his peers knew him, grew up like any small-town boy in Fredonia, New York, located about seventy-five miles southwest of Buffalo. He was only four when his father died in 1846. The latter had been quite a man—a physician, a justice of the peace, and a part-time merchant. The cause of his premature death is not a matter of record.

Will Cushing's mother saw to it that the boy attended Fredonia Academy, where he was an average student. If he excelled in anything, it was mathematics and English. Upon his graduation in 1856, he moved to Washington to become a page in the United States House of Representatives. Proving himself an adept politician at the age of fifteen, he won an appointment to the Naval Academy. Thus, in 1857, the six-foot-tall, blond, and wiry, though frail, young man became Midshipman Cushing. He was subject to recurrent headaches and respiratory infections.

In his second year at the Naval Academy, Will stood third in a class of thirty-seven in the subject of gunnery and ninth in general order of merit. Even so, he was not to graduate. Pranks—though scarcely more than the norm for an underclassman—compounded by his Spanish professor's running vendetta against him resulted in Cushing's forced resignation on March 23, 1861. It was not quite three weeks before the firing on Fort Sumter.

The academy's venting of petty pique seemed both a slap at the Congress that had appointed him and a waste of public funds. But Will did have his champions, especially Lieutenant Commander Charles W. Flusser, a professor. Flusser managed, on April 1, an appointment for Cushing as a master's mate, a junior rank of some responsibility even though the pay was low—forty dollars a month. Cushing was assigned to the USS *Minnesota*—soon to become Admiral Goldsborough's flagship—riding majestically at anchor off Fort Monroe.

Within three months, the nineteen-year-old Cushing was given command of two prize ships: a schooner and a bark. In late summer, he was a member of a raiding party that burned ten craft and captured one schooner in the backwater around Hampton Roads. He seemed to have acquired the killer instinct early on; he wrote his mother of "the supreme pleasure of burning one of the vessels with *my own* hands!"

By the spring of 1862, Cushing was a veteran of naval operations in the Tidewater area of Virginia. Attached to the converted steamer *Cambridge*, he was occupied with boarding and inspecting suspected blockade-runners, a duty attended with obvious peril. Should a vessel turn out to be a privateer, he risked being taken prisoner or being shot on sight.

On March 8, the day the *Merrimack* ran amuck, the *Cambridge* served as a tug, towing larger warships out of range of the furious ironclad. Cushing, in fact, was slightly nicked by shrapnel from one of the Confederate ship's many guns, but he missed the epochal encounter with the *Monitor*, since the *Cambridge* was ordered that Saturday night to Beaufort, North Carolina.

By August, manifestly pleased with Cushing's performance, the navy promoted him to the rank of lieutenant and granted his request for duty as executive officer on Flusser's *Commodore Perry*. In October, the former ferryboat was steaming up the Blackwater River, above Pamlico Sound, in support of ground forces attacking Franklin, Virginia. It was a brisk action, as Flusser would report to the Navy Department: "We kept up a fire of great guns and musketry. With the forward IX-inch gun I threw shells in the direction of Franklin; with the forward 32-pounder poured grape and canister into the wood on our left; with the after 32-pounder and field gun gave them the same on the right, and shelled the bluff. . . . At 10:15 we started down, getting a terrible fire from the bluff. The enemy continued to fire at us from every available point. . . . They also attempted to block the river in our rear, by felling trees, through which obstructions we pushed with a heavy head of steam."

The cost of this "excursion" was two dead and ten wounded, two of whom would later succumb. Flusser made mention of the "great gallantry" of Lieutenant Cushing, "who ran the fieldpiece [an army cannon mounted on wagon wheels] out amid a storm of bullets, took a sure and deliberate aim at the rebels, and sent a charge of canister among them that completely silenced their fire at that point."

Flusser postscripted, "He is the fighting man of the North Carolina sounds."

Cushing's reward came quickly; he was given command of the iron gunboat *Ellis*, which had been captured from the Confederates. As a leader of raiding parties, Cushing proceeded to destroy vital salt works and other installations, stores of cotton and tobacco, and the schooner *Adelaide*, when she was only twelve miles from the safety of Wilmington. In seizing another schooner, the *Jacksonville*, he found on board a consignment of slaves, whom he freed at once. His luck ran out in late November 1862, however, when the *Ellis* came too close to shore batteries and was sunk.

The "fighting man of the North Carolina sounds" continued his aggressive amphibious role in early 1863 as he made hit-and-run forays among South Carolina's strongholds. After relieving Richard Renshaw as captain of the *Commodore Barney*, he pressed his attacks until the ferryboat was too holed by artillery to be serviceable.

Barney was ordered to Baltimore for overhaul in June, affording Cushing a chance to renew old contacts in Washington. Gideon Welles, whom he had previously met, greeted him with warmth. Cushing was always ready to volunteer advice on winning the war, and the navy secretary decided to

William Barker Cushing.

introduce him to President Lincoln. Cushing found the president "rather subdued and sad" over Union reverses. Lincoln thought things were going pretty well at sea and upon the rivers, but he simply could not seem to find the right generals. (With the fall of Vicksburg in just a few more days, he would know he had found one in Grant.)

Later in the summer of 1863, after his older brother, Alonzo, had been killed at Gettysburg, Cushing returned to the *Barney* and duty off the Carolinas. That winter, he received his largest warship, the *Monticello*, a 655-ton, 11-knot screw steamer. He soon attempted his boldest venture yet: the capture of General Louis Hébert, the engineer who commanded the Cape Fear Department. It was the sort of military impudence that had been the province of the Confederate cavalry—the capturing of ranking officers asleep in their quarters.

Cushing knew that Hébert worked out of Smith's Island, the location of the Cape Fear headland, at the mouth of the river leading into Wilmington. On February 29, 1864, Cushing set out with twenty men in two small boats, rowed silently under the guns of Fort Caswell, and landed near the tiny town of Smithville (now Southport). There, the raiders enlisted the services of two willing slaves, who led them to Confederate headquarters.

The headquarters proved surprisingly unguarded. Cushing kicked open an inside door to find a tall man wearing a nightcap and nightgown holding a chair menacingly above his head. "I had him on his back in an instant with the muzzle of a revolver at his temple and my hand on his throat," the naval officer would recall.

But he had not caught Hébert, who was away in Wilmington. Cushing's prisoner was merely the general's adjutant, a junior officer named W. D. Hardman. Before returning to the *Monticello*, his lesser catch in tow, Cushing penned a note: "I deeply regret that you were not here when I called."

Two months later, in April, Cushing learned of the death of his friend and benefactor, Lieutenant Commander Flusser, aboard the *Miami* by fire from the Confederate ram *Albemarle*. Grief hardened into a resolve for revenge. Cushing found himself writing scenarios for the destruction of the *Albemarle* to any and all Washington officials who would listen. But the summer of 1864 was distinguished by operations on a grand scale: Sherman was knocking on the portals of Atlanta, and Grant was digging in around Petersburg for the final assault on Richmond. One ship, even a big enemy ship, had to be considered in relation to greater concerns.

Mindful of the fate of *New Ironsides* and *Housatonic*, Cushing decided that the simplest tactics would likely be the most effective. His answer was a torpedo, delivered not by a submarine, since none was obtainable, but by a vessel that would anticipate the torpedo boats of two twentieth-century wars. He resolved to obtain small, swift steam launches and spar torpedoes armed with at least a hundred pounds of powder. Then, in the dark, he would dash in and explode a charge below the water line and beneath the armor plating of his foe.

How could he fail?

Admiral S. P. Lee had initially approved Cushing's plan, but he had since been relieved as commander of the North Atlantic Blockading Squadron by Admiral Porter, who looked upon the expedition as "a forlorn hope." He could not decide if the young officer with the exemplary record made sense or not. Like Sherman, however, Porter was concerned with the broad canvas. At worst, the squadron stood to lose only a small boat or two if Cushing pushed ahead. "I have no great confidence in his success," Porter wrote to Commander W. H. Macomb of the *Shamrock*, a double-ender in the Roanoke Squadron, "but you will afford him all the assistance in your power, and keep boats ready to pick him up in case of failure."

It must have seemed to Porter like Joe Bailey and the Red River all over again. Only the cast, the background, and, of course, the objective differed.

Meanwhile, life had settled down to a humdrum aboard the *Albemarle*. She was at anchor off Plymouth, gathering river vegetation and scum on her keel from inaction. Her engines were turned over infrequently for lack of coal. She was undermanned, and the morale of those who comprised her meager company was low. Captain J. W. Cooke, who after great expenditure of effort had sunk only one ferryboat, had been relieved by none other than John Maffitt. Duty aboard the *Albemarle* proved at once too dull for Maffitt, however, since he cherished the sport of blockade-running as others might women or fine bourbon. In September, Maffitt wangled command of the new iron-hulled steamer *Owl*, built in England for the Confederacy.

The *Albemarle*'s third captain was Lieutenant Alexander F. Warley, a professorial-appearing officer with a neatly trimmed moustache who had commanded the 387-ton ironclad *Manassas* on the Mississippi; he had rammed the *Brooklyn* during Farragut's capture of New Orleans. Warley, graduated in 1846 from the first class at Annapolis, could not fathom why he had received no orders to go out on the attack. He was in a quandary as to whether he should take it upon himself to scrounge some coal and ammunition, borrow soldiers idling on the shore, and go thumping back down the Roanoke. Perhaps such indecisiveness was responsible for keeping Warley, almost twenty years out of the Naval Academy, a lieutenant. He would recall gloomily: "When I took command . . . I found her made fast to the river bank nearly abreast of the town of Plymouth. She was surrounded by a cordon of single cypress logs chained together, about ten feet from her side. There was no reason why the place might not be recaptured any day; the guns commanding the river were in no condition for use, and the troops in charge of them were worn down by ague, and were undrilled and worthless."

The anchorage was unfavorable from both offensive and defensive standpoints. Shallow and rather swift, the river was only a hundred yards across in some places, affording poor maneuverability for the elephantine *Albemarle*. The pinpoint town of Plymouth offered no substantial buildings that could be commandeered as strongholds. The only exception was the handsome, old, brick and stone Grace Episcopal Church, whose spire dominated the otherwise nondescript town. The Confederates, however, stopped short of using the house of worship as any manner of bastion.

Relief troops marched in during the latter part of October, even as rumors spread of "a steam launch having been seen in the river." Warley paid a call on the new army commander and bluntly informed him that "the safety of the place depended on the *Albemarle*, and the safety of the *Albemarle* depended on the watchfulness of his pickets."

The officer appeared to understand, at once arranging a "picket" of twenty-five men equipped with rockets and a cannon aboard a small schooner being used as a work vessel in the attempt to raise the *Southfield*, sunk in April by the *Albemarle*.

"The crew of the *Albemarle* numbered but 60," Warley continued, "too small a force to allow me to keep an armed watch on deck at night and to do outside picketing besides. Moreover, to break the monotony of the life and keep down ague, I had always out an expedition of ten men, who were uniformly successful in doing a fair amount of damage to the enemy."

"Monotony" was but part of the penance aboard the *Albemarle*. Her heavy hull—without ports except for those designed for the guns—and her armor plating made her a stifling iron box. The men mused whether the heat, some days, were sufficient to bake bread. Her so-called fo'c'sles were unbearable ovens. When they fired up her boilers, *Albemarle* was purgatory. Desertions were commonplace.

The captain remained on the alert. More and more nervous as time passed, he would remove his pince-nez for repeated sightings through his binoculars.

The evening of October 27 was "dark and slightly rainy." Warley doubled the watch "and took extra precautions." He recalled being especially uneasy, though he was not fully certain why. Shortly before 3:00 A.M. on the twenty-eighth, he was up and peering out into the murk. Nothing was to be seen. The only sounds were the occasional coughs of those on watch. It was too early for the first call of the roosters from the many poultry pens.

On October 25, Cushing returned to the Roanoke Squadron from Norfolk, where he had assembled his little "fleet." It had been a rough trip, part of the route through the imperiled Dismal Swamp Canal. He had lost two of his three boats—one grounded and surrendered to Confederate guerrillas, while the other sank in rough seas.

Porter, aghast, wrote, "Cushing's condition when he reported on board the flagship [*Malvern*] was most deplorable. He had been subjected to the severest exposure without shelter, for over a week, had lost all his clothes except what little he had on, and his attenuated face and sunken eyes bore witness to the privations he had suffered. Officers and crew had subsisted on spoiled ship's biscuit and water, and an occasional potato cooked before the boiler fire."

The next day, the twenty-sixth, several Union ships were lazing on picket duty near the mouth of the Roanoke River. They included the big double-ender *Otsego*, the squadron "flag" *Shamrock*, the ferryboat *Commodore Hull*, and lesser craft. Master's Mate Thomas S. Gay aboard the *Otsego* watched the approach of a small steam launch until it hove to alongside.

"Ahoy there!" came the call from a lanky, blond lieutenant. Will Cushing was making the rounds of the vessels, seeking volunteers for a most unusual "expedition," to be undertaken by a single 30-foot steam cutter. He described the exact nature of his operation succinctly: "To endeavor to destroy the rebel ram *Albemarle!*"

Cushing could have obtained all the volunteers he needed from his own *Monticello*, but he wanted the expedition to be representative of the Roanoke flotilla. He recruited Gay and two other officers from the *Otsego* and three officers and eight men from various other ships. There were fifteen in all, Cushing included.

One veteran from the Smithville foray and other "expeditions of peril," as Cushing phrased it, could not stay out of this one. He was tough, brawny Master's Mate William L. Howorth, who possessed a signal lack strangely common among sailors—he could not swim a stroke. Neither could Master's Mate John Woodman of the *Commodore Hull*, though Mate Gay of the *Otsego* was an exception. He was a strong swimmer.

Cushing outlined the challenges: a river, the Roanoke, 150 yards at its widest point; "several thousand soldiers" occupying Plymouth and forts along the banks (the young officer was not above wildly exaggerating the little garrison actually present); and sentries stationed on the wreck of the *Southfield*. "It seem[s] impossible to surprise, or to attack with hope of success." Then, with a touch of the theatric, Cushing observed that "impossibilities are for the timid!" and that "all obstacles" could be "overcome."

That night, Cushing and a few of his group with like tastes dined on champagne and terrapin. When he learned of the feast, Porter was piqued. A ham and eggs—and whiskey—man, the admiral may have been out of sorts because he was not invited.

At 11:00 P.M. on October 27, a Thursday, the lieutenant's launch, equipped with its spar torpedo, cast loose from the *Otsego*. A cutter in tow with two officers and ten men had been added to the force. Its mission was to attack and capture whatever pickets were on the wreck of the *Southfield*. All were armed with revolvers, cutlasses, and hand grenades in the event that Cushing decided to storm his target.

Throttling back the steam pressure, Cushing glided past the *Southfield*, no more than twenty yards abeam. The Confederate sentries must have been asleep. Since he had apparently attained his first objective—surprise—Cushing then decided to land at Plymouth's "lower wharf" and approach the ram from the banks. It was at that point that Lieutenant Warley aboard the *Albemarle* spotted the strange silhouette approaching.

The launch had just passed a stronghold known as Fort Race, according to Master's Mate Gay, and was "within hailing distance of the ram." The cutter was cast loose and ordered to take the *Southfield*. In the rain and darkness, there was confusion as to the exact position of the raiding party. Even while Cushing was "sheering in" his craft close to the wharf, Gay reported, a light appeared that they "took to be aboard the *Albemarle*," but astern, rather than ahead of, the launch. "On turning around, we were hailed from the ram. We made no answer. We were hailed again, making no answer, but still getting in a fair position."

Warley "rang the alarm bell." Since he could not depress his big guns at such close range, he ordered musket fire and grape from a small stern gun.

Steering for "the dark mountain of iron in front of us," Cushing had the impression that the enemy was "much confused," and he resolved to exploit that factor to its utmost advantage. "A heavy fire was at once opened upon us, not only from the ship, but from men stationed on the shore. This did not disable us, and we neared them rapidly. A large fire now blazed upon the bank, and by its light I discovered the unfortunate fact that there was a circle of logs around the *Albemarle*, boomed well out from her side with the very intention of preventing the action of torpedoes." Though Warley had placed the breadth of the boom at ten feet, Cushing estimated it at three times that figure.

At least one of his men had been wounded, Cushing wrote, while "three bullets—the air seemed full of them—struck my clothing."

He steered parallel to the log boom to examine it more carefully, then "sheered off for the purpose of turning, a hundred yards away, and going at the booms squarely, at right angles, trusting to their having been long enough in the water to have become slimy—in which case my boat, under full headway, would bump up against them and slip over into the pen with the ram.

"This was my only chance of success, and once over the obstruction my boat would never get out again. As I turned, the whole back of my coat was torn out by buckshot, and the sole of my shoe was carried away. The fire was very severe. In a lull of the firing, the captain hailed us, again demanding what boat it was. All my men gave comical answers, and mine was a dose of canister from the [12-pound] howitzer."

According to Gay, however, Cushing did more than fire. He sang out, "Leave the ram, or I'll blow you to pieces!"

It was much in character.

"In another instant," Cushing continued, "we had struck the logs and were over, with headway nearly gone, slowly forging up under the enemy's quarterport. Ten feet from us, the muzzle of a rifle gun looked into our faces, and every word of command on board was distinctly heard.

"My clothing was perforated with bullets as I stood in the bow, the heel jigger [part of the controls of the torpedo boom] in my right hand and the exploding-line in the left. We were near enough then, and I ordered the boom lowered until the forward motion of the launch carried the torpedo under the ram's overhang. A strong pull of the detaching-line, a moment's waiting for the torpedo to rise under the hull, and I hauled in the left hand, just cut by a bullet.

"The explosion took place at the same instant that 100 pounds of grape, at 10 feet range, crashed

Artist's depiction of the launch used by Cushing to sink the *Albemarle*.

among us, and the dense mass of water thrown out by the torpedo came down with choking weight upon us."

The *Albemarle* was doomed.

Warley ascertained at once that the torpedo had "smashed a large hole in us just under the waterline, big enough to drive a wagon in!"

Understandably, "everything" aboard the little launch was "in the greatest excitement," according to Gay. He had the impression that the little craft was "backed off," but Cushing was certain it was too disabled from water and shot to be moved.

The *Albemarle*'s captain called twice to the attackers to surrender. Cushing shouted at his men not to do so, but to save themselves instead. Then, throwing his sword, revolver, shoes, and coat overboard, Cushing leaped into the river. "It was cold long after the frosts. . . . The water chilled the blood, while the whole surface of the stream was plowed up by grape and musketry, and my nearest friends, the fleet, were twelve miles away . . . so I swam for the opposite shore. As I neared it, a man [Fireman Samuel Higgins] of my crew gave a great gurgling yell and went down."

Gay, along with several others, "sprang overboard" shortly after Cushing disappeared into the dark waters. He had not been swimming long when he "fell in with Mate Howorth [Cushing's veteran shipmate] on a log unable to proceed farther without assistance. Having a life preserver with me, I gave it to him and returned to the boat to procure another, not knowing how far I might have to swim, and at the same time I destroyed two boxes of ammunition and several carbines."

In the water a second time, Gay felt deeply chilled. "After a severe struggle," he wrote, "I regained the circle of logs where I found several of the crew, with a boat from the ram."

The war was over for Mate Gay. For all practical purposes, it was over for Lieutenant Warley as well. Vainly, Warley shouted orders for the *Albemarle*'s pumps to be manned and her furnaces stoked. They were apparently cold. He held forlorn hopes that sufficient steam could at least be raised to work "the donkey engine," which would operate the pumps, but "the water gained on us so fast that all exertions were fruitless, and the vessel went down in a few moments, merely leaving her shield and smokestack out."

Thrashing to keep afloat, Cushing was considerably surprised to hear his name being called from one of the *Albemarle*'s boats. Not bothering to speculate as to how the enemy knew of him, he struck out into the blackness with renewed vigor to avoid capture.

"This time, as I struggled to reach the bank, I heard a groan in the river behind me. Although very much exhausted, [I] concluded to turn and aid . . . the swimmer." Cushing thus came upon Master's Mate John Woodman from the *Commodore Hull*.

"Knocking his cap from his head, I used my right arm to sustain him and ordered him to strike out. For ten minutes at least, I think, he managed to keep afloat when, his physical force being completely gone, he sank like a stone."

The lieutenant kept on, swimming, he hoped, in the general direction of Plymouth, but, according to his account, "not making much headway, as my strokes were now very feeble, my clothes being soaked and heavy, and little chop-seas splashing with choking persistence into my mouth every time I gasped for breath."

Cushing had little idea how long he had been in the water when his feet touched soft mud. He lay semiconscious, half in the water and half on the riverbank, "not forty yards from one of the forts," until dawn. When the sun came out "bright and warm," he saw that the area was swarming with Confederate troops and sailors, the latter from the *Albemarle*, he suspected. In fact, two officers passing close to Cushing's swampy refuge speculated on the events of the night, wondering "how it was done."

He spent the morning moving slowly through the cypress swamp, lacerated again and again by "a network of thorns and briers that cut into the flesh at every step like knives." At noon, he encountered a slave and bribed him with twenty dollars in soggy greenbacks and "some texts of Scripture" to venture into town for news. When the man returned at about 2:00 P.M., he brought enough information so that, in Cushing's mind, "there was no longer doubt that [the *Albemarle*] had gone down."

Later in the afternoon, it was the lieutenant's good fortune to come upon a picket party of seven soldiers eating their supper and, for the moment, forgetting their small skiff tied to a cypress root. Cushing crept to it as silently as possible, cast it loose, and was away.

"Hour after hour I paddled, never ceasing for a moment, first on one side, then on the other, while sunshine passed into twilight that was swallowed up in thick darkness, only relieved by the few faint star rays that penetrated the heavy swamp curtain on either side. At last I reached the mouth of the Roanoke and found the open sound [Albemarle Sound]."

Steering by a star, Cushing finally saw the outline of the Federal fleet at anchor. He shouted "Ship ahoy!" several times before attracting attention.

The picket vessel *Valley City*, one of the original fleet in Pamlico Sound, lowered its boats, which cautiously circled Cushing, not knowing whether his vessel was a Confederate torpedo craft. It was "some time," by Cushing's calculations, before it was decided that the strange skiff was not bent on harm.

On board the *Valley City*, Cushing told of his successful exploit while sipping brandy. Then, as he would recall, "rockets were thrown up and all hands were called to cheer ship."

The captains of the other vessels were summoned to the *Valley City* to formulate a plan for attack up the river. Word was sent ashore to the army. By midmorning, the forces were off for Plymouth.

Warley's objectivity far exceeded his capacity for success and his luck. He concluded that "a more gallant thing [than the destruction of his own ship] was not done during the war." Though he was certain that Plymouth should be abandoned, he volunteered his crew to aid in its defense. After sinking the old schooner—the vessel that had assisted in the efforts to raise the *Southfield*—in the channel near the wreck where she had worked, he salvaged two 8-inch guns and some shells from the *Albemarle* and set them in position near the town.

"I did not have to wait long," Warley wrote. "The fleet steamed up to the obstructions, fired a few shells over the town, steamed down again, and early next morning were in the river and opened fire. . . . The fire of the fleet was concentrated on us [the two 8-inchers] and one at least of the steamers was so near that I could hear the orders given to elevate or depress guns.

"When I felt that by hanging on I could only sacrifice my men and achieve nothing, I ordered our guns spiked and the men sent round to the road by a ravine."

Thus, within seventy-two hours of the destruction of the ram, Plymouth's defenders lost heart without the big vessel's protection, and the town was again occupied by the Union. The commander of the Federal forces asked that the bells of Grace Church be "rung out!"

Cushing received the thanks of the Navy Department. President Lincoln asked Congress to express its august appreciation in a formal resolution, yet a Medal of Honor was never mentioned, even though it had been bestowed on some for exploits far less daring—an entire regiment won the coveted medal for duty no more hazardous than guarding the White House, for example. Had Cushing been a Briton in the service of Her Majesty, he would undoubtedly have earned an earldom and some such title as "Cushing of Albemarle."

The death of Commander Flusser, however, had been avenged.

In January, Cushing participated in the final assault on Fort Fisher, which had for so long guarded the approach to Wilmington. He took possession of encircling batteries that had been abandoned by their defenders. (Nearly bagged as an unexpected bonus in the assault was John Maffitt, who veered off his *Owl* moments before entering the channel under the guns now manned by Union forces. Heading down the coast for Charleston, Maffitt was intercepted off Rattlesnake Shoal. His small vessel was almost perforated, and a dozen crewmen were wounded, but the veteran blockade-runner's luck held. He made port, only to flee seaward once more before Sherman's conquering army.)

Cushing also revisited the town of Smithville. Again, General Hébert was gone. It would prove an enduring frustration to the aggressive young lieutenant that he never managed to meet the Confederate commander vis-à-vis.

Appomattox was only months away. Unlike many, perhaps the majority, of his shipmates, Cushing remained in the service, where he commanded various vessels. But his health deteriorated; he suffered further headaches and respiratory infections. What was the matter with him? The surgeons could not diagnose his ailment or ailments. Cancer, perhaps? Tuberculosis?

As with so many who gave so much in the Civil War, Cushing's flame was as ephemeral as it was brilliant. In 1874, as a lieutenant commander, he died suddenly.

He was thirty-two years old.

Artist's rendering of the *Alabama*.

U.S. Naval Historical Center

"OLD BEESWAX" AND THE *ALABAMA*

*"She sat upon the water with the lightness
and grace of a swan."*

JUST *WHAT* WAS THE RIDDLE OF RAPHAEL HARWOOD SEMMES?

Why did this aristocratic individual whose lineage was intertwined with the founding of the nation come to hate the United States with an all-consuming vitriol?

One of the most senior officers in either the Union or the Confederate navy, Semmes was old enough to have been the father, but not quite the grandfather, of William Barker Cushing. Born in September 1809 in Charles County, Maryland, just seven months after the birth of Abraham Lincoln, Semmes was of French-American, Catholic descent. Benedict Joseph Semmes had come over with Lord Baltimore in 1640 aboard the *Ark and Dove*. A descendant on his mother's side, Arthur Middleton, was a signer of the Declaration of Independence.

Raphael Semmes grew up much as an orphan. His mother died when he was very young and his father, Richard, when he was ten. Raphael and his brother Samuel went to live with an uncle, also named Raphael, in Georgetown, the District of Columbia. The young Raphael would recall, among the few pleasant memories of his life, "the Potomac in whose waters I used to swim and fish." He helped in the operation of his uncle's wood yard.

Raphael became a tall teenager, well over six feet, with a shock of red hair and a florid complexion. More imposing than handsome, with a hawklike, dour expression, he evoked attention—so much so

Captain Raphael Semmes aboard the CSS *Alabama* at Simonstown (Cape Town) in August 1863.
His first officer, Lieutenant John McIntosh Kell, is in the background.

U.S. Naval Historical Center

that President John Quincy Adams appointed him a midshipman in 1826. He had been nominated by another uncle, Benedict Semmes, a farmer and a member of the Maryland legislature who would be elected to the United States Congress in 1829.

Semmes was in no way at a loss for words in chronicling his later life and venting combustible thoughts on the Federal government, but he offered no hint of why a lad from a landbound family of businessmen, farmers, and lawyers should seek the seas. It wasn't an easy choice in those days unless one aspired to the captaincy of a merchantman. The Naval Academy in Annapolis was almost two decades on the horizon. Midshipmen—more the product of tradition than of a formalized program—went back to colonial days, when sons of the affluent were honored with berths on British men-o'-war.

The Revolutionary War effectively ended that opportunity. The War of 1812 made it final. Schools for midshipmen were established around the turn of the century in Norfolk, New York, and Boston. One of some four hundred applicants, Raphael Semmes took his oral examinations at Barnum's Hotel in Baltimore. There were so many young men that the group spilled over into the lower barroom. Raphael, along with the other aspirants, was compelled to commit to memory a rambling, quasi-grammatical compilation of "duties," which included in part:

1.   No particular duties are assigned to this class of officers.

2.   They are promptly and faithfully to execute all the orders for the public service which they shall receive from their commanding officer.

3.   The commanding officer will consider the midshipmen as a class of officers meriting in a special degree their fostering care; they will see therefore that the schoolmaster performs his duties toward them by diligently and faithfully instructing them in those sciences appertaining to their profession, and that he use his utmost care to render them proficient therein.

4.   Midshipmen are to keep regular journals and deliver them to the commanding officer at the stated periods in due form.

As one historian observed, the rank of midshipman "was not treated as . . . a very dignified grade, the Navy regulations sandwiching it in between masters-at-arms and the ship's cooks."

Semmes was a good student. In the early 1830s, as a "passed midshipman," he was appointed "in charge of chronometers," with his duty station or stations not clearly specified. His days were sufficiently flexible to enable him to take trips to Cumberland, Maryland, to read legal tomes in the law offices of his brother Sam. Raphael took an especial liking to the vagaries of international and admiralty law.

In 1835 came his first formal sea duty, on board the *Constitution*. Two years later, he was promoted to lieutenant, which was then a rank of considerable prestige. That same year, 1837, Semmes married Anne Elizabeth Spencer of Cincinnati. During the next decade, he was based at the Norfolk and Pensacola navy yards, commanding several ships, including the brig USS *Somers*.

Under another captain, *Somers* had become the only United States naval vessel on which mutineers were hanged. Three of the condemned plotters, including the son of the secretary of war, had been executed at sea in 1842. Although Semmes was an advocate of lashes as a disciplinary expedient—"All with the cats" enlivened the pages of his logbooks—he was too knowledgeable of the law to preside over a capital court-martial.

In 1847, during the blockade of Vera Cruz in the Mexican War, *Somers* was stranded in a gale and lost with more than half her crew. If Semmes did not emerge from the disaster smelling quite like a rose, he was at least absolved of responsibility.

It is generally believed that during this period Semmes grew, cultivated, and shaped his finely pointed, shocking, red moustache, which would stamp him with the sobriquet "Old Beeswax." None, however, not even those closest to him, ever so addressed the formidable officer. He was already a martinet, by the measure of some.

Raphael Semmes was distinguished by more than his moustache. By the 1850s, his personality and his manner were set—he was vain, opinionated, hot-tempered, arrogant, and aloof. It may have been his inability to entertain contrasting viewpoints that kept him "grounded" during the decade before the Civil War, even though he was promoted to commander.

Adopting Alabama as his state, Semmes practiced law in Mobile. He also served as secretary of the Lighthouse Board; the Navy Department apparently did not consider humor and a sense of camaraderie prerequisites for such a post. Thus, when Alabama seceded, Semmes was well-positioned geographically to offer his services to the provisional Confederacy in Montgomery. His resignation from the United States Navy was accepted rather speedily. Semmes became one of the first officers in the South's then nonexistent navy.

In civilian clothes and as incognito as was physically possible, Semmes traveled north at the end of February 1861. He paused in Washington on March 4 to witness the inauguration of President Lincoln before going on to New England. There, on instructions from Jefferson Davis, he purchased percussion caps and thousands of pounds of powder. Semmes never revealed the names of these "impartial" Yankee traders.

In June 1861, with the rebellion two months in progress, Semmes, who had been commissioned a captain in Richmond's navy, was given command of the *Sumter*, a mail steamer that had plied a mundane course between New Orleans and Havana in peacetime. *Sumter* had been appropriated from the Federal government, as had most of the Confederacy's inventory of everything from ships and port installations to guns and even clothing.

The Federal navy might have considered itself fortunate to be rid of the tempestuous officer, but its

Southern counterpart was glad to have him aboard. On July 3, the eve of Independence Day, Semmes made his first capture, the *Golden Rocket*. Hunting remained good, and with each "kill" the coals of Semmes's obsessive hatred glowed to white heat. His journals were filled with venom: "Future generations will be astonished at the folly and fanaticism, want of principle and wickedness . . . among the Puritan population of the North. A people so devoid of Christian charity, and wanting in so many of the essentials of honesty, cannot be abandoned to their own folly by a just and benevolent God. . . . The hyenas of the North will receive their reward under the inevitable and rigorous laws of a just government of the world."

He wrote that his "countrymen of New England . . . were outheroding Herod in carrying on against us a vindictive war filled with hate and vengeance," with the result that "the milk of human kindness which had begun to well up in my heart disappeared." It seemed, by any measure, a remarkable conclusion.

A deeply religious man, he would postscript: "The Almighty, for a wise purpose, hides future events from the eyes of mortals, and all we can do is to perform well our parts and trust the rest to His guidance. Success, as a general rule, attends him who is vigilant and active, and who is careful to obey all the laws of nature."

Success, indeed, attended the cruise of the *Sumter*. In less than a year's time, she effected seventeen captures. Six, heavy with cargo, were burned, while two were ransomed and the remainder released in Cuban ports. The raider was finally blockaded in Algeciras, Spain, by two of the Federal navy's most powerful cruisers, the chain-armored, propeller-driven sloops *Kearsarge* and *Tuscarora*.

But the cats had pounced too late. The mouse was gone. "Old Beeswax" was awaiting a brand-new and far more formidable command. "Hull No. 290," the *Enrica*, was being built at Cammell Laird's yard in Birkenhead, England, in bland disregard for neutrality laws or even "niceties." This was a curious bit of merchandising—Great Britain did not even recognize the Confederate States diplomatically, yet was willing to supply her with a powerful man-o'-war. Building a merchant vessel or a fishing sloop might have been a different matter.

"Hull No. 290" was 220 feet long and at least 1,040 tons, with twin 300-horsepower engines connected to oversize bronze propellers that could drive her at speeds upwards of 15 knots. She was also bark-rigged, and her amplitude of sail could propel her almost that fast without power. She could bunker 300 tons of coal, meaning that with an assist from her canvas, she would be able to cruise for half a year without touching port.

Stowed discreetly below were her guns: the latest 100-pound Blakely pivoted rifle, to be mounted forward; one 8-inch solid-shot cannon; and six 32-pounders for broadsides. She was armed to hold her own with any opponent save an ironclad or a chain-armored vessel. Her architects probably intended that the ship's speed would compensate for her lack of armor plating.

When delivered in international waters at the end of July 1862, "Hull No. 290" became CSS *Ala-*

bama, as she had long been designated in Richmond's files. As she swept majestically beneath the hills of Porto Playa, the Azores, which were dazzling in color that early August, it was the beginning of a childlike romance akin to the glimpsing of a lovely young face across a classroom.

"She sat upon the water," Raphael Semmes would pen, "with the lightness and grace of a swan."

Alabama was truly a beautiful vessel. One might speculate that her designers and builders could not have effected such a creation without sympathy for the cause "Hull No. 290" was destined to serve. They were scarcely neutral, in thought or deed.

Alabama entered commission in the Confederate navy with a crew of eighty and a Georgian, John McIntosh Kell, as executive officer, or first lieutenant. Bewhiskered, portly, gregarious, and friendly, Kell was the 180-degree opposite of his captain in both physique and personality. He had been court-martialed by the United States Navy for refusing to obey an order; he had been dismissed and then reinstated before he decided to resign his commission.

The crew was a melting pot of Southern pilots and seamen from Savannah, Charleston, and New Orleans, with a sprinkling of Yankee renegades who were "among . . . the best sailors," by Kell's measure; there were even a few volunteers from a British ferry crew. The latter had supposedly been inspired by Semmes's rousing diatribe against the "subjugation" of the South by the North and his lauding of the struggle of the "oppressed against the oppressor." It is doubtful, however, that the Liverpool tars, among the toughest in the world, knew what Semmes was talking about. Promise of better pay, shore leave, women, and rum was what "signing on" meant to them.

On September 5 came *Alabama*'s first prize, the Edgartown whaler *Ocmulgee*. Hoisting the United States flag, Semmes took the ship by surprise. He removed the thirty-seven crewmen before burning her. Shortly thereafter, he overhauled the unsuspecting *Ocean Rover*, out of New Bedford, and applied the torch, operating all the while blandly in or near Portuguese territorial waters.

In his first month, Semmes destroyed twenty merchant or fishing vessels, more than he had recorded in the *Sumter* in almost a year's time. He wrote, with bitter humor, that he was "peopling" the island of Flores in the Azores with the crews of his destroyed captures, until there were "nearly as many Yankee sailors as there were original inhabitants."

At the burning of the New Bedford whaler *Elisha Dunbar*, Semmes observed that "the scene [was] wild and picturesque beyond description. The black clouds were mustering their forces in fearful array. . . . The sea was in a tumult of rage; the winds howled, and floods of rain descended. Amid this turmoil of the elements, the *Dunbar*, all in flames and with disordered gear and unfurled canvas, lay rolling and tossing upon the sea."

It seemed to hint of the "tumult of rage" lurking within the writer's own soul.

Semmes crossed the Atlantic to winter in the warm caress of the Caribbean, capturing another score of vessels by mid-December. The California-bound *Ariel*, 1,295 tons, was one of his victims. She was owned by Commodore Vanderbilt and carried at least five hundred women and children.

Word was conveyed to Semmes of the "great state of alarm" on board the *Ariel*. He at once dispatched his "handsomest young lieutenant," a clean-shaven, sunken-eyed Georgian, Richard F. Armstrong, who soothingly assured the women that they had "fallen into the hands of southern gentlemen under whose protection you are entirely safe. We are by no means ruffians or outlaws."

While Semmes harbored scant affection for Vanderbilt, he nonetheless sent the *Ariel* on her way. It was a particularly hard decision, since he understood that there were Union naval and marine personnel on the liner.

Lieutenant Armstrong brought back New York, Boston, and Washington newspapers from the *Ariel* that alluded to the "pirate ship *Alabama*" and the "pirate Semmes." This did more than infuriate Semmes. It hurt his feelings. How could a "southern gentleman" be mistaken for a pirate?

Semmes did not know that *Ariel*'s big sister, the mighty *Vanderbilt*, was already boiling out into the Atlantic, baying on the trail of the *Alabama*. She had arrived in Hampton Roads too late to take on the *Merrimack*, and she had also missed the *Florida* in the Caribbean by a matter of hours.

Vanderbilt's shored-up bow was packed with cotton bales, which served to make her a formidable ram. So much lumber was stowed in her hull that she was as close as humanly possible to being unsinkable. She was joining such powerful warships as could be spared from the coastal blockade— among them the *Kearsarge* and the *Tuscarora*—to hunt down the Bible-thumping captain above whose wheelhouse was inscribed: "God helps those who help themselves."

Anchored on Christmas day off the Arcas Keys, west of the Yucatan Peninsula in the Gulf of Mexico, the Confederate captain experienced momentary compassion. Grieving that his men were "terribly pressed in this ruthless and wicked war," he allowed them sport ashore—fishing, swimming, sunning, and whatever else they desired. But Semmes speedily reined in his emotions. He ordered a seaman into irons for allegedly getting drunk, forbade his chief bosun's mate to return to England via a "neutral" coaling bark that came alongside, and logged his satisfaction that he had "jerked [other recalcitrant seamen] down with a strong hand." Among the punishments were lashes with the "cat" and a diet of bread and water.

So much for the spirit of Christmas.

In early January 1863, Semmes cruised the Gulf of Mexico on the lookout for Federal warships and transports. Thus, on the eleventh, he encountered Commander Blake and the *Hatteras* (see chapter 2).

After depositing his prisoners in Jamaica and effecting repairs on the *Alabama* through the generosity of the British, Semmes continued his prowling in Caribbean and South American waters. He found time to muse on the Gulf Stream, which flows northward from the Gulf of Mexico. Coming to the conclusion that the Gulf of Mexico must eventually become "dry ground" because of the perpetual, massive loss of water to the Gulf Stream, he evolved his own theory of "an under-current from the north, passing into the Gulf of Mexico, under the Gulf Stream, rising to the surface when heated, and thus swelling the volume of the outflowing water."

So much for hydrography.

On January 25, he overtook and burned the sailing vessel *Golden Rule*. From newspapers found aboard her, Semmes learned the good news that the Confederate cruiser *Florida* had escaped through the blockade of Mobile, that the *Monitor* had foundered off Hatteras, that General Sherman was bogged down in the Yazoo, and that the USS *Cairo* had been sunk by a torpedo in that same Mississippi tributary.

For the next four months, the *Alabama* ran amuck, burning or ransoming vessels at will. The *John S. Parks* became her thirty-fifth victim. Semmes anchored briefly at the lonely penal island of Fernando de Noronha, 225 miles northeast of Brazil, "a broken, picturesque, volcanic rock, in mid-ocean, covered with a pleasing coat of verdure . . . [but] awfully hot when the sun shines."

He disposed of upwards of a dozen more victims during the early summer of 1863 before setting course for Simonstown (Cape Town). Semmes dropped anchor there, in the shadow of the Cape of Good Hope, on August 5, only to learn that the *Vanderbilt* had just put to sea. Thus, the big converted liner was maintaining an unblemished reputation for narrowly missing her quarries. Before sailing, her commander, Charles H. Baldwin, had confided to the Royal Navy in Simonstown that he could easily overtake the *Alabama* and crush her by ramming. The comment was relayed to Semmes, who tended to agree with Baldwin's assessment. Semmes had just received news of the fall of Vicksburg and of Lee's repulse at Gettysburg. If he saw these reverses as omens for the end of the Confederacy, he did not confide this to his diary. He was more concerned with the pragmatics of the moment, such as avoiding the *Vanderbilt*, even though he dubbed her "that huge old coal box."

"We were not disposed to try issues," noted John Kell, the executive officer, "so one night about 11 o'clock while it blew a gale of wind from the southeast we hove anchor and steamed out of Simon's Bay."

Although Semmes knew that hunting was good in the South Atlantic and the Caribbean, he resolved to head through the Indian Ocean for the East Indies; he had an aversion to retracing old courses. When he heard that the 997-ton sloop USS *Wyoming* might be waiting for him in the Sunda Straits, Java, he took stock. Deciding that the *Alabama* could hold her own, he kept on.

The "pirate," as most in the North considered him, had destroyed but one additional ship by November 10, when he sailed boldly through the Sunda Straits flying the Stars and Bars. But the *Wyoming*, his presumed nemesis, was nowhere in sight, and for good reason. She had limped back to the Pacific, badly needing repairs after blundering into a gunboat and Japanese shore batteries off Honshu. There appeared no obvious provocation for the angry exchange, but *Wyoming* was out of action all the same.

Before putting into Singapore the week of Christmas 1863, Semmes burned two California clippers—*Winged Racer* and *Contest*. The war had been harsh on those towering, stately ships. The famed *Stag*

VANDERBILT. 19-15-4

RAY.

Artist's conception of the USS *Vanderbilt*. Having missed her appointments with the *Merrimack* and the *Florida*, she pursued the *Alabama* halfway around the world, only to come up empty again.

U.S. Naval Historical Center

Hound had been sunk by the *Florida* off Brazil. Fleet of keel by the standards of two decades past, they could not outrun Civil War raiders, which would claim fourteen of their number.

Semmes was tired. In his mid-fifties, he was twice the age of a number of generals in both armies. The hardships of the swashbuckling life were more for youngsters like Lieutenant Charles Williams Read, who had aroused Portland, Maine, that June. Semmes wrote, "The very roar of the wind through the rigging with its accompaniments of rolling and tumbling, hard, overcast skies, etc., gives me the blues!"

He went ashore like any tourist in Singapore, "which was a fishing village half a century ago, [but] now contains a hundred thousand inhabitants." He noted that "crowds gathered to look curiously upon [the *Alabama*]. . . . These crowds were themselves a curiosity to look upon, formed, as they were of all the nations of the earth, from the remote East and the remote West." He proceeded to record an inventory of the goods passing through the busy port, from pepper and tin ore to hides and raw silk. Then, in character, Semmes turned to political considerations of the British Empire, lavishing praise upon the policies that bound "her colonies to her with hooks of steel." He seemed to have forgotten that his prime purpose in life was liberating the South from her own oppressors.

So much for Her Majesty's colonialism.

Semmes celebrated Christmas Eve by firing the bark *Texan Star* in the Malacca Straits, northwest of Singapore. She was sailing low, heavy with a cargo of rice. Two days later, he came upon the *Highlander* and the *Sonora*, both in ballast. Their masters indicated that the *Alabama* had been expected for some time and that, in a way, it was a relief to have it over with.

Then, masquerading as the USS *Dacotah*, the Confederate ship was scolded by a British bark: "It won't do! The *Alabama* is a bigger ship than you, and they say she is iron-plated besides." Whatever name was on her fantail, the *Alabama* was crying for overhaul.

"Her boilers were burned out, and her machinery was sadly in need of repairs," noted John Kell. "She was loose at every joint, her seams were open, and the copper on her bottom was in rolls." He was seconded by Semmes, who wrote, "My ship is weary, too, as well as her commander and will need a general overhauling by the time I can get her into dock."

In February, as *Alabama*, bound for England or France, was raising the island of Madagascar, off the east coast of Africa, the CSS *Florida* gave the Union navy the slip once more. This time, she crept out of Brest, France, in heavy rain and mist. Captain John Ancrum Winslow had positioned his *Kearsarge* off the breakwater for several weeks, certain he had bottled up the Confederate raider *this* time.

A fifty-three-year-old North Carolinian, Winslow was blind in one eye, heavy, and rather stooped, in marked contrast to the tall, erect Raphael Semmes. The two officers, in fact, had served together in the Mexican War. Both had been commended for bravery, and both had lost a ship. Winslow had run the small gunboat *Morris*, captured from the Mexicans, onto a reef. Semmes and Winslow had joked with each other about not paying closer attention to navigation. It was perhaps the last time Semmes found anything funny.

Comparable in tonnage—about 1,031—to the *Alabama*, though not quite as fast, the *Kearsarge* was vastly superior in firepower, with a main battery of two 11-inch smoothbore Dahlgren semipivot guns. The Confederate ship's largest gun was but 8 inches. An even more important advantage of the steam sloop was the 1½-inch-thick chain armor draped over her sides.

Passing Napoleon's remote island of final exile, St. Helena, in early April, the *Alabama* "jogged along leisurely under topsails" northward through the Atlantic, according to Semmes's account. She sank her final two ships, the *Rockingham* and the *Tycoon*, in the last week of the month. The former, once abandoned, was used for target practice. Many of the raider's shells, deteriorated from long months in hot, humid climes, failed to explode.

What Semmes termed "the long chase" was over. He had stopped some three hundred ships, burned fifty-seven, and ransomed an additional fourteen, for a record that stands unbroken a century and a quarter later. It is also of note that not a single life was lost in the *Alabama*'s extended rampage.

On June 11, 1864, the *Alabama* dropped anchor in the harbor off Cherbourg, France. Semmes prepared a letter for the Confederacy's naval emissary in Paris, Flag Officer Samuel Barron, asking for repairs and asking also to be relieved of command, since his "health [had] suffered so much."

He proved an unwelcome guest. The French Ministry of Marine, aware that the navy of the United States was now superior to France's, wanted to know why the Confederate captain did not choose to put into Le Havre, which had more dry docks than Cherbourg, or, better still, why he did not go to England, or Holland, or anywhere else that would have him. Of course, Semmes could always request the permission of Emperor Napoleon III for repairs, but that would take considerable time, since His Majesty was away in Biarritz languishing in the baths. The emperor was still pondering his gambit in Mexico, with Archduke Ferdinand Maximilian the principal pawn.

Semmes did not wish to return to Liverpool or any other British port. He had learned that sentiment was swinging away from the Confederate States, thanks in large measure to the tough stand taken by Charles Francis Adams, the United States minister to the Court of St. James. More important from a pragmatic standpoint was the obvious fact that the United States was overcoming the rebellion. Grant was closing in on Richmond and Sherman encircling Atlanta.

While Semmes was thus debating whether to interrupt Napoleon's ablutions, Captain Winslow was welcoming an early-morning visitor aboard the *Kearsarge*, at anchor in the Schelde, off Flushing, the Netherlands. United States Consul William L. Dayton had electrifying news: The *Alabama* was in Cherbourg!

By the time the consul finished his second cup of coffee and was assisted back into his launch,

Winslow had steam up and was pounding out of the Schelde. On June 14, the *Kearsarge* swept into Cherbourg and past the *Alabama*, close enough for Winslow to recognize both Semmes and his second-in-command, John Kell.

Winslow then sent an officer ashore to request that any prisoners held on the Confederate ship be transferred to the *Kearsarge*. Seemingly confused by the whole accelerating episode, the French refused on the pretext that such a switch would constitute "an augmentation of military force."

Winslow next steamed outside the breakwater and dropped anchor. He was within three miles of the entrance.

Semmes, "tired of running from that flaunting rag . . . Old Glory," informed Kell, "I am going out to fight the *Kearsarge*!"

The executive officer knew it was suicide. Even if the ship and crew had not been depleted by the long cruise of almost two years, Kell was aware that the *Alabama* would still have stood no chance against the *Kearsarge*'s guns and chain armor. The fighting qualities of the respective captains, evenly matched or not, were much beside the point.

Like a gentleman whose honor had been challenged, Semmes dispatched a request to the Confederate representative: "I desire you to say to the United States consul that my intention is to fight the *Kearsarge*. . . . I beg you she will not depart before I am ready to go to sea!"

Winslow, who received the "invitation" the next morning, had no thoughts of leaving. He was ready.

By Friday, June 17, the news was in the Paris papers that the American warships *Kearsarge* and *Alabama* were going to slug it out, perhaps to the death, off Cherbourg. The sidewalk cafés buzzed with excitement. There had not been such an opportunity to observe bloodletting since the good old days at the Place de la Concorde. And this event would offer the bonus of being more sporting.

If the French fleet left something to be desired, not so the wonderful system of railroads. Special trains were chartered to leave for Cherbourg late Saturday afternoon and early Sunday morning. Several thousand hastened to buy tickets, then went home to pack their picnic baskets with wine, cheese, bread, and all sorts of tasty things in preparation for their departure from the Gare du Nord.

Sunday morning, June 19, 1864, dawned bright, beautiful, and calm. The excursion trains, bearing an unexpectedly heavy crowd of more than fifteen thousand, tooted into dockside. In a holiday mood, the Parisians poured out onto the breakwater, upon balconies and red terra-cotta rooftops, and even into the riggings of ships. Many captains, no minor opportunists, were charging admission. Any places relatively high in the generally flat area were at a premium, even though no one, including the captains of the two ships, knew how far at sea the battle might be fought.

There were family groups, the parents holding their panniers, the children clutching dolls and other toys. Most were in their Sunday best, with jaunty berets, floppy hats, light silk scarfs, and parasols. They

---

presented a bright, joyous, sparkling picture under the dazzling summer sun, against a background discord of ringing church bells.

They watched *Alabama* up anchor shortly before 10:00 A.M. and gather speed as she moved out of the harbor. She was accompanied by two so-called neutral consorts—the ironclad frigate *Couronne*, flying the Tricolor, and the steam yacht *Deerhound*, owned by English millionaire John Lancaster.

On the *Kearsarge*, Winslow had ordered the church flag hoisted above the ensign as he started the traditional service of the Episcopal church on the quarterdeck. While he was reading the confession—at about 10:15—he was interrupted by his quartermaster, who bellowed, "She's coming!"

There would be no divine service that day. Guns were loaded and side chains checked. The anchor was hauled up, and *Kearsarge* steered somewhat seaward, aiming at a likely battleground seven miles from land, outside France's territorial waters. Winslow was certain that the *Alabama*, slowly materializing over the gentle morning swells, was not attempting to elude him. But he did speculate over Semmes's eagerness to offer battle against such odds.

Past the breakwater, the two consorts dipped their colors in salute and dropped astern. The captain of the *Alabama* then stood atop a gun carriage on the aft deck and addressed his crew with a touch of the Nelson mystique: "Officers and seamen of the *Alabama*: you have at length another opportunity of meeting the enemy. . . . The flag that floats over you is that of a young Republic, which bids defiance to her enemies, whenever and wherever found. Show the world you know how to uphold it!" He continued some moments before concluding with the order: "Go to your quarters!"

In character, the aggressive Semmes took the initiative. As he would report to Flag Officer Barron, "We were distant about one mile from each other when I opened on him with solid shot, to which he replied in a few minutes."

Actually, taking a hit through the rigging of the *Kearsarge*, Winslow kept moving toward his adversary for half a mile without opening fire. He sat calmly on a little chest on the quarterdeck beside the rail, telescope in hand, in easy speaking distance of his quartermaster and the hatch to the engine room. The bell signals were within reach, and he was close to the gunnery officer. Given to shortness of breath, the captain preferred to be seated.

As Winslow would report, his strategy was to fight close in and stay between *Alabama* and the shore, to prevent her from running back into Cherbourg. Thus, he circled the Confederate ship at full speed, pouring shot into her "broadside to broadside." The result was worse than dismaying to Semmes, whose weaker firepower could not penetrate the chain armor of the *Kearsarge*; though she rode high because of low coal bunkers (less than 120 tons), her sides were well-protected.

"Mr. Kell!" Semmes shouted in abject frustration. "Use solid shot. Our shell strike the enemy's side and fall into the water!"

Unretouched photograph of the USS *Kearsarge* off the Portsmouth (New Hampshire) Navy Yard shortly after her return from European waters in 1864.

U.S. Naval Historical Center

One shell, however, lodged in the *Kearsarge*'s rudderpost, but it failed to explode. It might have spelled the end of the fight had the missile not been defective.

The firing continued "rapid and wild," according to Winslow, shell alternating with solid shot as the combatants steamed in concentric circles. The closeness of the battle resulted in a continuous, deafening din and a thick, acrid miasma of dark smoke. The combination of smoke and distance made for very poor viewing from shore.

"The enemy's 11-inch shells were now doing severe execution upon our quarterdeck section," Kell conceded. "Three of them successively entered our eight-inch pivot gun port; the first swept off the forward part of the gun's crew; the second killed one man and wounded several others; and the third struck the breast of the gun carriage and spun around on the deck. . . . Our decks were now covered with the blood of the dead and the wounded and the ship was careening heavily to starboard from the effects of the shot holes on her waterline."

Semmes endeavored to flee to Cherbourg, just as Winslow had anticipated he might if the battle went against him. But the *Kearsarge*, like a mastiff, remained grimly, furiously between the *Alabama* and sanctuary. There was no escape.

"Our bulwarks are . . . shot away in sections," Lieutenant Arthur Sinclair, sailing master of the *Alabama*, wrote in his reconstruction of the battle. "The spar deck is by this time being rapidly torn up by shell bursting on the between decks, interfering with working our battery; and the compartments below have all been knocked into one.

"The *Alabama* is making water fast, showing severe punishment; but still, the report comes from the engine room that the ship is being kept free to the safety point. She also has now become dull in response to her helm, and the sailtrimmers are ordered out to loose the headsails. . . . We are making a desperate but forlorn resistance."

Then, Sinclair continued, "an 11-inch shell enters us at the waterline, in the wake of the writer's gun and, passing on, explodes in the engine room, in its passage throwing a volume of water on board, hiding for a moment the guns of this division.

"Our ship trembles from stem to stern from the blow. Semmes at once sends for the engineer on watch who reports the fires out, and water beyond the control of the pumps."

Semmes then ordered Kell: "Go below, sir, and see how long the ship can float!"

Passing through the wardroom en route to the engine compartment, Kell found a "sight . . . indeed appalling. There stood Assistant Surgeon [David Herbert] Llewellyn at his post, but the table and the patient upon it had been swept away from him by an 11-inch shell which opened in the side of the ship an aperture that was fast filling with water." The executive officer hastened back to the quarterdeck to advise Semmes, "We cannot float 10 minutes!"

As Kell would recall, the captain replied in a strong but somber voice, "Then, sir, cease firing, shorten sail, and haul down the colors! It will never do in this 19th century for us to go down and the decks covered with our gallant wounded!"

There next arose some confusion, since Winslow was "unable to ascertain whether [the *Alabama*'s colors] had been hauled down or shot away." When he saw "a white flag . . . displayed over the stern, our fire was reserved."

Then, Winslow noted, "she again opened on us with two guns on the port side. . . . This drew our fire again." When he saw the white flag once more, he ordered cease fire a second time.

Boats were lowered from the *Alabama*. One, bearing wounded, came alongside the *Kearsarge* to request assistance. Captain Winslow inquired, "Does Captain Semmes surrender his ship?"

"Yes" was the reply from Master's Mate George Fullam, an Englishman, who then asked permission to return for more wounded, pledging to surrender himself and those with him.

Meanwhile, Kell had ordered: "All hands save yourselves!" He urged them to grab a spar or anything that would float and jump overboard. Lieutenant Sinclair, however, lingered. He later reported that "the scene was one of complete wreck. The shot and shell of the enemy had knocked all the compartments into one; and a flush view could be had fore and aft, the water waist-deep, and air bubbles rising and breaking with a mournful gurgle at the surface. . . . The spars were wounded woefully, some of them toppling, and others only held by the wire rigging. The smokestack was full of holes, the decks torn up by the bursting of shell, and lumbered with the wreckage of woodwork and rigging and empty shell-boxes. Some sail was set; and the vessel slowly forged ahead, leaving a line of wreckage astern, with the heads of swimmers bobbing up and down amongst it."

The *Kearsarge* hove to just a few hundred yards starboard of the derelict. Her boats were put over, her guns still trained. The *Deerhound* was already at the scene—one that was, according to Kell, "a mass of living heads striving for their lives." The *Deerhound*'s boats were picking up survivors as fast as possible. Semmes was among the water-drenched lot.

About an hour and a half after the firing of *Alabama*'s opening broadside, the Confederate raider made her last plunge, about four and a half miles off the Cherbourg breakwater. She settled "stern foremost," according to Kell, "launching her bows high in the air. Graceful even in her death-struggle, she in a moment disappeared from the face of the waters."

Semmes, aboard the *Deerhound*, would pronounce his own amen: "She could swim no more, so we gave her to the waves."

Some 173 projectiles had been fired by the Union sloop, about half the number fired by her opponent. Nine crew members had been killed by enemy fire—including Assistant Surgeon Llewellyn—and ten drowned on the *Alabama*, with at least twenty-one wounded. The *Kearsarge* listed but one fatality and two wounded.

The *Deerhound* picked up 114 survivors in addition to Semmes, leaving a mere 50 prisoners for the Federal navy. In accepting sanctuary—and the protection of the Union Jack—aboard the British yacht, the commander of the *Alabama* may thus have broken faith with his "bargain" for surrender, as tendered by Master's Mate Fullam, and, by implication, with the sparing of his life by his foe.

While the *Deerhound* set course for the Thames and the *Kearsarge* for Holland, the sightseers from Paris began to board the excursion trains. Their picnic baskets were empty. The children were tired, their dolls hanging limply in their hands. There was an atmosphere of anticlimax, perhaps disappointment. A legend of invincibility had preceded the *Alabama* by many months.

Only the *London Times* appeared satisfied, pronouncing the engagement a "magnificent spectacle." Almost three weeks later, the news crossed the Atlantic. On a first page packed almost solidly with details of the battle, the *New York Times* announced: "THE PIRATE SUNK OFF CHERBOURG BY THE *KEARSARGE*."

Winslow was lionized and promoted to commodore upon his return to the United States. Semmes remained in London editing his impassioned journals for a British publisher, Saunders Otley and Co. Their unusually succinct title was *Cruise of the* Alabama *and* Sumter. But the war was not over for the captain.

He returned to the South in the autumn by way of Havana and Shreveport. Eluding General Sherman's octopus-like armies was not easy, but Semmes nevertheless reached Richmond in January 1865. He must have known that the end was near when he accepted his admiral's commission and the command of the James River Squadron, which consisted primarily of converted tugs and small river craft.

Despair and desertions haunted his crew. With the evacuation of Richmond on April 2, the admiral of three months' standing fired his squadron. The ironclad *Virginia II* blew up, according to Semmes, "like the shock of an earthquake. . . . [It] shook the houses in Richmond and must have waked the echoes of the night for 40 miles around. The spectacle was grand beyond description."

It was also the death agony of his last command.

A diehard like Jefferson Davis, Semmes commandeered a train, tore down fence posts for fuel, and rattled westward with a most unusual potpourri of generals, colonels, ordinary soldiers, sailors, and a few frightened government clerks. He arrived in Danville, Virginia, on April 4, missing by a matter of minutes a raiding party from General Phil Sheridan's cavalry that tore up the tracks. Danville became the temporary seat of the Confederacy after Lee's surrender at Appomattox on the ninth.

It was unusual for an admiral, but Semmes proceeded to organize a ragtag band of soldiers and sailors into a defense force on the perimeter of Danville. They dug trenches and set up artillery pieces in earthen breastworks. When Danville had to be evacuated, Jefferson Davis and a small personal party including his wife, Varina, started for Georgia. Semmes continued only as far as Greensboro, North Carolina.

The proud sea raider finally gave up. He signed formal surrender and parole papers on May 1 with representatives of Sherman's army. The young Federal officers who thereby witnessed his signature appeared quite in awe of the tall, proud admiral with the distracting red hair.

For Raphael Semmes, the war was over at last.

THE ILL-FATED *SULTANA*, HELENA, ARKANSAS, APRIL 27, 1865

Certainly the last photograph of the *Sultana*. Note the incredible overcrowding. The original caption is in error. The *Sultana* exploded above Memphis early in the morning on the twenty-seventh.

U.S. Naval Historical Center

Chapter 11

WHAT SANK THE *SULTANA*?

"It looked like a huge bonfire in the middle of the river."

ADMIRAL SEMMES WAS EN ROUTE TO GREENSBORO to seek terms from General Sherman while the big Mississippi steamer *Sultana* was making her way upriver.

The 1,700-ton, two-year-old sidewheeler was jammed solid with at least twenty-three hundred souls, well over twice her listed capacity, plus more than fifteen hundred horses, cows, and pigs. The passengers poured onto her at Vicksburg, many of them hungry, ragged, sweating prisoners from the pestilential camps of Andersonville, Georgia; Macon, Georgia; and Cahaba, Alabama. Victory had set them free. Their number was augmented by an overflow of soldiers from nearby Camp Fisk who struggled to obtain discharge papers and shoulder aboard. Two companies of armed infantry had also been ordered onto the *Sultana* to protect her from guerrillas along the banks and to guard a group of Confederate prisoners who were suspected of crimes. Twelve ladies of the Christian Commission crowded into the last available cabin, thankful that they did not have to travel overland. Northern bushwhackers vied with Southern diehards to render travel through the back roads of most of the Southern states wholly unsafe for man or woman.

With so many soldiers, sutlers (hawkers of various wares), and other camp followers wanting to go home now that "the cruel war" was over, steamers the length of the Mississippi from New Orleans northward were swamped with hordes of would-be passengers. Masters were faced with far more potential fares than they could possibly accommodate. They had to request armed guards at the piers to keep the boisterous, pushing mobs off the gangplanks.

Thus, while some "Billy Yanks" were stomping aboard and others were held at dockside by phalanxes with bayoneted rifles, the *Sultana*'s grizzled chief engineer, Nate Wintringer, scratched his head over his problems, the most pressing of which was a leak in the new "experimental" boiler. It was hard to patch up a boiler without going into a shipyard, where engineers probably would have replaced the whole unit.

The best that Wintringer and his assistant, Ed Clemmans, could do was screw soft iron plugs into the more obvious holes and tighten metal straps the girth of larger areas, such as around the seams. Good man, that Clemmans, Chief Engineer Wintringer often thought—Clemmans neither drank nor swore. Wintringer could think of no other engineer on the entire Mississippi with a similar pedigree of sobriety and restraint.

While the engineers fussed and sweated in their greasy domain, two other steamers arrived in Vicksburg—the *Pauline Carroll* and the *Olive Branch*. Neither appeared as hopelessly overcrowded as the *Sultana*, whose passengers wondered why there could not have been a more equitable division among the three riverboats.

Although Wintringer was not wholly satisfied with his repairs, Captain J. Cass Mason ordered steam up for Helena, Arkansas. There, much of the bulk cargo—a hundred hogsheads of sugar for ballast—was unloaded. Who needed more ballast? Some of the livestock was also led ashore, though the odor remained in full miasma. A number of the soldiers aboard the *Sultana* earned a few dollars and eased their boredom during the unloading by serving as stevedores.

The master's carefulness in casting off from the dock at Helena impressed at least one of his passengers, Lieutenant Joseph Taylor Elliott of Indiana, one of those released from Andersonville; Elliott heard Mason cautioning the travelers not to crowd to one side of the boat.

The *Sultana* paddled into Memphis at dawn on April 26, 1865. The remaining hogsheads of sugar were trundled onto the wharf, along with additional cows, horses, and pigs. A dozen mules were tugged aboard and into the ship's cattle pens, however, as the quartermaster at Cairo, Illinois—the next stop—had telegraphed ahead for those cussed but essential quadrupeds of many jobs.

Then the coal barges came alongside to satisfy the voracious appetite of the sidewheeler's inefficient furnaces. The *Sultana* would need every chunk she could bunker to make Cairo. Wintringer and Clemmans again hammered and tightened the "experimental" boiler that had occupied so much of their attention.

The two companies of armed infantry assigned to protect the *Sultana* and guard the Confederate prisoners relaxed during the day's layover in Memphis. Some went ashore in search of timeless soldiers' pleasures, with the accent on liquor and women, while others caught up on their sleep on the hard decks. Memphis, snatched from the Confederates in mid-1862, had remained strongly garrisoned by Federal troops. Fort Pickering, for example, was just up the river. The *Sultana*'s guards figured that their prisoners would not try to escape. Where could they go?

That they should keep an eye on the coal coming aboard or on other aspects of security never occurred to them, even though the occupation forces were well aware of the "bad losers" still wandering the city. Memphis had never been 100 percent secure. Certainly, communications being what they were, it was unlikely that any officer stationed in Memphis was aware that General Benjamin Franklin Butler's communications ship, *Greyhound*, had been sabotaged recently in the James River by explosives placed in her coal bunkers. The war was over, and complacency was in the air. Just two short weeks past, no one—certainly not his guards—had thought that President Lincoln was walking into danger when he entered Ford's Theater.

On the other hand, Colonel I. G. Kappner, the commander of Fort Pickering, remained obsessed with the idea that guerrillas might materialize from shore and river to wreak all manner of violence upon his confines. That very Wednesday morning, for example, he had mustered Company A, Third Colored Artillery (Heavy), whose men were then performing a great deal of sentry duty. Whatever Kappner told them, his worthies had come away with the idea that they should shoot at anything that moved. That was fine with them. They were bored and wanted to see some action. The night watches were interminable, and the sentries tended to doze off.

Most of the *Sultana*'s passengers drifted ashore. A very few decided that they would wait for the next boat and proceeded to find themselves rooms or houses of prostitution where they could tarry a night or two. Another option was to continue north by rail and wagon, but that was a tedious, time-consuming, and not altogether safe alternative.

Among the passengers who went ashore was Joe Elliott, who was seeking "amusement" and some time in which to "cool off." His nemesis ever since Vicksburg had been a Captain McCoy of Ohio, a fellow Andersonville prisoner. Not only had the two men exchanged "some very unpleasant words" over possession of a double-decker cot, according to Elliott, but the "words" had at least twice degenerated into physical combat. Their shipmates had separated them each time.

A small minority made the best of their situation. "A happier lot of men I think I never saw," wrote Chester D. Berry, twenty-one, of South Creek, Pennsylvania. A choir singer and avid churchgoer, Berry loved spirituals and "old time hymns." By untiring perseverance, he corralled others of like inclinations aboard the *Sultana*. "All went gay as a marriage bell," he wrote. "The most of them had been a long time in prison, and the prospect of reaching home made them content to endure any amount of crowding. . . . The main thought that occupied every mind was home, the dearest spot on earth."

He had found himself a cot inside one of the passenger compartments shared by dozens. The conditions were dirty, smelly, and tightly packed, but if Berry had faithfully appraised the situation, the passengers were nonetheless in good spirits. Of course, his most recent basis of comparison was Andersonville. He had been captured at Fredericksburg early in the war and had suffered from typhoid in addition to the expected hardships of any Southern prison.

Berry had heard gossip to the effect that "while the boat lay at Memphis, someone had gone up the river" to prepare for her destruction. He had shrugged this off as "talk." He also conceded, however, that it was "a grand opportunity for guerrillas, if they [knew] . . . that there was such a boatload of prisoners coming up the river. . . . They could plant a battery on the shore, sink the boat, and destroy nearly all of the prisoners on board."

Others like Otto Barden of Wooster, Ohio, were inhabiting gratings in recesses of the engine room despite the shattering noise, the grease, and the steam. Perhaps the heat acted as an anesthetic for Barden, who claimed the dubious distinction of having been captured by General Nathan Bedford Forrest's tough cavalry.

P. L. Horn, also of Wooster, defied the jungle of heads, arms, and booted legs to spread his bedroll on the top deck near one of the cinder-belching stacks. At least he obtained some night air, mingled with the soot and the sparks showering down upon him and his mates.

Gaslights were shedding their familiar, nostalgic glow over Memphis's streets when the soldiers began to straggle or stagger back aboard the *Sultana*. The engineers were not satisfied with either the boiler or the engines, but Captain Mason could not recall an engineer ever pronouncing the machinery fit in all respects to propel any vessel. If he waited for the "grease monkeys" to say they were ready, he might never cast off from any dock.

Nevertheless, it was almost midnight before coaling was completed, steam was up, and the majority of his passengers were on the steamer. One of the captains of the armed infantry reported to the master that "most" of his company had answered muster. Mason squinted into the blackness. A light rain was falling. Then he volunteered to the army captain that he planned to sell his interest in the *Sultana* "*if*" she reached Cairo.

As Mason walked away, the army captain found himself thinking that the master's remark was curious indeed. Further reverie was interrupted by two throaty blasts of the sidewheeler's whistle, as lines were hauled onto the slippery decks. *Sultana* pulled away from Memphis and into midstream.

Chester Berry's group finished a final chorus of "Sweet Hour of Prayer" as they stared at the rapidly vanishing lights of Memphis. They would have been compelled to stop anyhow, since a rough, unkempt knot of soldiers nearby had threatened them bodily harm if they did not shut up. Joe Elliott was again arguing with McCoy over the cot, but Otto Barden, in the engine room, and P. L. Horn, on the upper deck, both slept through the departure like babies.

Well past midnight on Thursday, April 27, the *Sultana*, grossly overloaded, was wallowing opposite

Tagleman's Landing. Near the rough, shaky wharf, the converted sidewheeler USS *Essex* lay silently at anchor. Battle-scarred from the Vicksburg action, she was scarcely fit for duty more demanding than that presently assigned. Ensign James H. Berry, the *Essex*'s young executive officer, had just been relieved by Ensign Jim Earnshaw and was preparing to hit the sack. Earnshaw logged "a large side-wheeler, prominently illuminated." He noted the time meticulously—2:00 A.M.

Ashore, the sentries of the Third Colored Artillery swung their arms against the chill and dampness. After their briefing, they gazed suspiciously at the large, dark silhouette thumping upriver. Was it *friendly*? They remembered what Colonel Kappner had told them.

Ahead, to port, wavered the misty outlines of Paddy's Old Hen and Chickens Islands, no more than half a mile off the eastern bank of the Mississippi. There, the frogs of spring croaked their throaty chorus.

In the *Sultana*'s engine room, Clemmans had just relieved Chief Wintringer. The needles of the many gauges seemed to speak their normal, mute pattern. Not so mute were the wheezing pistons and grinding shafts, some eight inches in diameter, which drove the huge wheels.

The transition from quiet night on the river to cataclysm came wholly without warning and had but one common denominator: shock!

"Hot steam, smoke, pieces of brickbats, and chunks of coal came thick and fast. I gasped for breath," recalled Otto Barden of the scene near his engine-room grating.

In the same area, Chief Engineer Wintringer "stood bewildered for a moment, then saw the river perfectly alive with human beings struggling in the water, and the cry from all quarters, 'put out the fire!' which was getting good headway."

Hot water awoke Chester Berry as it soaked his blanket, compelling him to the conclusion: "I had better move. . . . I sprang to the bow of the boat and turning, looked back upon one of the most terrible scenes I ever beheld. The upper decks of the boat were a complete wreck and the dry casings of the cabins, falling in upon the hot bed of coal, were burning like tinder."

On the upper deck, P. L. Horn first thought he was in a railroad wreck—a few weeks previously, he had survived a prison train smash-up near Athens, Georgia. He was in a good position to abandon ship, and taking off his shoes and coat, he did just that. Plunging off the side toward the inky, black water, Horn would remember thinking that "the Confederates had blown up the vessel."

Near Horn on the upper deck, William H. Norton of Summit County, Ohio, paused to listen in strange fascination to "that awful wail of hundreds of human beings burning alive in the cabins and under the fallen timber."

Topsides near the bronze bell, twenty-two-year-old J. P. Zaizer of Limaville, Ohio, was awakened by one of the stacks falling down, splitting in two as it did so. One half knocked the bell onto the deck with a doleful clap, while the other crushed "Sgt. Smith who had laid by us." Without further thought, Zaizer jumped overboard.

Joe Elliott had paused in his continuing donnybrook with McCoy to doze off—for a matter of seconds. He dreamed he was "in the regions of eternal torment." Suddenly aware that these "regions" were terribly real, not the province of nightmare, he observed with shock that many soldiers were still asleep. He "turned around and made for the stern of the boat," he recalled, "hardly knowing what I was doing."

Aboard the *Essex*, Ensign Berry was awakened when his watch officer, Ensign Earnshaw, pounded on his door. Earnshaw informed the executive officer that a steamer had blown up nearby and was burning furiously, showering sparks high into the night. "I ordered all the boats manned," Berry would report, "and I went in the cutter. . . . We went out into the middle of the river. The morning was very dark . . . and the weather overcast, and the shrieks of the wounded and drowning men was the only guide we had."

Believing that the "whole river" was illuminated by the blaze, Otto Barden paused momentarily by the engine-room hatch—the top of which had been blown off—in an effort to keep others from falling in. "I stood there until the fire compelled me to leave," he recalled. "I helped several out of this place." Then he started for the wheelhouse. "I tried to get a large plank, but this was too heavy, so I left it and got a small board and started to the wheel to jump into the water.

"Here a young man said to me, 'you jump first, I cannot swim!' This man had all his clothes on. I had just my shirt and pants on. I said to him, 'you must paddle your own canoe, I can't help you.' Then, I jumped and stuck to my board."

Engineer Wintringer found that "there was such a mass of confusion and such a complete wreck of the boat that nobody, apparently, could get out of the position they were in. I managed to get hold of a shutter and saw that the fire would soon force me off the boat; I took my chances and jumped into the river."

Chester Berry rationalized that "a few pails full of water would have put the fire out, but alas, it was ten feet to the water and there was no rope to draw with; consequently, the flames swept fiercely through the light wood of the upper decks. . . . I went back to where I had lain and found my bunkmate, Busley, scalded to death; I then secured a piece of cabin door casing, about three or four inches wide, and about four feet long; then going back to the bow of the boat I came to the conclusion I did not want to take to the water just then, for it was literally black with human beings, many of whom were sinking and taking others with them.

"Being a good swimmer, and having board enough to save me even if I were not, I concluded to wait till the rush was over."

P. L. Horn went down twice before he managed to maintain his head above water by kicking and dog-paddling. His impression that he was in a train wreck was quickly corrected. "How far or how high I was blown into the air I do not know," he reported, "but I remember that my feet first struck the water and with the exception of being slightly hurt on my left side I suffered but little from the shock."

Grabbing hold of a portion of the *Sultana*'s deck stairway, which was floating past, Horn and a number of others clung "with a death grip." Then, of all things, a mule, "another floating waif of this disaster swam along and dumped us all into the river, compelling us all to exert our strength to regain our hold." The swift current also compelled the men to relax their grip, and only "with the greatest difficulty [did] they . . . recover it again."

Soon Joseph McKelvey, who had been sleeping next to Horn on the steamer, grabbed hold of the stairs. Horn asked him if he were hurt. "Yes," McKelvey replied, "scalded from head to foot!"

Bill Norton, Horn's fellow Ohioan, reported that as he "arose to the surface, several men from the boat jumped upon me and we all went down together. Others leaping on us forced us down until I despaired of ever reaching the surface again; but by a desperate struggle, I succeeded in getting out from under them and reached the surface. I tried to swim through the crowd of men but could not.

"One man caught hold of me but I managed to get away from him, and not knowing what to do or which way to go I instinctively turned toward the burning boat. Reaching that and swimming alongside, I found the ring which is used in tying up the boat. I had no sooner caught hold of it than a drowning man clasped his arms around me in a death grip. I told him he must let go, but it was of no use."

Still aboard the flaming wreck, Joe Elliott stumbled through a curtained-off women's cabin, only to be greeted by an angry: "*What* do you want in here, sir?"

He told the woman that there was "something wrong with the boat" and then hurried on his way toward the stern. "I climbed up to the hurricane deck. Throwing myself across the bulwark around the deck, I looked forward toward the jackstaff. The boat's bow was turned toward the Tennessee shore, one of the boat's chimneys was down, and all the men were in commotion.

"As I started back, realizing that it was not a dream, I heard the men calling, 'don't jump, we are going ashore!' I answered, saying that I was going back to where I came from. On getting back and looking down into the river, I saw that the men were jumping from all parts of the boat into the river. Such screams I never heard—twenty and thirty men jumping off at a time, many lighting on those already in the water—until the river became black with men, their heads bobbing up like corks, and many disappearing never to appear again.

"We threw over everything that would float that we could get hold of, for their assistance; and then I, with several others, began tearing the sheeting off the sides of the cabin, and throwing it over."

About that time, a soldier from the Tenth Indiana Cavalry asked Elliott, "Have you seen my father?" Just as Elliott said he had not, the older man appeared, and father and son embraced. By then, the fire was "jumping along from one crosspiece to another in a way that made me think of a lizard running along a fence.

"I now made up my mind to leave the boat, and walked around the right side of the cabin to the wheelhouse," Elliott continued. "I feared that it was too far to jump, and on looking over to see what the distance was, I saw one of the fenders hanging just behind the wheelhouse, I lost no time climbing over the side of the boat and 'cooning it' down to the lower deck. . . . Casting my eyes around, I could see nobody, and stepping to the edge of the boat and looking to see that the river was free from any poor struggling soldier, I dived off."

Otto Barden went down so far that he was forced to let go of his board and was "strangled twice before I reached the top," as he recorded. "Then the young man [who had said he could not swim] caught me and strangled me twice. By this time I was about played out. I then reached the wheel, and clung to it until I tore off all my clothes, with the intention of swimming with one hand. I looked around and recognized Fritz Saunders, of my regiment, by my side."

Barden saw two doors under the paddle wheel. One contained glass panels. He discarded it. Then he noticed a solid wooden one, which he and Saunders took. As they moved away, "a man swam up and laid across the center of [the door they had rejected]. And even as he did so, the wheel housing burned through and fell over door and occupant.

"I said to Saunders, 'let's go to the right, it is nearer to the shore.'" Saunders saw a boat, and the two decided to paddle for it instead. They met "three young men clinging to a large trunk; they grasped our door; that put us all under the water. I gave the trunk a kick and raised on the door and brought it to the surface of the water.

"Then, I said, 'boys if you don't keep your weight off of the door, then you must steer the trunk yourselves.' By this time, I was cold and benumbed and was in a sinking condition, but having presence of mind, I reached and got my board and called aloud to God for help. I rubbed my arms and got the blood in circulation again."

Chester Berry, concerned that his poor physical condition was not up to the herculean demands of the night, was one of the last to quit the furiously burning *Sultana*. He heard a level of "swearing, praying, shouting and crying" that exceeded anything that had ever before stunned his ears, "much of it . . . followed by petitions to the Almighty, denunciations, by bitter weeping." He came across one man "wringing his hands as if in terrible agony, continually crying: 'o dear, o dear!'"

When Berry asked if he were hurt, the man replied that he could not swim. "I've got to drown. O dear!"

Berry showed the distraught man his piece of cabin-door casing and told him to get one for himself. "Put it under your chin," he advised, "and you can't drown." The man argued that he had already found one and that it had been taken away from him. "Well, then, get another," Berry admonished.

"What would be the use?" the other persisted. "They would take it away from me. . . . I've got to drown!"

Thoroughly disgusted, Berry gave him a shove and shouted, "Drown, then, you fool!"

Berry then jumped and "struck out for some willows that I could see by the light of the burning boat, they appearing to be about one-half mile distant." When he looked back, he witnessed much the same sight as had Otto Barden—the crashing of one of the fiery wheel housings. Berry, however, saw a man on top of the flimsy structure burning to death.

Some survivors were already being plucked from the night waters of the Mississippi. Horn, for one, was picked up by a small river steamer that raced to the scene.

Also assisting in rescue efforts were boats from the USS *Tyler*, laid up in Memphis for repairs. One of her officers, William H. C. Michael, would recall the moment that "the *Tyler*'s crew, half-clad . . . pushed off into the stream. The wails, cries and prayers could be heard, but the morning fog made it impossible to see any object distinctly. Even when we had reached the nearest to us it was impossible to see the struggling men from whom the cries for help ascended. . . . Surrounded by piteous prayers for help, and yet unable to save a single soul!

"The fog lifted a little and we were able to escape the confusion of the wails and moans and prayers and pick up as many as our boat could hold. These were landed as quickly as strong arms and willing hearts could pull ashore, and again we were in the midst of the heart-rending scene.

"Thus we worked till all was hushed upon the surface of the river."

Ensign Berry of the *Essex* had by then arrived in a small boat. The first survivor he encountered was so "chilled and benumbed" that he could not speak. The second died in minutes. The naval officer set course for Fort Pickering to unload. Rowing in, his skiff was fired upon. Berry kept on anyhow, and accosted the sentry who appeared to have fired the shot. He was only obeying orders, the sentry asserted, to "shoot at anythin' that moved." Berry, who did not log his full reply, informed the soldier of what had happened on the river and that he "was picking up drowning men!" The sentry stared at him in silence as he pushed off again, having emptied his boat. Soon, Berry was hauling in survivors "who were so benumbed that my boats' crews were obliged to handle them as if they were dead men."

Otto Barden was lucky. He reached shore, grabbed a tree growing on one of Paddy's Old Hen and Chickens Islands, and hung on.

Bill Norton broke the death grip of the drowning man, but his troubles were not over. He was not only numbed, as were all who hit the river, but he was experiencing debilitating stomach cramps as well. "It seemed as if I could go no further," he recorded, "but if I stopped swimming I found myself sinking. . . .

"I could hear the cries of those that were burned and scalded screaming with pain at every breath, and men all along the river were calling for help. Away in the distance, floating down . . . was the burning boat with a few brave men fighting the fire with buckets of water. Looking to my left, I thought I could see the trees through the darkness. This gave me new courage, and I turned in that direction and soon some brush struck me in the face.

"A little farther on I was washed up against a log which had caught in the young cottonwood trees."

Joe Elliott went down so far in water "colder than Greenland's icy mountains" that he was certain he'd never resurface. "Then," he noted, "my drawers began to slip down around my feet, and it became necessary to get rid of them as soon as possible."

Like Horn, he came upon floating stairs. He figured they were the ones that had led from the cabin deck up over the wheel housing to the hurricane deck. Another man already astride the stairs invited him aboard after he politely inquired if Elliott thought it would support two.

From the stairs' eminence, Elliott watched the last moments of the incandescent *Sultana*: "It looked like a huge bonfire in the middle of the river. As the flames ascended, mingled with smoke, and shed their peculiar light on the water, we could see both sides—bluffs on one side and timber on the other, and with no sensation as to the moving current.

"It was more like one of those beautiful lakes that I have seen in Minnesota, and if it had been only a painting it would have been grand; but alas! it was all real. . . .

"The men who were afraid to take to the water could be seen clinging to the sides of the boat until they were singed off like flies."

Suddenly, with a great hissing, the flaming *Sultana* vanished before his eyes. The shrieks and cries from inside her ceased.

She was gone.

Elliott stroked on minus his drawers. He was soon passed by a man "bobbing up and down in a way that reminded me of the frog in the game of leap-frog." He called out to the man, only to receive the reply: "Don't touch me! I'm on a barrel."

Next, Elliott and his fellow passenger on the stairs encountered a man "on the end of a large log." The three joined forces, somehow holding the stairs and the log together with their hands and feet. Idly wondering what had happened to his archenemy, McCoy, Elliott "made no further exertions to get on shore, but floated on down the river with the current. . . . I remember passing Memphis, and seeing the gas lights burning in the streets. . . . I heard the splash of an oar and tried to call for help, but my voice seemed to have left me.

"It was some such feeling as when one tries to call out in a nightmare."

Chester Berry, holding his piece of wood and thrashing in what he thought was the direction of the shoaly islands, became "despondent" of saving himself and lapsed into a meandering reverie, in which he was "transported . . . to the old house at home. . . . I was wending my way slowly up the path from the road gate to the house, but, strange for me, when I reached the door, instead of entering at once, I sat upon the step."

His mother was a devout Christian, and although his father was no less so, he was deaf and dumb. Thus, Berry's mother was compelled to lead the family in prayer and hymn. At nine o'clock every evening, the family had its hour of prayer. If a member happened to be absent, he or she was prayed for.

Now, gulping huge mouthfuls of the foul Mississippi, Berry imagined that it was nine o'clock and that he was the object of his family's beseechings. "Mother, by the help of God, your prayer shall be answered," he believed he called aloud. Ahead, he thought he saw "the bow light of the gunboat [*Essex*]."

His namesake, Ensign Berry, however, continued to experience difficulties with the shore sentries. As he attempted to bring in another load of survivors, a shot "came whistling over our heads," he recalled. Seeing a sentry raising his musket, Berry shouted angrily that he wished to see the man's officer—at once! The officer was produced.

"I told him," the young naval officer would report, "that these boats were not skiffs, that they were a man-of-war's gig and cutter, and again reminded him of what had happened and of the drowning men whose cries he could not help hearing. . . . He said he had as much humanity as anyone, and in firing at me he had only obeyed orders."

Baffled and still furious, Ensign Berry put back into the river.

Missing the *Essex*, Chester Berry came upon a tree "whose roots were now fast in the bed of the stream, upon which I climbed and was nearly asleep when a number of men from the boat came along and climbed upon it, also. Their united weight sank it low into the water, whose icy coldness coming upon my body again awakened me. Then, to more fully arouse me, a man got hold of my board and tried to take it away from me," claiming it was his. Their brief tug of war ended in Berry's grabbing firm hold of the board. He floated off and "gave [himself] up to sleep." And thus, slumbering, Chester Berry was picked out of the river by sailors from the steamer *Pocahontas*.

Otto Barden was rescued from his tree by the same ship. Nearby was a man who had been clinging all night to a trunk from the *Sultana*'s baggage rooms. He was dead. Bill Norton was saved by a canoeist who paddled out from the Arkansas shore. Joe Elliott, though swept past Memphis, was still in range of the *Essex*'s busy boats, one of which hauled him aboard. He, too, complained that he had been fired upon from the shore as he floated downstream. Chief Engineer Wintringer was rescued from a large plank he had shared with four others, one of whom slipped off moments before salvation.

Not a hint was ever found as to the manner of Captain Mason's demise. It was presumed that he was among the last to quit his flaming command.

Eleven of the twelve women from the Christian Commission were lost, including a bride and her husband. One woman refused to jump, fearing that her presence in the water would add to the panic when male swimmers sought to rescue her. It was said, without confirmation, that the sole survivor was a Mrs. Harvey Ennis, who had boarded at Memphis. She rode to shore on the back of a mule. Her husband—a navy lieutenant—her child, and her sister were all drowned.

As army Surgeon H. H. Hood sought to commandeer cots and medical supplies en masse in Memphis, he pronounced the condition of the survivors "pitiable."

There were fewer than 700 of them, not even a third of those who had been aboard. Thus, more than 1,600 perished that rainy night on the Mississippi. Such a toll remains unequalled in American waters and off our shores. (As points of comparison, approximately 1,500 died on the *Titanic*, and 1,198 on the *Lusitania*.)

For the survivors, the memory would haunt them the remainder of their lives. Many bore physical scars. Chester Berry, for example, had fractured his skull, and he languished several months in a Memphis hospital. When he walked into his home in South Creek, Pennsylvania, in midsummer, his mother collapsed. He had been reported dead at the time of the disaster.

Others succumbed to burns after lingering for agonizing months. A few, unable to stand the continuing torment, found one of the service revolvers or muskets that still abounded in the land and ended their pain.

Yet others turned to poetry. Bill Norton began a meandering requiem:

On sails the steamer through the gloom,
On sleep the soldiers to their doom.
And death's dark angel—oh so soon,
Calls loud the muster roll . . . !

But what, or *who*, was the villain in the catastrophe?

Chief Engineer Wintringer had no idea what had happened. He could not testify that the "experimental" boiler had burst, for he did not know. Most river steamers, outrageously overworked throughout the war, steamed without exploding in spite of leaky boilers. Anyhow, high-pressure steam remained several decades in the future.

Marine investigations and a few court-martials adjourned without coming to any conclusions. Significant, perhaps, were the rumors of sabotage or outright "torpedoing" (mining) that had followed the *Sultana* all the way up from Vicksburg.

Lieutenant Michael of the *Tyler* would write some years after the war: "Admiral Porter and many other well-informed officers connected with the Mississippi Squadron believed that the explosion was caused by coal loaded with powder by one of the many fiends in human form who had banded themselves together and taken an oath to destroy Federal gunboats and transports whenever and wherever it could be done. I have a list of the names of men who had thus sworn to do such work.

"In 1888, William C. Streator, on his deathbed in St. Louis, stated that a noted Confederate blockade runner and smuggler of mails, by the name of Robert Lowden, known during the war by the alias of Charles Dales, concocted and carried out the demonish plot. Streator says that Dales told him after the war that while the *Sultana* was lying at the wharf taking on coal the night previous to the disaster he smuggled aboard a lump of coal charged with powder. This he laid on the coal pile in front of the boilers for the purpose of destroying the boat and wrecking [sic] vengeance on the ——— Yankees.

"This statement, taken with other evidence in my possession, . . . proves to me that the *Sultana* was blown up in the manner described."

Lieutenant Michael's theory is easily plausible. A cast-iron bomb resembling a large chunk of coal had been invented early in the war by Confederate Brigadier General Gabriel Rains, who had also introduced a crude type of land mine. These instruments of sabotage became such a concern to Union commanders that during the Vicksburg operation, Admiral Porter ordered that anyone seen carrying a lump of coal near any Federal man-o'-war be shot on sight. These "coal bombs" rarely sank ships, but they often ripped up furnaces and tore holes in vessels' sides.

What sank the *Sultana*?

The cause of the devastating explosion remains as profound a mystery as that surrounding Lincoln's assassination.

The shattered steamer persisted as a gruesome curiosity. Bones, skulls, and scorched bits of clothing were visible within the charred hull when the river was low. Some artifacts washed ashore, to be seized and preserved by the morbid.

A frugal reward of two hundred dollars for the body of Captain J. Cass Mason was never claimed, but eighteen thousand dollars in gold rumored to have been somewhere on board the *Sultana* inspired divers to probe the disintegrating wreck for several decades.

Then the Mississippi changed its course, and the sidewheeler's remains vanished altogether.

Yet the *Sultana*'s fiery demise was not to be the last war-related act in the wake of Appomattox.

The CSS *Shenandoah*. This extremely rare photograph, taken when she was in dry dock in Melbourne, does not show the big, British-built ship to full advantage. Her long yards (cross-spars on her lofty masts) testify, however, to her amplitude of sail.

Chapter 12

THE LAST TO KNOW

"Ten American flags were hauled down instantaneously with the hoisting of the flag of the South."

THIS CHAPTER IS A FIRST-PERSON account written by Lieutenant James I. Waddell of the CSS *Shenandoah*. It is taken directly from *Official Records of the Union and Confederate Navies in the War of the Rebellion*, ser. 1, vol. 3. Waddell's account of his postsurrender cruise of destruction is articulate, and it reveals much of the man—a tough, moustached, forty-year-old North Carolinian, a veteran of twenty-three years in the United States Navy who took part in the Confederate defense of Drewry's Bluff, south of Richmond, during General McClellan's ill-starred Peninsular campaign. Later, he was in command of the harbor at Charleston. That he was a man of quick temper was hinted at by his limp, the product of an old dueling wound. That he was chivalrous was illustrated in his act of allowing a lady from a ship he had captured to take off her personal possessions and books—all but *Uncle Tom's Cabin*, which he ordered tossed into the sea. The very name Harriet Beecher Stowe was anathema to James Waddell.

The *Shenandoah* took her name from the Shenandoah River and Valley in Virginia, and ultimately from the imaginative Indian name translated "Daughter of the Stars." She was constructed of finest-grade teak over an iron frame. Launched in 1863 as the *Sea King*, she was designed for transporting troops and supplies to India, and she was thus "spacious 'tween decks." By English measurements, her tonnage was comparable to that of the *Alabama*. American displacement yardsticks, however, put her at about 790 tons, some 200 tons less than her illustrious predecessor. At 230 feet overall, she was 10 feet longer than the *Alabama*. Her engines, on the other hand, could crank only 180 horsepower, compared with *Alabama*'s 300.

As Waddell himself sized her up, "Under the most favorable circumstances she could not steam over 9 knots," but she was "very fast under sail, and a pretty vessel." The *Shenandoah* packed so much canvas, in fact, that special winches were employed to hoist her towering, heavy topsails.

It should be noted that Waddell seems to have paid scant attention to the English press, which told in the months before he sailed of the fall of Vicksburg, the Southern rebuff at Gettysburg, and the capture of Atlanta. He could have surmised that the Confederacy's demise would occur in a matter of a few months. He was not a stupid man. He simply did not notice.

The ultimate aim of my cruise was the dispersion or destruction of the New England whaling fleet, as pointed out in the memorandum of the honorable the Secretary of the Navy (Mallory). . . . It was hoped that I would be able to greatly damage and disperse that fleet, even if I did not succeed in utterly destroying it.

I left Liverpool, England, in the Confederate supply vessel *Laurel* on Sunday morning, the 9th of October, 1864, for Funchal, island of Madeira, taking with me all the officers but one detailed for my command.

A few picked men selected from the crew of the late CSS *Alabama*, who were specially retained, accompanied me and constituted the nucleus of the new force which I should have to organize at the place of rendezvous.

. . . The sun rose full of fire; a messenger was dispatched for a customs official to repair on board with the vessel's papers, and while the customs boat was being pulled off to us, accompanied by bumboats and fishing smacks, whose purpose it was to coax in the way of trade the last farthing out of thriftless Jack, that black steamer came in sight . . . from the north with flags flying from her mastheads which were recognized and answered from our steamer, and the cry arose from the shore boats which surrounded us, "Otro *Alabama*," i.e., another *Alabama*.

The fires had been kindled in [the *Laurel*'s] furnaces at daylight, and steam was ready; chain had been hove in to a short stay, and the vessel's quiet swing to a single anchor only increased our restlessness to follow the black steamer.

The customs officials being settled with and all strangers seen out of the *Laurel*, her anchor was tripped at 10 A.M. and she stood to sea in chase of the steamer, whose engines were slowed to enable us to come up rapidly. The 19th of October, 1864, was fine; the atmosphere clear and bright, and a wind blew from the southwest. So soon as the *Laurel* had approached sufficiently near the stern of the steamer I saw there three words, in large white letters, and I read through my lorgnette "*Sea King*—London."

An idea flashed across my brain—Is she to be a sea king? I ordered the *Sea King* to be telegraphed to follow the *Laurel* [to] refuge on the north side of the Deserters [the Desertas Islands], where I found a smooth sea, no interruptions, and a good but deep anchorage for negotiations and work. The first Lieutenant, William C. Whittle jr., of Virginia, had taken passage in the *Sea King* from London, as her purser, and joined me at this juncture of affairs.

The *Shenandoah* was commissioned on the ocean on the 19th day of October, 1864, under the lee and on the north side of the . . . Deserters . . . only a few miles distant from and in sight of Madeira. . . . In thirteen hours the consort [*Laurel*] had discharged every conceivable outfit intended for the *Shenandoah*, and was only delayed for such passengers as she was compelled to receive on board. I felt I had a good and fast ship under my feet, but there was a vast deal of work in as well as outside of her to be done, and to accomplish all that a crew was necessary.

It became my effort to ship the crew of the late *Sea King*, now the *Shenandoah*, and as many of the crew of the consort as possible and the men were called to the quarterdeck of the *Shenandoah*. . . . I informed them of the changed character of the *Sea King*, read my commission to them (made my first speech), pictured to them a brilliant, dashing cruise, and asked them to join the service of the Confederate States.

Only twenty three out of fifty five men were willing to venture on such service, and a large majority of those shipped for six months only. Those who declined service in the *Shenandoah* were directed to go on board the *Laurel*. My feeble force was then ordered to lift an anchor, which proved too heavy; the officers threw off their jackets and assisted in lifting it to the bow, and the little adventurer entered upon her new career, throwing out to the breeze the flag of the South.

I was truly afloat. . . .

[Waddell then had to attend to housekeeping chores. The decks had to be cleared of all manner of stores, from food and tackle to ammunition and clothing. Gunports had to be sawed and decks and bulwarks strengthened for the heavy guns. The carpenter was faced with a particular problem—he could find no helper. None of the small crew admitted to being able to do so much as drive a nail.]

The steamer was supplied with Enfield rifles, cutlasses, and revolvers, and there on the deck in huge boxes lay the guns and carriages. Though impatient to see them mounted and their grim faces projecting beyond our wooden walls, of what great use could they be in defense of so vulnerable a vessel? True, their appearance would go a long way toward reconciling an unarmed foe, but a short scrutiny inboard developed clearly our entire incapacity for contending against a regularly appointed man-of-war.

[The captain must have denigrated his firepower with tongue in cheek. Although Waddell did not commit to paper what he had, J. Thomas Scharf noted in his *History of the Confederate States Navy* that the *Shenandoah*'s battery consisted of four 8-inch smoothbores, two Whitworth 32-pounder rifles, and two 12-pounders. Except for the *Alabama*'s rather revolutionary Blakely pivoted gun at the bow, the *Shenandoah*'s armament compared very favorably with her famed predecessor's. Thus, her "incapacity" was considerably less than Waddell professed to believe.]

I concluded to take the offensive immediately. The deck was cleared of such articles as belonged below, the gun boxes lashed to and near the sides where the ports were designed to be cut, and having a partially clear deck, I could, with the aid of an Enfield rifle, investigate a stranger's nationality and, if of the kind I was in search, appropriate her. The crew was not sufficiently numerous to manage the vessel easily.

[Waddell converted his rudely furnished starboard cabin into a powder magazine. He had little choice, since the hold and the decks alike were crammed with coal. He covered the explosives with tarpaulins and started the process of moving. The expedient was in harmony with the unusual proportions of the command itself—twenty-four officers to twenty-three men.]

The novel character of my political position embarrassed me more than the feeble condition of my command, and that was fraught with painful apprehensions enough. I had the compass to guide me as a sailor, but my instructions made me a magistrate in a new field of duty, and where the law was not very clear to lawyers. Managing a vessel in unsettled, stormy weather and exposure to the dangers of the sea was a thing I had studied from my boyhood; fighting was a profession that I had prepared myself for by the study of the best models; but now I was to sail and fight and to decide questions of international law that lawyers had quarreled over with all their books before them. I was in all matters to act promptly and without counsel.

On the 22nd of October, four days after the vessel had been commissioned, the guns were all on their carriages. . . . The carpenter had succeeded in discovering a man who could lend him a hand in his department, and two ports were cut on either side of the deck. Other ports were to be cut, and the fighting bolts were first to be found before they could be driven. By some strange accident they escaped the observation of the gunner, and were found a few days afterwards in a beef barrel, stowed with the provisions in the hold. The gun tackles could not be found, and it soon became a matter of certainty they never were put on board.

There was a plenty of rope, but no blocks suitable for gun tackles; the absence of them rendered the battery totally useless. I had nothing left me but to look to the enemy to supply the deficiency. I had been directed to live off his supplies, and I suppose inanimate as well as animate objects were embraced in those directions.

The guns were on the carriages, and as the fighting bolts and gun tackles could not then be found, they were secured fore and aft the deck, close to the ship's side, and in the absence of bolts, straps were run through scuppers and toggled outside of the vessel, to which the guns were secured. The deck then became more cheerful. . . .

Several officers slept on the deck in the absence of berths, and wash-deck buckets were resorted to in the place of basins. The furniture in my cabin [apparently not the cabin in use as a powder magazine] consisted of one broken plush-velvet bottomed armchair, no berth, no bureau, no lockers for stowing my clothing in, no washstand, pitcher, or basin. The deck was covered with a half-worn carpet, which smelt of dogs or something worse. It was the most cheerless and offensive spot I had ever occupied. The apartments assigned the commissioned officers were in little better condition, except the room of the executive officer, which was comfortable, and as to the apartment of the steerage officers, it was filled with iron tanks holding bread, and there was no furniture of any kind for it.

Under all those trials our condition created merriment rather than sadness. It seemed to me I was the only anxious person on board. . . .

On the 25th of October, the powder was removed to a small apartment under my cabin, the deck of which was very little below the surface of the ocean, and divided from the steerage deck by a strong, open latticework, which was rendered more secure by heavy canvas tacked to the partition.

By the 26th of October, enough coal was removed from the berth deck to fill the side bunkers, from which a supply [had been] drawn for steaming since the 19th instant. The removal of such a quantity of coal developed a large, spacious, and finely ventilated deck, upon which it was designed to berth the crew, and the coal which could not be accommodated in the side bunkers was thrown well aft on that deck. . . .

The ship had now reached a low latitude, and was constantly receiving heavy rain and violent squalls of wind, and to our horror the decks were discovered to be leaking like sieves and the seams of the hull were sufficiently open to admit a fine spray as a sea had spent itself on her sides. Lieutenant Chew, an intelligent and promising young officer, erased *Sea King* from the stern of the *Shenandoah*.

On the 27th of October, 1864, the *Shenandoah* took the offensive and entered upon her first chase, and, in compliment to the stranger she was in chase of, crossed for the first time her royal yards [set a main staysail]. She rapidly overhauled the chase, which proved to be the *Mogul*, of London. Immediately after separating from that vessel, she entered upon another chase and overhauled her quickly; she also was British.

[On October 30, Waddell captured and scuttled the bark *Alina*, out of Searsport, Maine, bound for Buenos Aires with a cargo of railroad iron. He obtained from her the needed block, tackle, and rope, as well as kitchenware and a mattress for his cabin. Five seamen and a coal passer were cajoled into shipping on the manifest of the raider. Waddell then sank the *Alina* by knocking holes below her water line. In so doing, he observed that burning, Semmes's favorite method, tended to make the prize a beacon.

[On November 5, he captured his second victim, the American schooner *Charter Oak*, out of Boston, bound for San Francisco. In addition to her captain, logged only as "Gilman," Waddell took aboard the captain's wife, her sister—widowed after Harpers Ferry—and the sister's son as passengers. He fixed up his starboard cabin as "guest" quarters and invited the four to mess with him in the wardroom. Confiding to his log his "compassion" for women, Waddell presented Gilman's wife with two hundred dollars in gold seized from her husband.

[After capturing and burning the schooner *Lizzie M. Stacey*, also of Boston, on November 13, Waddell sailed the *Shenandoah* across the equator on the fifteenth. He helped arrange the traditional ceremony starring King Neptune and invited his involuntary passengers, representing three destroyed ships, to join in. He allowed them all a peek at "the line" through his telescope, across which a fine thread had been placed. Sure enough, there was the equator.

[On December 4, Waddell captured the whaling ship *Edward*, out of New Bedford, off the Brazilian coast in sight of lonely Tristan da Cunha Island. He appropriated her beef, pork, fish, biscuits, oil, canvas, tackle, and similar necessities. After burning the whaler—thus contradicting his earlier resolve— the merchant raider landed his captives on the island. He left them an estimated six weeks' rations and entrusted them to a "Yankee" who called himself the "governor" of the sparsely populated out-cropping.

[On December 29, Waddell overtook and destroyed the bark *Delphine*, out of Bangor, Maine. "A tall, finely proportioned woman of 26" identified as a Mrs. Nichols was the passenger from the *Delphine* whose copy of *Uncle Tom's Cabin* was jettisoned by William Whittle, the former purser on the *Sea King* who was now the *Shenandoah*'s executive officer. Waddell next rounded the Horn and set course for Australia.

[The American consul at Melbourne, apparently a very active emissary, induced a number of the *Shenandoah*'s crew to desert. In addition, Waddell began receiving anonymous letters threatening the destruction of his ship. The captain's request for police protection elicited a wholly unforeseen reaction. On February 14, 1865, "all the militia at Melbourne . . . turned out under arms, and artillery companies," Waddell reported, were "sent to the beach to threaten the *Shenandoah*." He could only conclude, with mingled hurt and surprise, that the authorities were "inimical to the South," a far cry from the attitude in Great Britain. Waddell resisted what he construed as attempted mass searches of his command, finally agreeing to a perfunctory daily visit by a customs official. All in all, the Confederate captain was happy to cast off from Melbourne in March. Not until April 1 did he encounter new prey, and on that date he sank four ships flying the United States flag.]

In all the course of my sea life I never enjoyed more charming weather; the sun shone with splendid brilliancy, and the moon shed her peculiar luster from a dark-blue vaulted sky, while the vast mirror below reflected each heavenly body and flashed with sprightliness as the great ocean plow tore the waters asunder, and for ten consecutive days I would stand for hours on her deck gazing on that wonderful creation, that deep liquid world.

The track of vessels bound from San Francisco and many from the west coast of South America to Hong Kong lay between the parallels in north latitude of 17° and 20°, because the trade wind is better there than a more northerly route would find them, and the track for vessels bound to San Francisco and other ports along the west coast of America from the China coast lay between the parallels of 39° and 45° because west wind prevails [west of the California and Oregon coasts].

I spent several days in cruising along those frequented paths, but did not see a sail; the delay was, however, not without its reward, for the old boatswain had time to see things in his department in good condition for hard knocks. After the vessel had reached the parallel of 43° N. the weather became cold, foggy, and the winds were variable and westerly in direction, but unsteady in force, and that ever-reliable friend of the sailor, the barometer, indicated atmospheric convulsion—change in weather. [The *Shenandoah*] was prepared for a change of weather, which was rapidly approaching; the ocean was boiling from agitation, and if the barometer had been silent I would have called the appearance of the surface of the deep a famous tide rip.

A black cloud was hurrying toward us from the northeast, and so close did it rest upon the surface of the water that it seemed determined to smother and blot out of existence forever the little vessel; and there came in it a violence of wind that threw the vessel on her side, and she started like the affrighted stag from his lair, bounding off before the awful pressure. Squall after squall struck her, flash after flash surrounded her, and thunder rolled in her wake, while every timber retorted to the shakings of the heavens. It was a typhoon; the ocean was as white as the snowdrift. Such was the violence of the wind that a new maintopsail, close-reefed, was blown into shreds.

Aeolus soon emptied his wrath upon the bosom of Neptune, and in ten hours the *Shenandoah* was making northing again.

Two days after that fearful typhoon we received another from the same quarter, but it was more civil and lasted a shorter time. The weather continued so threatening I felt as if the uncertainty and violence of the weather, the constant threatening sky, and agitated sea would never allow the vessel to get north of the parallel of 45°. That gale, like its predecessors, had worked to the westward, and the vessel began her northing again. On the 17th of May the ship was north of the parallel of 45°, and the weather, though cold, looked more settled.

[The war had by then been over some five weeks.]

On the 20th of May the Kurile Islands, covered with snow, came in sight, and on the forenoon of the 21st steamed under staysails into the Sea of Okhotsk and ran along the coast of Kamchatka under sail. There is a strong current setting along the Pacific side of the Kurile Islands, which helps to form the Sea of Okhotsk to the northeast.

On the 29th of May captured and burned the whaling bark *Abigail*, of New Bedford. When the *Abigail* was discovered, the *Shenandoah* was skirting an extensive field of floe ice, and beyond another she was seen standing toward us; I therefore awaited her arrival, and learned that her captain mistook the steamer for a Russian provision vessel going to the settlement of Okhotsk to supply the Russian officials. A vessel goes there twice a year for that purpose. The *Abigail* was valued at $18,000.

Several of the *Abigail*'s crew joined us, and among them a New Bedford man, a genuine down easter. The captain was frightfully astonished at his situation; could hardly realize his misfortune; he had before fallen into Admiral Semmes' hands, and his vessel was destroyed and, although he had gone almost out of the world to secure a paying voyage, he had failed again. He had been away from home for three years when he was captured by me.

I continued as far as the mouth of Ghijinsk Bay, but found it so full of ice the steamer could not be entered. Then I stood along the land of eastern Siberia as far as Tausk Bay; then she was forced away by the ice and started for Shantaski Island, but found ice in such quantities before she reached the one hundred and fiftieth meridian of east longitude she was forced to the southward with ice almost in every direction and apparently closing on her. That ice varied from 15 to 30 feet in thickness, and although not very firm, was sufficiently so to seriously injure the vessel if neglected. I desired to reach Shantaski Island (called Green Island), for the fishing is there and in the bays southwest of it.

Within twenty days the ship had run from the tropics into snow and ice, from excessive heat to this excessively cold climate, and yet there was nothing more than catarrhs among the crew, from which they soon recovered. I had been without a stove, and the *Abigail* supplied the requisition. The caution resorted to [to] prevent sickness was an order preventing unnecessary exposure of the crew: consequently the vessel was kept under easy sail.

The men were required by the surgeon, Charles E. Lining, an intelligent gentleman and excellent physician, to clothe themselves warmly and keep themselves dry. Extra rations of grog and hot coffee were served at regular hours, and the surgeon's assistant, Dr. Fred J. McNulty, a good fellow, inspected the food for the crew before and after prepared. Indeed, the medical gentlemen can not be complimented too highly for their excellent discretion in preserving the sanitary condition of the vessel. . . .

[Similarly, combating the subarctic gales and ice floes demanded the highest skills of a ship handler and navigator. Waddell wrote of seas striking the far edge of the floes and "throwing sheets of water 20 feet high . . . a majestic sight, resembling an infuriated ocean wasting itself against an ironbound coast."

[On June 22, off Cape Navarin, Siberia, on the Bering Sea, some two and a half months after Lee's surrender, Waddell captured five vessels, including the *William Thompson*, "the largest whaler out of New England." He invited Captain Howe of the *Milo*, out of New Bedford, to come aboard with his papers.]

I asked for news. He said the war was over. I asked for documentary evidence; he could not supply it;

he believed the war had ended, from what he had heard. I replied that it was not satisfactory, but that if he could produce any reliable evidence, I would consider his impressions.

He then said: "I took your command for a telegraph steamer which we have been expecting to lay a cable between Russian America and eastern Siberia." He was informed that I was willing to ransom his vessel if he accepted my conditions. He reflected a little and then said: "I see how it is; I will give bond and receive all prisoners you may put on board."

I received his register and bond and directed him to return to his vessel and send all his boats with full crews to the steamer for prisoners and to keep her fore-topsail aback.

The boats came to the *Shenandoah*, and she steamed in pursuit of two vessels which seemed to be in communication. I resorted to the stratagem with the *Milo* of drawing her crew away to prevent her escape, for if I had not removed her crew her captain could have forced me to ransom another vessel, which would have been clever in him. A breeze had sprung up, the vessels had taken alarm, and I knew that the work before me required promptitude and management, or the rascals would have a good joke on me. The captains had communicated and entered their vessels in the floe.

The *Shenandoah* ran close to and parallel with the floe and separated the barks, each being distant a mile, and fired at the one farthest in the ice, which made her heave to. Her consort then tacked and stood out of the floe for the Siberian coast with a good wind. I fired a second time at the bark which was hove to, and her captain interpreted it to mean stand out of the floe, and submitted to the prize boat which was in pursuit of her. She proved to be the *Sophia Thornton*, and her captain and officers were received on board the steamer.

[Waddell finally succeeded in rounding up his captives, which had fled like sheep before a predator. A remark by Captain Williams of the *Jireh Swift* that the Confederacy should have sent a cruiser to destroy the whaling fleet two years earlier inspired a lengthy diatribe in Waddell's journals concerning "Yankee character . . . fat contracts and immense Government expenditures." Bonded for forty-six thousand dollars, the *Milo* was packed with prisoners from the other whalers and dispatched on her way to San Francisco with Waddell's hope that "the Richmond government might hear of my whereabouts and what the steamer was doing."]

On the 23rd of June captured the brig *Susan Abigail* [not to be confused with the previous *Abigail*], of San Francisco and from that city, with California papers containing a number of dispatches, and among them was one that stated the Southern Government removed to Danville and the greater part of the Army of Virginia had joined General Johnston's army in North Carolina, where an indecisive battle had been fought against General Sherman's army; also that at Danville a proclamation was issued by President Davis, announcing that the war would be carried on with renewed vigor, and exhorting the people of the South to bear up heroically against their adversities.

I questioned the captain of the *Susan Abigail* upon the general opinion in San Francisco about the military condition of American affairs, and he said: "Opinion is divided as to the ultimate result of the war; for the present the North has the advantage, but how it will end no one can form a correct opinion; and as to the newspapers, they can not be relied upon." The *Susan Abigail* gave the latest information from America, and she fell into my hands before she had communicated with any vessel; indeed, the *Shenandoah* was the first vessel she had seen since she had left San Francisco.

Three of the *Susan Abigail*'s crew joined the *Shenandoah*, which was evidence that they did not believe the war ended; and they had been paid their advance, so they had nothing to lose by returning to San Francisco; they were not urged to ship, but rather sought service in the *Shenandoah*.

On the 25th June, put the ship under steam in chase of and captured the *General Williams*, New London; burned her. She was valued at $44,740. . . . On the 26th of June chased and captured . . . six Yankee whale vessels, and burned the whole of them except the *General Pike* which was ransomed for the sum of $30,000. . . . Within 48 hours, the *Shenandoah* destroyed and ransomed property to the value of $233,500. . . .

On the 27th June, ship under sail with a head wind, and eleven sail in sight, all to windward. I felt no doubt of their nationality, and to attempt the capture of any one of them while the wind blew would be the loss of the greater part of them. Lowered the smokestack and continued in the rear of the whalers, keeping a luff and retarding her progress as much as possible, so as to arouse no suspicions among the Yankee crowd ahead. On the 28th at 10:30 A.M. a calm ensued; the game were collected in East Cape Bay, and the *Shenandoah* came plowing the Arctic waters under the American flag with a fine pressure of steam on. Every vessel hoisted the American flag.

I had heard of the whale ship *James Maury* when at the island of Ascension, and after reaching the Arctic Ocean heard again of her, and also of the death of her captain, whose widow and two little children were on board. While the boats were being armed, preparatory to taking possession of the prizes, a boat from the whale ship *Brunswick* came to the steamer, and the mate in charge of the boat, still ignorant of our nationality, represented that the *Brunswick* a few hours before had struck a piece of ice, which left a hole in her starboard bow 20 inches below the water line, and asked for assistance, to which application Lieutenant Whittle, the executive officer, replied, "We are very busy now, but in a time we will attend to you."

The facetiousness of that reply coaxed a smile from me.

The mate thanked Mr. Whittle, and he was asked which of the vessels was the *James Maury*; he pointed to her. The *Brunswick* was lying on her side, her casks of oil floating her well up, and her captain, seeing his vessel a hopeless wreck, had offered (I was told) his oil to any purchaser for 20 cents per gallon. The *Brunswick*'s boat returned. The *Shenandoah*, being in position to command the fleet with her guns, hoisted our flag, and the armed boats were dispatched to take possession of certain vessels (she had only five boats), with orders to send captains with their ship papers to the steamer.

Ten American flags were hauled down instantaneously with the hoisting of the flag of the South. The eleventh still hung to the vessel's gaff, and seeing someone on deck with her gun, I sent Mr. Whittle to capture her and to send her captain on board. That bark was the *Favorite*, of Fair Haven, and her captain was unable to take care of himself from drunkenness. His vessel was without a register, liable to seizure in profound peace by the police of the sea. . . .

All the captains and mates were more or less under the influence of liquor, and some of them swore their sympathy for the South, while others spoke incoherently of cruisers, fire, and insurance. A drunken and brutal class of men I found the whaling captains and mates of New England. The boarding officer of the *James Maury*, Lieutenant Chew, sent her mate to me, who represented the widow to be in a very distressed condition with her two little children; that she was very sad, and that the remains of her husband were preserved in a cask of whisky. I sent a message to the unhappy woman to cheer up; that no harm should come to her or the vessel; that I knew she was an owner in the vessel, and that the men of the South never made war on helpless women and children. . . .

[Waddell thus eclipsed Semmes's record by burning nine and bonding two vessels valued at half a million dollars, all within a span of eleven hours on June 28. Flames lit up the subarctic gloom. "An occasional explosion on board of some one of the burning vessels informed me of the presence of gunpowder or other combustibles," Waddell wrote, "and a liquid flame now and then pursued some inflammable substance which had escaped from their sides to the water, and the heavens were illuminated with the red glare, presenting a picture of indescribable grandeur, while the water was covered with black smoke commingling with fiery sparks. Discharges . . . often resembled distant artillery."

[The crews, totaling 336 persons, sailed off in the two ransomed ships—the *James Maury* and the *Nile*. Almost three months after the capitulation at Appomattox, they would prove the *Shenandoah*'s last victims. Thus, she had made thirty-eight captures, releasing six on bond. Of the thirty-eight, only thirteen had been effected *before* the end of hostilities. In Waddell's estimation, the time had arrived to quit the waters. He was fearful that word of his rampage among the whaling fleet had reached United States Navy patrols. The illumination of the sky by his bonfires would appear to have been telltale enough. Another factor was the *Shenandoah*'s rudder, which was sustaining damage from the constant pressure of the ice.]

Two days before the steamer left Bering Sea, a black fog closed upon us and shut out from our view the sky and all objects 50 yards distant; still she pressed her way toward the Amoukhta [Amukta] Pass, or the one hundred and seventy-second meridional passage of the Aleutian Islands, which are stretched from the Alaska Peninsula, the extreme southern land of Russian America [which was to become United States territory in two more years], in a semi-circular course toward the coast of Kamchatka, and a cursory glance at a map representing that part of the world shows alternate land and water for a distance of 20° of longitude. When the dead reckoning gave the steamer a position near the Amoukhta Pass, through which I intended she should enter the North Pacific, the fog continued thick and gloomy, but she dashed along on her course trusting to accuracy of judgment and a hope that the fog would lift. . . .

[The passage] only required a little nerve. When I expected the ship to be about the center of the pass, much to my relief land was seen off either beam, and the position of the ship was accurately discovered or ascertained by taking cross bearings. That feeling of security against a danger which is overcome is truly delightful to the senses. It was my first great experience, for it involved the safety of the ship and the lives of all on board. The ship was safe.

Again in the North Pacific Ocean, with fine weather, and the Aleutian Islands astern, I felt an unbounded sensation of freedom on the surface of that vast expanse of water where those who can take care of ships feel at home, and when looking back in that direction where we had seen such hard and dangerous service I involuntarily breathed away dull care; and why not? It was my home for twenty years; my early ideas were associated with the ocean and ships and all that sort of thing; I felt no longer trammeled by icebergs, floe, and land; no longer to hear the masthead lookout cry "Ice ahead!" We had run out of a gloomy vapor into a bright, cheerful, sparkling ocean, and as soon as a hot sun thawed the frosty timbers and rigging of the craft, she would be more than a match for anything she might [meet] under canvas.

It was the 5th of July when the Aleutian Islands were lost sight of, and the ship sought the parallel for westerly winds to hasten her over to the coast of Lower California and Mexico to look after the steamers running to and from Panama for San Francisco. . . .

On the 2d of August got up steam in chase of a bark, and in a short time came up with and boarded the British bark *Barracouta*, of and bound for Liverpool, thirteen days from San Francisco. The sailing master, Mr. Irvine S. Bulloch, was the boarding officer, and through that officer I received a few papers in which the surrender of the several Southern generals in the field and the capture of President Davis was announced.

[Master Bulloch, not one to idly toss out words, pronounced his own succinct amen: "The war is a thing of the past!"

[The following remarks are taken from an entry in the logbook of the lieutenant of the watch dated August 2, 1865, and signed by D. M. Scales: "Having received by the bark *Barracouta* the sad intelligence of the overthrow of the Confederate Government, all attempts to destroy the shipping or property of the United States will cease from this date, in accordance with which the first lieutenant, William C. Whittle, jr., received the order from the commander to strike below the battery and disarm the ship and crew."

[Surgeon Lining, a South Carolinian, noted that a petition was sent to Waddell requesting that the ship be navigated to the nearest English port. The captain, Lining recorded, assembled "all hands aft and made a very pretty little speech." Waddell did not, however, immediately inform his men that he intended to sail the many thousands of miles to Liverpool.]

. . . The intelligence of the [outcome] of the fearful struggle cast a deep stillness over the ship's company and would have occupied all my reflection had not a responsibility of the highest order rested upon me in the course I should pursue.

I first thought that a port in the South Atlantic would answer all my purposes for taking the ship, but upon reflection I saw the propriety of avoiding those ports, and determined to run the ship for a European port, which involved a distance of 17,000 miles—a long gantlet to run and escape. But why should I not succeed in baffling observation or pursuit? There was everything to gain and only imaginary dangers.

The ship had up to that time traversed over 40,000 miles without accident. I felt assured a search would be made for her in the Pacific, and that to run the ship south was of importance to all concerned. Some nervous persons expressed a desire that the steamer should be taken to Australia or New Zealand, or any near port, rather than attempt to reach Europe. I could not see what was to be gained by going in any other direction than to Europe. . . .

The run down to Cape Horn was expeditious, and before reaching the pitch of the cape, in fine weather, several American vessels passed us going to the westward. One vessel only was standing as we were, to the east, and that English vessel ran away from the *Shenandoah*. I attribute her defeat to the condition of the copper on her bottom, an unpleasant circumstance, for it might require all her fleetness to escape a Federal cruiser.

The wind was northwest on the Pacific side, and for several hours before doubling the cape under topgallant sails the ship ran 15 knots. . . .

She passed unpleasantly near the Shag Rocks [off the South Georgia Islands, east of the Falklands] during darkness in boisterous and cold weather. Day after day icebergs and dangerous blocks of ice were near the ship. We were without a moon to shed her cheerful light over our desolate path, and the wind blew so fiercely that the ship's speed could not be reduced below 5 knots. . . .

Some of the icebergs were castellated and good representations of fortifications and sentinels on guard. Although the nights were painfully dark, she escaped injury. Did you ever see darkness so black that it seemed tangible or seemed impenetrable to light?

When the senses dwell upon such an envelopment the eye feels oppressed by the black weight, and a feeling of suffocation is produced. These outer struggles of our vessel were in accord with the deep, dark, and gloomy thoughts that now filled our minds; we were without a home or a country. . . .

[*Shenandoah* transited the equator on October 11, 1865, and set course across the North Atlantic for England, keeping a respectful distance from the many ships sighted.]

On the afternoon of the 25th of October, when she had crossed the trade belt and was running out the northern edge of it in light air, the ship just fanning along, a masthead lookout cried, "Sail ho!"

The cry of "sail ho!" carried apprehension to the hearts of many; the dreaded Federal cruiser might be at hand, and what then? The cry brought many to their feet who were indulging repose, and an enquiring glance conveyed their anxiety of mind; for if a Federal cruiser was to be found anywhere she would be in that region of ocean where most vessels bound to Europe would be intercepted. Glasses swept the northern horizon in search of the stranger, but she was visible from aloft only.

I sent a quartermaster aloft with orders to communicate to me only what he could ascertain from the appearance of the sail. He reported her under short sail with her mainsail up or furled, and that from the spread of her masts [she seemed] to be a steamer. She was standing a little more to the east of north than the *Shenandoah* was heading. The sun was thirty minutes high and the sky was cloudless. I could make no change in the course of [our] ship or the quantity of sail she was carrying, because such evolution would have aroused the stranger's suspicion.

After the sun had gone down, leaving a brilliant western sky and a beautifully defined horizon, I sent that quartermaster again aloft with orders similar to those he had previously received. He reported her to be a cruiser and he believed her awaiting in order to speak. The *Shenandoah* had come up rapidly with the sail and there seemed little chance of escaping communication. A danger was, she would approach too near during light. She could already be seen from deck, and darkness came on more slowly than I had ever before observed it. . . .

Darkness finally threw her friendly folds around the anxious heart and little ship, and closed the space between the vessels. What a relief! She could not have been 4 miles off.

The *Shenandoah*'s head was turned south and steam ordered. At 9 o'clock the moon rose while our sails were being furled, and the surface of the steamer aloft being greatly reduced by that maneuver, it would be difficult to ascertain where she lay.

The *Shenandoah* was 500 miles southeast of the Azores. . . .

[*Shenandoah*'s phenomenal luck continued. On November 5, she pushed into St. George's Channel, at the mouth of the Irish Sea, 122 days from the Aleutians, having "sailed a distance of 23,000 miles without seeing land," by Waddell's calculations. A pilot came aboard at the Liverpool Bar, making the interesting understatement that "the war had gone against the South." On the sixth, in the Mersey River, Waddell hauled down his flag as British customs officials took possession of the *Shenandoah* and a Royal Navy gunboat warped alongside. On the eighth, he surrendered himself, 10 officers, 14 "acting appointments," and 109 enlisted, all of whom were "unconditionally released." The great number of men aboard the *Shenandoah*, compared with the meager crew of 47 at the time of the ship's commissioning, may presumably be attributed to the presence of volunteers from captured ships.]

My baggage was very closely examined, but that proceeded more from my directions concerning it than any desire on the part of the officials to be impertinently inquisitive. I had neither thoughts nor stores to conceal from anyone. I presented my tumblers, decanters, and bedding, with a few trophies from the islands, to the wife of the lieutenant commanding. . . .

[The *Shenandoah*] was the only vessel which carried the flag around the world, and she carried it six months after the overthrow of the South.

The last gun in defense of the South was fired from her deck on the 22d of June, Arctic Ocean.

She ran a distance of 58,000 statute miles and met with no serious injury during a cruise of thirteen months.

Her anchors were on her bows for eight months.

She never lost a chase, and was second only to the celebrated *Alabama*.

I claim for her officers and men a triumph over their enemies and over every obstacle, and for myself I claim having done my duty.

POSTSCRIPT

The author's grandfather, a young naval surgeon in Porter's fleet before Vicksburg, sleeps in Arlington National Cemetery with many others who pushed forward the "war to save the Union."

In that goal they admirably succeeded. Lasting peace they could in no way assure. Thirty-three years after Appomattox, a number of them were back in uniform helping to defeat Spain in new, watery theaters of battle—Santiago de Cuba and the environs of Manila Bay. Confederate sailors had proven more formidable.

Not even the youngest in Farragut's, Porter's, or DuPont's fleets could rally to the colors in 1917 to fight the kaiser. And the very few surviving in 1941 read with the greatest difficulty the news of Japan's attack on Pearl Harbor.

The author served for five years in the United States Navy in World War II. He considered himself fortunate, in comparison with Admiral Selfridge, to have been sunk but once. Invited to the next conflict—Korea—he politely declined.

Then, Vietnam. The wars did not stop. What has it all been about? Who were the victors and who the losers?

Were the sacrifices at Mobile Bay or in the Roanoke River, at Guadalcanal or Normandy, or in the waters off Inchon, Korea, for nothing? Were they the building blocks for a better tomorrow, or were they merely expedient, ephemeral answers to momentary challenges?

Thomas Wolfe wrote an uncharacteristically light short story entitled "Only the Dead Know Brooklyn." By the same token, and as an amen, perhaps only our naval dead know the answers to those several questions.

BIBLIOGRAPHY AND ACKNOWLEDGMENTS

Almost two decades fled before historians took up their pens in significant numbers to acknowledge that there had, indeed, been a Civil War at sea. Naval action had quickly been forgotten. The nostalgic (especially the journalists among them), the bereaved, and the merely morbid had directed their attention to battlefields and cemeteries. In the North, platoons of war correspondents were rushing into print the memories of the headiest years of their lives. George Alfred Townsend published his *Campaigns of a Non-Combatant* (New York: Blelock and Co.) in 1866. On the other side of the conflict, Edward A. Pollard, a Richmond editor, produced his *Southern History of the War* (New York: Charles B. Richardson). It was a busy year. With the guns scarcely cold, John S. C. Abbott published *The History of the Civil War in America* (New York: Henry Bill). And Benson J. Lossing issued the first installment of his three-volume series, *The Pictorial History of the Civil War* (Philadelphia: George W. Childs). Featured were sketches, most of them inspired by photographs. The remaining volumes appeared in 1867 and 1868.

Charles B. Boynton hurried out his *History of the Navy During the Rebellion* (New York: D. Appleton and Co.) in 1867; and, that same year, J. T. Headley produced *Farragut and Our Naval Commanders* (New York: E. B. Treat and Co.). Otherwise, there were only sporadic reminiscences of one nautical event or another, such as Edward P. Lull's *History of the United States Navy Yard at Gosport*, which appeared between cardboard covers in 1874. The United States Government Printing Office (GPO) in Washington did the honors.

Finally, in 1883, Charles Scribner's Sons of New York published a three-volume series entitled *The Navy in the Civil War*. Vol. 1, *The Blockade and the Cruisers*, was written by James Russell Soley, an English professor at the Naval Academy; Vol. 2, *The Atlantic Coast*, was written by Daniel Ammen, who had served as a young naval officer during the war; Vol. 3, *The Gulf and Inland Waters*, was written by Alfred T. Mahan, a little-known forty-three-year-old lieutenant commander who had served aboard the *Seminole* during the Sabine Pass debacle.

Soley, a prolific and authoritative naval historian, went on to write a long chapter entitled "The Union and Confederate Navies" for vol. 1 of that bible of rebellion researchers, *Battles and Leaders of the Civil War*, published originally by *Century* magazine. Under the joint editorship of Robert U. Johnson and Clarence C. Buel, this ambitious undertaking appeared in four volumes between 1884 and 1887. Ammen, in an obvious attempt to squeeze more mileage out of his original research, went on to write *The Old Navy and the New* (Philadelphia: J. B. Lippincott, 1891). In 1890, Mahan published *The Influence of Sea Power on History, 1660–1783* (Boston: Little, Brown and Co.). It sent such saber rattlers as imperial Germany and Japan scurrying to their naval drawing boards.

If there was not exactly a spate of naval and other military lore in the 1880s, there was at least an ample offering. In 1885, Admiral Porter's chatty *Incidents and Anecdotes of the Civil War* (New York: D. Appleton and Co.) proved a counterpoint to Soley's scholarly work. The aged admiral was less free with facts and figures in *The Naval History of the Civil War* (New York: Sherman Publishing Co., 1886). Then the ever-curious, versatile naval officer turned to romantic fiction. He did not have much time; he died in 1891. His trove of papers, numbering some seven thousand items, reposes in the Manuscript Division of the Library of Congress. It is, however, as frustrating as it is vast. Porter's handwriting is close to illegible.

Into the first decade of the twentieth century, living memory persisted, as veteran after veteran sought to commit to paper—before it was too late—what they had seen at Mobile Bay or Manassas, Albemarle Sound or Atlanta, regardless of whether the minutiae attending their months or years in uniform were dimmed by creeping age.

A signal exception to the effects of time on the human brain was Thomas O. Selfridge, whose active postwar career included a role in the building of the Panama Canal. In April 1917, in his eighty-second year, he was not wholly understanding when the Navy Department declined his offer to serve in the nation's latest war. In 1924, G. P. Putnam's of New York published his *Memoirs*. But Selfridge had waited a bit too long. He died that year on February 4 in a house in Washington near that of Woodrow Wilson, who had expired the previous day. The friendly old admiral never saw his bound copies.

Several thousand Union and Confederate veterans survived into the 1930s. Some were even able to march—slowly—in Memorial Day parades. By then in their eighties and nineties, they had once been drummer boys or privates who had lied about their ages. They were less than articulate not only because of their years but because they had scarcely

been situated so as to understand the various strategies of the Civil War. They had nothing to communicate, whether by the written or spoken word.

As a cub reporter just before the outbreak of World War II, this author had the privilege of seeing some of those very old men, even of grasping their chill, bony hands. They were deaf, some of them almost blind. Interviews were out of the question.

But they were alive. They breathed. They were palpable proof that there had once been a terrible conflict between the states.

And now, the printed page remains the sole key to those dramatic years, 1861 to 1865.

The author is indebted to two scholar-researchers in the Office of Naval History, Department of the Navy, for numerous contributions—Dean Allard and Charles R. Haberlein. One of the former's many leads revealed the *Idahoe* folder in the National Archives. His office published the handy *Civil War Chronology, 1861–1865* (Washington, D.C.: Department of the Navy, 1971). "Chuck" Haberlein, photographic curator *extraordinaire*, presides over a treasure-trove of naval art and photographs dating back to the Revolutionary War. He can instantly identify ships from the scant evidence of a spar or a gunport.

INTRODUCTION

As *the* major naval operation of the war, the blockade was accorded proportionately extensive documentation. For example, no fewer than seventeen volumes (vols. 5-21) of ser. 1 of the *Official Records of the Union and Confederate Navies in the War of the Rebellion* (Washington, D.C.: United States War Department) address the blockade, and vols. 22-27 deal with blockading operations in western waters. James Russell Soley helped launch this vitally important encyclopedia of the Civil War at sea. The thirty volumes appeared between 1894 and 1922. Two new wars had come and gone in the meantime, the Spanish-American War and World War I.

One interesting and nonofficial source should be mentioned at the outset—a visionary bit of publishing, the *Rebellion Record*, released in eleven volumes between 1861 and 1868. It was first produced by G. P. Putnam's, then, after 1863, by D. Van Nostrand, both in New York. Edward Everett, the author and man of letters, was the editor until his death in 1865. The hardcover counterpart to *Leslie's Illustrated Weekly Newspaper* and *Harper's Weekly* (both of which are almost required reading for any Civil War research), the *Rebellion Record* is a compilation of news stories, articles, essays, official orders, speeches, pamphlets, and almost anything pertaining to the rebellion. It remains a remarkable document.

Among the treasures of basic research material on the blockade are these:

Almuzi, John J. "Incidents of the Blockade." In War Paper #9. Washington, D.C.: Military Order of the Loyal Legion of the United States, Commandery of the District of Columbia.

Bradlee, Francis B. C. *Blockade Running During the Civil War*. Salem, Mass.: Essex Institute, 1925.

Chadwick, F. E. "The Federal Navy and the Blockade." In vol. 6, *The Navies*, of Francis Trevelyan Miller's ten-volume series, *The Photographic History of the Civil War*. New York: Review of Reviews, 1911. Vol. 6 also includes descriptions of the Union and Confederate navies, a chapter on the ironclads, and material on the New Orleans assault and the Confederate cruisers, including the *Alabama*.

Cochran, Hamilton. *Blockade Runners of the Confederacy*. New York: Bobbs-Merrill, 1958.

DuPont, Samuel Francis. *A Selection from His Civil War Letters*. Edited by John D. Hayes. Ithaca, N.Y.: Cornell University Press, 1969. Vol. 2 of DuPont's three-volume collection of letters is *The Blockade*. DuPont effected the first successful amphibious expedition of the war by opening up South Carolina's strategic Port Royal Sound with an overwhelming force of seventeen warships and twenty-five supply schooners in November 1861. Twelve thousand troops under Sherman then assaulted Fort Walker on Hilton Head Island and the defenses of Port Royal and Beaufort. But the two officers failed to continue their momentum by driving down to Savannah, Georgia, only twenty miles south.

Hobart-Hampden, Augustus C. *Sketches from my Life*. New York: Outing Publishing Co., 1915.

Horner, Dave. *The Blockade Runners*. New York: Dodd, Mead, 1968.

Morgan, James M. *Recollections of a Rebel Reefer*. Boston: Houghton Mifflin Co., 1917.

Ross, Ishbel. *Rebel Rose*. New York: Harper and Brothers, 1954.

Scharf, J. Thomas. *History of the Confederate States Navy*. New York: Rogers and Sherwood, 1887.

Taylor, Thomas E. *Running the Blockade*. London: John Murray, 1912.

Wilkinson, John. *The Narrative of a Blockade Runner*. New York: Sheldon and Co., 1877.

Certain newspapers were geographically situated to provide information about blockade-running. These included the *Charleston Daily Courier*; the *Mobile Daily Advertiser and Register*; the Savannah papers *Herald* and *Daily Republican*; and the *Wilmington Daily Journal*.

The statement that participants in Civil War naval actions "died in earnest," though certain operations might appear to have been curious kinds of games, is an allusion to Plutarch's writings in the first century: "Though boys throw stones at frogs in sport, the frogs do not die in sport, but in earnest." British philosopher Sir Roger L'Estrange paraphrased the quotation in the seventeenth century, apparently without attribution.

Chapter 1   THE *MERRIMACK* IS COMING!

To say the least, a singular group of executives and lesser officials gathered in the White House that fateful Sunday in March. And they left in their passing a singular amount of documentation. On file in the Library of Congress are the personal papers of Samuel Portland Chase, John A. Dahlgren, John Hay, John G. Nicolay, and Gideon Welles. Welles's collection, the largest, includes more than 15,000 items, while Chase's includes some 12,500. Also at the Library of Congress are the papers of Captain Gustavus V.

Fox, who happened to be "covering" the story from Fort Monroe that weekend.

Thus, the hysteria of the morning was amply chronicled by those present, with the unfortunate exception of Edwin Stanton. He died in 1869, far too preoccupied in the postwar years in sparring with Andrew Johnson to answer many of the questions lingering after the rebellion. *Why*, for example, had the secretary of war been so anxious that Mary Surratt hang?

Chapter 1 was inspired by the author's book *Thunder at Hampton Roads* (Englewood Cliffs, N.J.: Prentice-Hall, 1976). Credit should again be given to the Mariners Museum in Newport News, Virginia, and to John Lochhead, then the librarian. That unique and colorful museum contains much valuable material on the historic battle and related intelligence. Artifacts recently retrieved from the wreck of the *Monitor* are on exhibit.

In 1968, David R. Smith climaxed years of fascination with the great event at Hampton Roads by publishing *The Monitor and the Merrimac, a Bibliography* (Los Angeles: University of California Library). Truly a labor of love, it contains references to books, magazines, and newspapers, as well as citations of government documents and unpublished articles and manuscripts.

Vol. 1 of *Battles and Leaders of the Civil War* includes the accounts of John M. Brooke, Frank Butts, R. E. Colston, Dana Greene, Henry Reaney, and Taylor Wood. Ser. 1, vols. 6, 7, and 8, of *Official Records of the Union and Confederate Navies* also contain useful information.

Other sources include:

Anderson, Bern. *By Sea and by River, the Naval History of the Civil War*. New York: Alfred A. Knopf, 1962. A former rear admiral, Anderson was an aide to the late Samuel Eliot Morison.

Browning, Orville Hickman. *The Diary of Orville Hickman Browning*. Edited by Theodore Calvin Pease and James G. Randall. Springfield: Trustees of the Illinois State Historical Library, 1925.

Chittenden, Lucius E. *Recollections of President Lincoln and His Administration*. New York: Harper and Brothers, 1901.

Dahlgren, Madeleine Vinton. *Memoir of John A. Dahlgren*. Boston: James R. Osgood and Co., 1882.

David, Donald E. *Inside Lincoln's Cabinet: the Civil War Diaries of Salmon Portland Chase*. New York: Longman's Green, 1954.

Fox, Gustavus Vasa. *Confidential Correspondence of Gustavus Vasa Fox, Assistant Secretary of the Navy, 1861–1865*. Edited by Robert Means Thompson and Richard Wainright. New York: De Vinne Press, for the Naval Historical Society, 1920.

Jones, Charles C. *The Life and Services of Commodore Josiah Tattnall*. Savannah, Ga.: Morning News Steam Printing House, 1878.

Jones, Virgil Carrington. *The Civil War at Sea*. Vols. 1 and 2. New York: Holt, Rinehart and Winston. Jones's assiduously researched work was published in three volumes between 1960 and 1962. It became the first major naval history of the war to emerge since the previous century, and it reflects, editorially, the measured balance of time. The extensive bibliography in each volume leaves nothing to be desired. The three volumes by Jones, an acquaintance of this author, provided general background and opportunities for cross-checking several chapters in this book.

Knox, Dudley W. *A History of the U.S. Navy*. New York: G. P. Putnam's, 1936. The Civil War is but one part of Knox's authoritative study.

Lewis, Charles Lee. *Admiral Franklin Buchanan*. Baltimore: Norman Remington, 1929.

Naval History Division, United States Navy Department. *Monitors of the U.S. Navy*. Washington, D.C.: GPO, 1969.

Nicolay, John G., and John Hay. *Abraham Lincoln: a History*. New York: Century Co., 1890.

Schuckers, J. W. *Life and Public Services of Salmon Portland Chase*. New York: D. Appleton and Co., 1874.

Strong, George Templeton. *The Diary of George Templeton Strong*. Edited by Allan Nevins. New York: Macmillan Co., 1952.

Welles, Gideon. *Diary of Gideon Welles*. Boston: Houghton Mifflin Co., 1911.

Worden, John Lorimer. *The Monitor and the Merrimac, Both Sides of the Story*. New York: Harper and Brothers, 1912. The story is told by Lieutenants Worden and Greene of the *Monitor* and by H. Ashton Ramsay, chief engineer of the *Merrimack*.

Since White House press conferences were several decades on the horizon, the role of the newspapers that Sunday was distinctly peripheral. Concern over the *Merrimack*, however, was reflected in several dailies, including the *Baltimore Sun*; three New York papers, the *World*, the *Herald*, and the *Tribune*; the *Norfolk Day Book*; and the *Washington Evening Star*.

Chapter 2   THE FIGHTING FERRYBOATS

On April 6, 1910, Dr. Stephen Ayres, a former navy surgeon, read a paper before the Ohio Commandery of the Military Order of the Loyal Legion of the United States. It was titled "A Sketch of the Life and Services of Vice-Admiral Stephen C. Rowan, U.S. Navy." Rowan had by then been deceased for twenty years, and with him, seemingly, had died much of the living memory of the role of ferryboats in the Civil War.

Thus, at least for the period of Dr. Ayres's presentation, the plucky little terriers of the shallows paddled again. The monitors and the ponderous ironclads, great steam frigates such as the *Hartford*, and even impressive hospital ships like the *Red Rover* had plowed through many memoirs, whether books, periodicals, newspaper features, or papers like the surgeon's. But ferryboats?

Charles W. Flusser's headstone weathered at the Naval Academy cemetery. Who, the plebes could rightfully ask, was Flusser? And what were his ships?

Even those naval histories or commentaries that listed the ferries by name rarely identified them by their true pedigrees. They were simply "gunboats" or, more humiliating yet, "2d-," "3d-," or even "4th-class" ships. *Official Records of the Union and Confederate Navies* well documented their actions through countless dispatches, orders, and reports, especially in ser. 1, vols. 6–10, 13, 14, 16, 18, 19–22, 24, and 27. But rarely were they identified other than by name—the USS *Westfield*, for example. Some clues are to be found in ser. 2, vol. 1, a catalog of Union and Confederate warships—their original names, locations, sizes, prices, dispositions, etc. But all listings are not definitive, as the type of vessel is not invariably given. Often, the researcher has to

attempt a determination with reference to the original owner, such as a local transportation company.

A year following Dr. Ayres's reading, Francis Trevelyan Miller's *Photographic History of the Civil War* appeared, with a new recognition by Admiral Chadwick in vol. 6: "Manned by brave men who rendered yeoman service for the Federal cause, many of these small craft sank into oblivion, overshadowed by the achievements of the great monitors and ironclads which were eventually provided by the Navy Department for service along the shore." In vol. 1 of *Battles and Leaders of the Civil War*, Brigadier General Rush C. Hawkins and General Ambrose Burnside, the expedition commander, wrote on the "Early Coast Operations in North Carolina." Yet the ferryboats, seldom named, emerged as "steamers," "gunboats," or "light-draught vessels."

In 1957, John Perry published his *American Ferryboats* (New York: W. Funk). He entitled one chapter "Amateur Warships: Ferryboats in the Civil War." His motives were correct, though his labeling was a bit off-target. For the most part, the ferryboat crews fought like professionals, certainly with a fury and courage the equal of that of their counterparts aboard the big men-o'-war. With paper-thin hulls and superstructure and imperfect armaments, the ferryboats fought oblivious to their inherent contradictions.

There had never been anything like the squadrons of ferryboats that steamed into the Civil War, flags flying. And there has been nothing quite like them since. Documented history has sadly slighted their role, and it is a pity.

Chapter 3   THE ORDEAL OF CAPTAIN NEWCOMB

For some years, the author had heard rumors of a singular voyage on western waters—one involving a river captain with a boatload of shady ladies who proved about as easy to disembark as a cargo of hornets. As previously noted, Dean Allard of the Office of Naval History finally steered the author to the Judicial, Fiscal, and Social branch of the National Archives, the guardian of the *Idahoe* file. Not only does the file contain John Newcomb's plaintive letter to the secretary of war, but the original orders that sent him steaming away from peaceful security toward an unsought adventure as well. As time passed, the Quartermaster Corps came to feel less than proud of the gambit in wartime Nashville. Rather than being deposited in the *Official Records of the Union and Confederate Navies*, where posterity could peruse them, the orders ended up—of all mundane places—in the Office of the Third Auditor, General Accounting Office.

The author is indebted to these administrators and researchers at the National Archives: John Krauskopf, Terry Matchett, Tamara Melia, and William Sherman. He also wishes to thank Beth Gerber of the Cincinnati Historical Society and James A. Hoobler of the Tennessee Historical Society.

These publications proved helpful:

Appleton's Annual Cyclopedia and Register of Important Events. New York: D. Appleton and Co., 1863–64. Referenced under "Tennessee."

"Captain Newcomb and the Frail Sisterhood." *American Heritage* 33 (June-July 1982): 98–99.

Egerton, John. *Nashville, the Faces of Two Centuries*. Nashville: Plus Media, 1979.

Fisher, Horace Cecil. *The Personal Experiences of Colonel Horace Newton Fisher in the Civil War*. Boston: privately printed, 1960.

Lynch, Amy. "Nashville's Love Boat." *Nashville Magazine* 11 (February 1984): 62–64.

Maslowski, Peter. *Treason Must Be Made Odious: Military Occupation and Wartime Reconstruction in Nashville, Tennessee, 1862–65*. Millwood, N.Y.: KTO Press, 1978.

Morgan, Julia. *How it Was: Four Years Among the Rebels*. Nashville: Methodist Episcopal Church South, 1892.

United States Congress. House. *Document 337. Quartermaster's List*. 40th Cong., 2d sess., 1869. Washington, D.C.: GPO.

The War of the Rebellion. A Compilation of the Official Records of the Union and Confederate Armies. Ser. 1, vols. 23 (part 2) and 52. Washington, D.C.: GPO.

Wiley, Bell I. *The Life of Billy Yank, the Common Soldier of the Union*. Indianapolis and New York: Bobbs-Merrill, 1951.

These newspapers provided information: the *Cincinnati Daily Commercial*, the *Cincinnati Daily Gazette*, the *Louisville Daily Press*, the *Nashville Daily Press*, the *Nashville Dispatch*, the *Nashville Republican Banner*, and the *New York Times*.

Chapter 4   THE HOAX THAT CAME TO STAY

Hoax and deception are as old as warfare itself. Gideon ordered a mere handful of soldiers to bang pitchers and plates together and blare their trumpets to hoodwink Israel's ancient foes, the Midianites, into believing they were confronted by formidable legions. The ploy worked. In the following century, the twelfth B.C., a crafty Greek named Epeus created a wooden horse to break a ten-year deadlock before Troy, according to classical mythology.

Centuries later, George Washington himself proved a master of the sly art of deception. In the first frosty days of 1777, his men broke camp in the night to attack Princeton, New Jersey. Left behind were a few troops to tend scores of blazing campfires. The British slept snugly under blankets, assured by their sentries that the Americans were themselves snoozing in warmth. Princeton was thus won.

Eighty-five years later, the Confederates were also lighting multiple campfires, emplacing "Quaker," or wooden, guns, and sounding bugles to create the illusion of preponderant forces. General John Bankhead Magruder, who gave the Union such trouble at Galveston, thoroughly confused and stalled General George B. McClellan by employing such tactics. With mere regiments against McClellan's divisions, he marched his troops around hills and in and out of wooded areas, where they could be counted many times over. One of Magruder's bands changed both its tunes and its costumery at each appearance.

General Sherman accomplished a nearly impossible act of deception by moving an army of at least seventy thousand out of the trenches enveloping Atlanta and marching in a wide arc southward. The defenders, thinking "Old Tecumseh" was retreating, held victory balls. Then, with the fury of an avenging angel, Sherman reappeared before Jonesboro, on the south side of the city. He swept into Atlanta after the Confederates' evacuation and accepted the city's surrender on September 2, 1864.

Though he preceded Sherman's gambit by a year, Admiral Porter had plenty of grist for venturing a hoax of his own. There was a certain desperation in the admiral's move, since his full fleet had not yet been assembled before Vicksburg. He needed anything that floated, including dummy ships.

The participants' accounts, North and South alike, are covered quite fully in ser. 1, vol. 24, of the *Official Records of the Union and Confederate Navies.*

The despair of Colonel Wirt Adams is preserved for posterity in *The War of the Rebellion. A Compilation of the Official Records of the Union and Confederate Armies*, ser. 1, vol. 24 (parts 1 and 3). The *Indianola* is also referenced in ser. 1, vol. 5.

Admiral Porter discussed the hoax in his *Incidents and Anecdotes of the Civil War*, as did James Russell Soley in his biography *Admiral Porter* (New York: D. Appleton and Co., 1903). An account is also to be found in vol. 3 of Virgil Jones's *The Civil War at Sea.*

The following provided general background:

Army Times Editors. *The Tangled Web, True Stories of Deception in Modern Warfare.* Washington, D.C.: Robert D. Luce, 1963.

Hoehling, A. A. *Vicksburg: 47 Days of Siege.* Englewood Cliffs, N.J.: Prentice-Hall, 1969.

Wayman, Norbury L. *Life on the River.* New York: Bonanza Books, 1969.

Chapter 5   THE "INVASION" OF PORTLAND, MAINE

The author's initial research into this episode was accomplished when he was an editor with the *Portland Telegram.* His article appeared in that newspaper on May 18, 1958.

In spite of Read's humiliation, the South did not wholly dismiss the possibility of landing troops along the barren Maine coast and burning ports such as Boothbay, Camden, Bar Harbor, and even Portland. In the summer of 1864, the Confederate cruiser *Tallahassee* (later the *Olustee*) was available, but she would have had to sally forth alone, without consorts or transports. The *Alabama* was at the bottom of the English Channel, off Cherbourg, France. The *Florida* was bottled up in South American waters (and was soon to be captured). All military efforts were being expended in the attempt to save Richmond from General Grant and Atlanta from General Sherman.

So Portland was spared once more.

An account of the "invasion" is contained in ser. 1, vol. 2, of *Official Records of the Union and Confederate Navies.* The newspaper *Daily Eastern Argus* and the following publications provided source material:

Goold, William. *Portland in the Past.* Portland: B. Thurston and Co., 1886.

Long, Barbara C. "When the Civil War Came to Maine." *Yankee* 43 (October 1979): 198–211.

Shingleton, Royce Gordon. *John Taylor Wood, the Sea Ghost of the Confederacy.* Athens: University of Georgia Press, 1979.

The Maine Historical Society, located on old Congress Street in Portland, is a must for researching almost anything pertaining to Maine or Portland. Such names as Jewett, Liscomb, and Caleb Cushing—keys to the high moments of the past century—continue to endure in the Pine Tree State.

Chapter 6   THE HOMICIDAL *HUNLEY*

The Civil War was unique in previewing weaponry, great and small, that would be perfected and standardized in future conflicts, especially World War I. There was Richard Gatling's revolving-barrel invention, which heralded the machine gun. The Spencer and Henry repeating, breechloading rifles made muzzleloaders obsolete, though they arrived too late to be a decisive factor. Thaddeus Lowe's balloon corps certainly foreshadowed aerial warfare, even if there is no record of the professor's ever dropping anything lethal from his baskets. The Confederates made great use of their "torpedoes" (mines), though the principle was hardly revolutionary. The *Monitor*'s armor and revolving turret rendered wooden ships with fixed cannon obsolete overnight. But the South's efforts to create submarines were perhaps the most visionary of all.

It is indeed fortunate that two officers shared their experiences through the printed word. Almost all the others involved in the South's underwater program who were articulate did not survive their particular Frankenstein. William A. Alexander wrote vividly and with a certain nostalgia. His reminiscences can be found in the *Richmond Dispatch* of July 21, 1902; they were reprinted in vol. 30 of the *Southern Historical Society Papers*, edited by R. A. Brock (Richmond, Va.: Southern Historical Society, 1902). Lieutenant William T. Glassell had chronicled the little *David*'s moment of glory in the same society's papers of 1877 (vol. 4).

In his *History of the Confederate States Navy*, J. Thomas Scharf was among the first historians to take serious note of the Confederate submersibles and their torpedoes. In addition to supplying diagrams of the submersibles, he contributed, no doubt through painstaking research, a box score of the damage done to Union vessels by the so-called torpedoes.

United States Navy messages concerning the *Housatonic* and *New Ironsides* may be found principally in ser. 1, vols. 15 and 16, of *Official Records of the Union and Confederate Navies*. Also included is a minor collection of Confederate correspondence, with at least one telegram from General Beauregard expressing his regret at the loss of Southern sailors.

Chapter 7   THE MAN WHO SAVED THE SHIPS

Joseph Bailey was a man of few words, as previously noted. Others, however, did chronicle his unusual feat. Even so, the Red River episode has been accorded relatively little space in the annals of history. That is surprising, since the miraculous rescue was a kind of Civil War Dunkirk.

The fragmentary clues to the man himself repose in the State Historical Society of Wisconsin, and they were generously shared with the author by reference librarian Geraldine Strey, who wrote, for example, "The Historical Society Museum possesses a sword and a punch bowl presented to Joseph Bailey by the State of Wisconsin in honor of his achievements. Supposedly, the sword and punch bowl were sold by Bailey's family to the Society after his death, when

his family was left in poor circumstances." Unwittingly, Strey thus introduced another question: *What* family? The impression had until then persisted that Bailey was a loner and a bachelor.

The best information available about Bailey's early years is in an article by E. C. Dixon entitled "Newport, Its Rise and Fall" in the *Wisconsin Magazine of History* (vol. 25, June 1942: 444-55), and in the *Dictionary of Wisconsin Biography*, edited by the state historical society (Madison: State Historical Society of Wisconsin, 1960). Among the references in local sources, as filed in the society's archives, are articles from three Wisconsin newspapers: the *Beloit News*, July 20, 1924; the *Boyd Herald*, June 8, 1916; and the *Kenosha News*, July 16, 1914.

As to Bailey's exploits during the Red River expedition, the most vivid account was furnished by General James Grant Wilson in an address before the New York Commandery of the Military Order of the Loyal Legion of the United States. It was published in the order's papers in 1891 under the title, "The Red River Dam."

Admiral Porter wrote of the dam in his *Incidents and Anecdotes of the Civil War*, as did Selfridge in his *Memoirs* and Alfred T. Mahan in his *Gulf and Inland Waters*, vol. 3 of Charles Scribner's Sons' *The Navy in the Civil War*. Selfridge also contributed the account of the Red River venture in vol. 4 of *Battles and Leaders of the Civil War*. Others writing in that volume included Confederate General Edmund Kirby-Smith and Lieutenant Colonel Richard B. Irwin, assistant adjutant general, Department of the Gulf.

The Red River campaign is covered in ser. 1, vol. 34 (part 1), of *The War of the Rebellion. A Compilation of the Official Records of the Union and Confederate Armies* and in ser. 1, vol. 26, of the *Official Records of the Union and Confederate Navies*.

Other sources include:

Boatner, Mark M., III. *Civil War Dictionary*. New York: David McKay, 1959. This is a most valuable book for all Civil War research.

Pratt, Fletcher. *The Civil War on Western Waters*. New York: Henry Holt, 1956.

Chapter 8   DAMN THE TORPEDOES!

George Taylor, ship's armorer, was quite deservedly awarded the Medal of Honor for his gallantry aboard the *Lackawanna* in extinguishing the powder-room fire with his bare hands.

But Confederate Admiral Franklin Buchanan, wounded for the second time in an historic sea battle involving ironclads, received no medal. He spent most of the remainder of the war in the United States Navy Hospital in Pensacola, Florida, where Confederate Dr. Daniel B. Conrad and Federal surgeons accorded him such excellent treatment that his leg was saved. Much like Jefferson Davis, Buchanan never fully made his peace with the Union. "He always complained of his bad luck in his two great actions," Dr. Conrad recalled. "In the first [aboard the *Merrimack*], he was struck down at the moment of victory, and in the last at the moment of defeat."

Dr. Conrad's articulate narrative "Capture of the CSS Ram *Tennessee* in Mobile Bay, August, 1864" is included in vol. 19 of the *Southern Historical Society Papers*. The durable surgeon was then living in Kansas City, Missouri. His recollections are also included in *Hero Tales of the American Soldier and Sailor* (Philadelphia: Century Manufacturing Co., 1899).

Union Dr. William F. Hutchinson's "The Bay Fight" was read before the Rhode Island Soldiers and Sailors Historical Society and is listed as Personal Narrative No. 8 in the society's papers (Providence: Sidney S. Rider, 1879).

The account of Lieutenant John C. Kinney, signal officer of the *Hartford*, is contained in vol. 4 of *Battles and Leaders of the Civil War*. The article by Commander James D. Johnston of the *Tennessee* is included among others on the subject in the same volume. Johnston's report is also contained in the *Official Records of the Union and Confederate Navies*, ser. 1, vol. 21, along with the reports of Farragut, Buchanan, and other participants in the great contest.

Quartermaster John H. Knowles's lashing of Farragut to the rigging is chronicled in *The Photographic History of the Civil War*, which otherwise treats the engagement very sparsely.

The rather sketchy letters of Percival Drayton, captain of the *Hartford*, were published by the New York Public Library in 1906. The captain died on August 4, 1865, almost a year to the day after Mobile Bay.

Eight years after his father's death, Loyall Farragut published *The Life of David Glasgow Farragut* (New York: D. Appleton and Co., 1879). Another book on Farragut is Charles Lee Lewis's *Our First Admiral* (Annapolis, Md.: Naval Institute Press, 1943).

Chapter 9   FIGHTING MAN OF THE NORTH
             CAROLINA SOUNDS

On a crisp, not-too-cold January morning, the author paused in Plymouth, North Carolina. The little town on the Roanoke River slumbers on, unchanged save for the addition of stores and warehouses, its lovely old Georgian homes and its dominating, stone Grace Episcopal Church still intact. One was left to speculate as to why such a small, peaceful place should have been so desirable in the eyes of Union strategists. An historical marker proclaimed: "RAM *ALBEMARLE* CONFEDERATE IRONCLAD WINNER OF NOTABLE VICTORIES UNDER CAPT. J. W. COOKE WAS SUNK 800 FEET NORTH NIGHT OF OCT. 27 1864." Omitted were the names of *Albemarle*'s other captains—Maffitt and Warley—and the circumstances surrounding her demise. The author was struck by both the swiftness and the narrowness of the river, which made William Barker Cushing's feat seem all the more remarkable.

Never at a loss for words, the young officer amply chronicled his exploit for the Navy Department. It rests in ser. 1, vol. 10, of the *Official Records of the Union and Confederate Navies*. Further documentation on Cushing is in ser. 1, vols. 3, 5, 6, 8, 9, 11, and 12, and in ser. 2, vol. 1.

Shorter accounts by Ensign Thomas S. Gay and Lieutenant Alexander F. Warley are in vol. 4 of *Battles and Leaders of the Civil War*.

Among the biographies of Cushing—most of them aimed at young-adult audiences—is *Lincoln's Commando, the Biography of W. B. Cushing*, by Ralph J. Reske and Charles Van Doren (New York: Harper and Brothers, 1957). A monograph by Theron W. Haight dealing with Cushing's early years was published in Madison in 1910 by the Wisconsin History Commission; it is entitled *Three Wisconsin Cushings*.

Cushing's diary is in the National Archives.

Chapter 10 "OLD BEESWAX" AND THE *ALABAMA*

Secretary of the Navy Welles found it impossible to let bygones be bygones. In December 1865, with the ink barely dry on the various articles of surrender, the cabinet officer had Raphael Semmes arrested on open charges, then brought to Old Capitol Prison. He was held there for several weeks before an irate General Grant joined equally incensed navy officers and members of Congress in demanding the release of the honorable and chivalrous warrior, who had already been paroled.

Semmes returned to Mobile to resume the practice of law and become one of that city's most distinguished citizens. Unlike the majority of the South's military and civilian leaders, however, "Old Beeswax" never reconciled himself to the South's loss. Judging from existing records, he never uttered a kind word for the United States government. Mobile continued to revere him for vexing the Yankees right up until that sad day, August 30, 1877, when the admiral "slipped his anchor" to meet his Maker. The *Mobile Register* "turned the rules" to border its columns in black, printing eulogies that might otherwise have been reserved for the passing of a statesman of international renown. Far more reserved, the Northern press conceded his correctness as a foe.

A French sonar ship located a hull thought to be that of the *Alabama* in October 1984. Clive Cussler, author of *Raise the Titanic* and organizer of a foundation for locating famous shipwrecks, told the author that he had also found the *Alabama* but was forbidden to work on it by the French government. He understands that French divers have brought up artifacts. Plans to raise the vessel have been put forward, and the *Alabama* may again be making headlines in the coming years, with the town of Cherbourg and the state of Alabama vying for the rights to her remains.

Records of the *Alabama*'s voyages are to be found in the "Cruisers" section of the *Official Records of the Union and Confederate Navies*, ser. 1, vols. 1–3. Additional information is in vol. 2 of *The Civil War at Sea* and in vol. 4 of *Battles and Leaders of the Civil War*, with accounts by John McIntosh Kell, Surgeon John M. Browne, and James Russell Soley.

Other sources include:

Clark, William H. *Ships and Sailors*. Boston: L. C. Page and Co., 1938.

Elliott, John M. *The Life of John Ancrum Winslow*. New York: G. P. Putnam's, 1902.

Gosnell, Harpur Allen, ed. *Rebel Raider. Being an Account of Raphael Semmes' Cruise in the CSS* Sumter. Chapel Hill: University of North Carolina Press, 1948.

Hoehling, A. A. *Epics of the Sea*. Chicago: Contemporary Books, 1977.

Krafft, Herman F., and Walter B. Norris. *Sea Power in American History*. New York: Century Co., 1920.

Sinclair, Arthur. *Two Years on the* Alabama. Boston: Lee and Sheppard, 1895.

Chapter 11 WHAT SANK THE *SULTANA*?

The mystery of the catastrophic fire aboard the *Sultana* remains as profound as that attending the somewhat similar loss of the *Morro Castle* off the New Jersey shore almost seventy years later. Lieutenant William H. C. Michael of the *Tyler* did not publicly speculate about possible causes until May 4, 1898, in a paper read before the Nebraska Commandery of the Loyal Legion, later published in *Civil War Sketches and Incidents* (Omaha: Military Order of the Loyal Legion of the United States, Commandery of the State of Nebraska, 1902). Admiral Porter was dead by then. Michael's claims about William C. Streator and Robert Lowden (Charles Dales) cannot be corroborated, since their names are not to be found elsewhere.

Six years earlier, in 1892, the durable Chester D. Berry had written the first full account of the Mississippi holocaust, entitled *Loss of the* Sultana (Lansing, Mich.: D. D. Thorp Co.).

In 1913, the accounts of Joseph Taylor Elliott and others were published under a rather obvious title, "The *Sultana* Disaster," in the *Indiana Historical Society Publications* (vol. 5, no. 3: 163–99). This was followed in September 1927 by an article by William B. Floyd in the *Wisconsin Magazine of History* (vol. 11: 70–76) entitled "The Burning of the *Sultana*."

James Elliott, grandson of Joseph Taylor Elliott, published *Transport to Disaster* in 1962 (New York: Holt, Rinehart and Winston).

John Means wrote a feature article on the subject that appeared on April 25, 1965, in the *Memphis Commercial Appeal*; a similar treatment appeared on May 28, 1969, in the *Memphis Press Scimitar*. News articles may also be found in May 1865 issues of the Memphis papers *Appeal*, *Avalanche*, and *Bulletin*. All are on file in the Memphis Public Library.

The *Sultana* is referenced in *The War of the Rebellion. A Compilation of the Official Records of the Union and Confederate Armies* in ser. 1, vols. 23, 34, 48, and 52; ser. 2, vol. 8; and ser. 3, vol. 5. Curiously enough, the navy ignored the sinking, with only a mention in ser. 1, vol. 25, of *Official Records of the Union and Confederate Navies* that the steamer was fired upon in 1862.

According to the Memphis Public Library, a small team has located the *Sultana* under a soybean field on the Arkansas shore but has not yet revealed its location, in an effort to protect the wreck from treasure seekers. Clive Cussler also believes that one of his teams has located the corpse of the *Sultana*.

Chapter 12 THE LAST TO KNOW

James I. Waddell remained in England, finding it difficult to disabuse himself of the conviction that the United States might hang him as a pirate. Not until President Ulysses S. Grant assured him in the early 1870s that he was welcome did he return. Hired by the Pacific Mail Line, he was given command of the new, 4,000-ton liner *San Francisco*, plying between Australia and California. Back in Melbourne in

1877, Waddell never completed the return leg of the vessel's maiden voyage. He stranded on an uncharted rock off the Mexican coast. Though all were saved, the ship was a total loss. The line exonerated him, and the old sea raider continued in its employ for a few more years, until, in semi-retirement, he took a job with the state of Maryland chasing down oyster pirates in Chesapeake Bay. He pursued that prey, which proved almost as defenseless as the New Bedford whalers, until his death in March 1886.

The *Shenandoah*, turned over to the United States government, was sold to the sultan of Zanzibar. She was stranded in a hurricane in 1872.

Great Britain had to reach deep into her purse for compensation for the damages inflicted by the *Alabama*, the *Shenandoah*, and the *Florida*, a third English-built ship. In 1872, an international tribunal representing five nations ordered Great Britain to pay Washington $15.5 million in gold. *Alabama* accounted for the greatest percentage, with *Shenandoah* second. Waddell's whalers simply did not possess the monetary value of the merchantmen hit by Semmes.

In addition to the primary source, *Official Records of the Union and Confederate Navies*, and William C. Whittle's account, "Cruise of the *Shenandoah*," in vol. 35 of the *Southern Historical Society Papers*, these publications treat the *Shenandoah*:

Horan, James D., ed. CSS Shenandoah, *The Memoirs of Lieutenant Commanding James I. Waddell*. New York: Crown Publishers, 1960.

Horn, Stanley F. *The Fabulous Cruise of the CSS* Shenandoah. New Brunswick, N.J.: Rutgers University Press, 1947.

Lining, Charles. "Cruise of the Confederate *Shenandoah*." *Tennessee Historical Magazine* 8 (July 1924): 102–11.

Morgan, Murray. *Dixie Raider, the Saga of the CSS* Shenandoah. New York: E. P. Dutton and Co., 1948.

Stern, Philip Van Doren. *The Confederate Navy—A Pictorial History*. Garden City, N.Y.: Doubleday and Co., 1962.

Index

McCoy (captain), 159–60
McKelvey, Joseph, 163
McNulty, Fred J., 178
Macomb, W. H., 128
Maffitt, John Newland, 3, 66, 128, 135
Magruder, John Bankhead, 31
Mallory, Stephen, 12, 74, 81, 172
Malvern, 129
Manassas, 128
Marion. See Morse
Mary Bowers, 8
Mason, Edwin C., 70
Mason, J. Cass, 158, 160, 167, 169
Maury, Matthew Fontaine, 79
Maximilian, Ferdinand, 93
Meigs, Montgomery C., 12, 17–19
Merrimack, 11–24, 106, 143
Merryman, James H., 68–70, 71–73
Metacomet, 113
Miami, 32–34, 127
Michael, William H. C., 165, 168–69
Middleton, Arthur, 137
Milo, 178–79
Minnesota, 11, 15, 20–22, 124
Mississippi, 61
Mixer, H. M., 58
Mogul, 175
Monitor, 8, 13, 15, 18, 20–24
Monongahela, 111, 115, 118
Monticello, 127
Morgan, James D., 41, 44
Morgan, James Morris, 4
Morgan, John Hunt, 38
Morris, 146
Morse, 27
Mound City, 100, 102
Mullany, J. R. M., 111

N

Napoleon III, 93, 147

Neosho, 101–2
Newcomb, John M., 41–46, 47–49
New Ironsides, 77–80, 83
Nichols, Mrs., 176
Nicolay, John G., 17–19
Night Hawk, 8
Nile, 181
Norton, William H., 161, 163, 165–68

O

Ocean Rover, 142
Ocmulgee, 142
Octorara, 109
Olive Branch, 158
Oneida, 111
Osage, 94–95, 97, 101
Ossipee, 115, 118–19
Otsego, 3, 129–30
Owl, 128, 135
Ozark, 102

P

Page, R. L., 111
Palfrey, J. C., 99
Parks, Thomas, 82–83, 87
Patrick Henry, 20
Paulding, Hiram, 19
Pauline Carroll, 158
Paul Jones, 77
Payne, John, 81–82
Petrel. See Alabama
Phelps, S. Ledyard, 95
Philadelphia, 52
Pickering, C. W., 85–87
Pioneer, 81
Pittsburg, 102
Pixley (brothers), 103
Pocahontas, 167

Stoney, Theodore, 80
Stormy Petrel, 8
Streator, William C., 169
Strong, George Templeton, 12
Strong, J. H., 115
Stubbs, J. D., 41, 44
Sullivan, James, 80
Sultana, 157–66, 168–69
Sumter, 140–41, 142
Surratt, Mary, 48
Susan Abigail, 179–80
Switzerland, 54

T

Tacony, 67
Taylor, George, 116
Taylor, Richard, 93–94, 100
Taylor, Zachary, 56
Tecumseh, 107, 110, 113
Tennessee, 106, 107, 111–19
Texan Star, 146
Thomas, George H., 47
Tibbets, Howard, 32
Titanic, 168
Titcomb, Elbridge, 67
Todd, John, 68
Tomb, James H., 80, 83
Trenholm, George, 80
Tuscarora, 141, 143
Tuscumbia, 51
Tycoon, 147
Tyler, 165

V

Valley City, 30, 134
van Brunt, Gershon, 20–22
Vanderbilt, Cornelius, 28, 142
Vanderbilt, 19, 143–44

Venus, 8
Vesta, 8
Vicksburg, 56
Virginia. See Merrimack
Virginia II, 153

W

Wabash, 83–84
Waddell, James I., 171–85
Warley, Alexander F., 128–29, 130–35
Watson, Baxter, 81
Watson, J. Crittenden, 114
Watson, Peter, 17
Weehawken, 78
Welles, Gideon, 17–18, 24, 58–59, 80, 125–27
Welles, William N., 33–34
Westfield, 27–28, 30, 31
Whitehall, 27
Whitehead, Robert, 88
Whittle, William C., jr., 173, 176, 180–81, 182
Wilkinson, John, 3, 4
Williams (captain), 179
Williams, Robertson, 71
William Thompson, 178
William Webb, 56, 57–58, 60, 61
Will o' the Wisp, 8
Wilson, James Grant, 98–100, 101–2
Winged Racer, 144
Winslow, John Ancrum, 146–53
Wintringer, Nate, 158, 161–62, 167, 168
Woodman, John, 130, 133
Wool, John E., 15
Worden, John L., 15, 20–22, 24
Wyoming, 144

Z

Zaizer, J. P., 161–62

Typeset in Galliard by the Composing Room of Michigan

Designed by Debra L. Hampton